International FrameNet Workshop 2020

Towards a Global, Multilingual FrameNet

Marseille, France
11 – 16 May 2020

Editors:

Tiago T. Torrent
Collin F. Baker
Oliver Czulo

Kyoko Ohara
Miriam R. L. Petruck

ISBN: 978-1-7138-1263-0

LREC 2020 WORKSHOP
Language Resources and Evaluation Conference
11–16 May 2020

International FrameNet Workshop 2020
Towards a Global, Multilingual FrameNet

PROCEEDINGS

Edited by:
Tiago T. Torrent, Collin F. Baker, Oliver Czulo, Kyoko Ohara and
Miriam R. L. Petruck

Proceedings of the LREC International FrameNet Workshop 2020: Towards a Global, Multilingual FrameNet

Edited by: Tiago T. Torrent, Collin F. Baker, Oliver Czulo, Kyoko Ohara and Miriam R. L. Petruck

For more information:
European Language Resources Association (ELRA)
9 rue des Cordelières
75013, Paris
France
http://www.elra.info
Email: lrec@elda.org

Introduction

This workshop continues the series of International FrameNet Workshops, based on frame semantics and FrameNets around the world, including meetings in Berkeley, California in 2013 (sponsored by the Swedish FrameNet group), in Juiz de Fora, Brazil in 2016 (sponsored by FrameNet Brasil), and in Miyazaki, Japan in 2018 (in conjunction with the LREC conference there). The last of these was specifically designed to bring together two sometimes separate groups of researchers, those concentrating on frame semantics and those concentrating on construction grammar, which Charles J. Fillmore and many of the same colleagues developed in parallel over a period of several decades. The call for papers of the current conference emphasized that the workshop would welcome studies of both theoretical and practical issues, and we are fortunate to have strong contributions of both types, sometimes within a single paper. A number of the papers arise out of the parallel annotation of Ken Robinson's TED talk "Do schools kill creativity?". This very popular talk has been translated (or at least subtitled) in a wide variety of languages. The attendees at the International FrameNet Workshop in 2016 decided that different groups would undertake Frame Semantic annotation for it, based on Berkeley FrameNet Release 1.7 as shared standard. These efforts have raised a number of important theoretical issues while also helping new FrameNet projects to get underway in several languages.

Three papers deal with expansion of FrameNets to new languages and content areas:

- Gargett and Leung describe the building of a new FrameNet for Emirati Arabic, and how they were able to use novel combinations of existing databases and tools to create an Emirati Arabic corpus and begin annotating it semiautomatically with frames and frame elements derived mainly from Berkeley FrameNet. They report encouraging numbers for inter-annotator agreement and good prospects for further automatic processing.

- Giouli et al. describe participating in the shared annotation task on the TED talk and the issues they encountered in trying to use the Berkeley FrameNet frames for Modern Greek. Some of these are simply gaps in the BFN lexical coverage, others are interesting issues related to differences between English and Greek.

- L'Homme et al. are building a multilingual frame semantic resource for the specialized terminology relating to the environment. They have created more than 100 new frames for this purpose and "slightly modified" 40 more in the process; they began with French and expanded to English, Spanish, Portuguese, and Chinese recently. They propose a general technique for FrameNet expansion in technical domains.

Two papers deal with how frame semantics applies across languages and what relation it has to differences in constructions across languages:

- Ohara concentrates on constructions, comparing constructions in English and in Japanese, also based on examples from the shared annotation task. In this study, she expands on earlier work comparing frames and constructions between English and Japanese children's books, and points out that the Japanese version of the TED talk is not exactly intended as a complete translation of the English version.

- Baker and Lorenzi describe a variety of techniques for aligning frames between FrameNets in different languages. For this purpose, the authors have created a tool to visualize the alignments and compare the techniques used, an effort that should aid in testing different combinations of alignment methods.

Three papers deal with practical application of frame semantics to other NLP tasks:

- Marzinotto projects FrameNet annotation from English to French using two cutting-edge NLP methods, attention-based machine translation and parsing based on BERT embeddings, using data from two French frame semantic resources, ASFALDA and CALOR. The study found that projecting annotation in this way slightly improves the performance of the parser.

- Lee et al. report on the creation of a database of Mandarin Chinese verbs, and how it was used to analyze the occurrences of verbs in Chinese language textbooks used in China across grades 1-12. They found that the distinction between core and non-core frame elements helps to predict the reading difficulty of the texts.

- Gruzitis et al., in a surprising change of direction, start from the Latvian FrameNet corpus, which also has a universal dependency layer and semi-automatically create a complete set of Propbank annotation for the same corpus; this process was found to be much easier than a mapping from Propbank to FrameNet would have been.

Four papers deal with connecting frame semantics to other types of meaning:

- Czulo et al. remind us that from early in the development of frame semantics, Fillmore conceived of the theory as encompassing both lexical frames where meanings are tied to specific lexical items and pragmatic frames (called "scenes" at that point) tied to the situational context of usage, rather than lexical items. The paper offers an update on the concept, with examples from the shared annotation task.

- Postma et al. describe a new approach to annotating both semantic frames and real-world references (based on Wikidata) on the same texts, creating rich possibilities for future work analyzing text coherence and variations in framing of news events. The authors have developed a tool which both assists and constrains the annotator in this process.

- Remijnse and Minnema also deal with real-world references, but for the problem of constructing narratives from news reports. The authors found that pragmatically inferred frames were needed to achieve coherence across documents.

- Belcavello et al. discuss a novel tool they have created for annotating multimodal data with semantic frames. The paper provides an example worked in detail about how the text, audio, and video can all be annotated somewhat differently, with attention to how they are actually temporally related in the data – here, a TV series about travel to different countries. The paper also illustrates how a highly elaborated set of ternary qualia relations can help to connect the annotations of the different modalities.

The Organizing Committee would like to thank the authors for submitting so many substantial papers and the reviewers for helping to select and improve those included here. We would also like to thank LREC for scheduling a full day for this workshop, so that we could cover the full range of relevant topics. As this preface is being written, the pandemic caused by COVID-19 makes it uncertain whether the workshop originally planned for May 16, 2020 in Marseilles in conjunction with the LREC conference will simply be postponed or will be converted into an on-line meeting. Still, we are eager to press ahead with the publication of the proceedings, so that these exciting papers can receive the attention they deserve.

Collin Baker, for the Organizing Committee

Organizers:

Tiago Timponi Torrent, FrameNet Brasil, Federal University of Juiz de Fora, Brazil
Collin Baker, FrameNet, International Computer Science Institute, USA
Oliver Czulo, Department of Translation Studies, Universität Leipzig, Germany
Kyoko Ohara, Japanese FrameNet, Keio University, Japan
Miriam R. L. Petruck, FrameNet, International Computer Science Institute, USA

Program Committee:

Hans Boas, University of Texas, Austin
Dana Dannells, Gothenburg University
Gerard de Melo, Rutgers University
Ellen Dodge, Google Inc.
Jerome Feldman, International Computer Science Institute
Maucha Gamonal, University of Leipzig
Laurent Gautier, University of Bourgogne
Normunds Gruzitis, University of Latvia
Karin Friberg Heppin, Apple Inc.
Richard Johansson, Gothenburg University
Dimitrios Kokkinakis, Gothenburg University
Marie-Claude L'Homme, University of Montréal
Russell Lee-Goldman, Google Inc.
Ely Matos, Federal University of Juiz de Fora
Sebastian Padó, University of Stuttgart
Michael Roth, University of Stuttgart
Josef Ruppenhofer, Institute for the German Language (IDS)
Nathan Schneider, Georgetown University
Simon Varga, University of Mainz
Alexander Ziem, Heinrich-Heine University Düsseldorf

Table of Contents

Conference Program

Saturday, May 16, 2020

09:00–09:20   Opening Session

09:00–09:20   *Welcome and introduction to the workshop*
Collin F. Baker

09:20–11:00   Oral Session 1: Theoretical Papers

09:20–09:45   *Beyond Lexical Semantics: Notes on Pragmatic Frames*
Oliver Czulo, Alexander Ziem and Tiago Timponi Torrent

09:45–10:10   *Finding Corresponding Constructions in English and Japanese in a TED Talk Parallel Corpus using Frames-and-Constructions Analysis*
Kyoko Ohara

10:10–10:35   *Towards Reference-Aware FrameNet Annotation*
Levi Remijnse and Gosse Minnema

10:35–11:00   *Frame-Based Annotation of Multimodal Corpora: Tracking (A)Synchronies in Meaning Construction*
Frederico Belcavello, Marcelo Viridiano, Alexandre Diniz da Costa, Ely Matos and Tiago Timponi Torrent

11:00–11:30   Coffee Break

Beyond lexical semantics: notes on pragmatic frames

Oliver Czulo, Alexander Ziem, Tiago Timponi Torrent

Universität Leipzig, Heinrich-Heine Universität Düsseldorf, Federal University of Juiz de Fora

czulo@uni-leipzig.de, ziem@phil.hhu.de, tiago.torrent@ufjf.edu.br

Abstract

FrameNets as an incarnation of frame semantics have been set up to deal with lexicographic issues (cf. Fillmore and Baker 2010, among others). They are thus concerned with lexical units (LUs) and conceptual structures which categorize these together. These lexically-evoked frames, however, generally do not reflect pragmatic properties of constructions (LUs and other types of non-lexical constructions), such as expressing illocutions or establishing relations between speaker and hearer. From the viewpoint of a multilingual annotation effort, the Global FrameNet Shared Annotation Task, we discuss two phenomena, greetings and tag questions, highlighting the necessity both to investigate the role between construction and frame annotation and to develop pragmatic frames (and constructions) related to different facets of social interaction and situation-bound usage restrictions that are not explicitly lexicalized.

Keywords: frame semantics, construction grammar, pragmatic frames, tag questions, greetings, pragmatics, multilinguality

1. Introduction

The past two decades have witnessed the development of framenets[1] for several languages (Borin et al. 2010; Burchardt et al. 2006; Ohara et al. 2004; Subirats Rüggeberg and Petruck 2003; Torrent and Ellsworth 2013, and others). Relying more or less on the original Berkeley FrameNet infrastructure and data (Baker and Sato 2003), those initiatives have built independent resources whose alignment is currently being pursued under the Multilingual FrameNet Project (Gilardi and Baker 2018). Because the resulting resources are very diverse in nature, in 2016, during the International FrameNet Workshop held in Juiz de Fora, representatives of various framenet projects involved in the multilingual alignment initiative agreed on engaging in a shared annotation task so as to assess the complexity of the differences found between each language-specific resource.

In the following, we address one of these attested differences, namely linguistically encoded pragmatic information. Just like in constructionist analyses (Cappelle 2017), frame-based approaches to linguistic meaning tend to neglect conventionalized pragmatic properties (as an exception, see Blyth and Koike 2014). However, as we will argue, they are essential to a plethora of frames and constructions.

The starting point of our investigation are results obtained in the Global FrameNet[2] Shared Annotation Task (Torrent et al. 2018) in which an original text and its translations into other languages are all annotated for the frames in Berkeley FrameNet Data Release 1.7. The annotation teams were allowed to create Lexical Units (LUs) for their languages, but not to change, or create new, frames. Hence, mismatches between frames and the LUs associated with them are parameterized in the system for further analysis. Among the relevant questions are the comparability and alignment of frames, annotation

standards and applications of FrameNet data. The shared annotation task is devised such that comparable texts or originals with their translations from different genres may be annotated in multiple languages. The comparison between these annotations should highlight various differences such as between the conceptual structures of frames in two languages or the structure of certain parts of a framenet (e. g. the types of relations between a set of frames). Moreover, the resulting data can be used in applications, such as designing machine translation metrics (Czulo et al. 2019) and multilingual annotation projection[3]. Nonetheless, the kinds of analyses and applications that can be derived from the data in the shared annotation task are restricted to the existence of some lexically-specified material evoking a given frame.

In this paper, building on this restriction, we make the case for the oftentimes neglected pragmatic nature of many frames. Particularly, we analyse greetings and tag questions as instances of multi-word expressions evoking a frame. We show that these units do not refer to entity-, state-, attribute-, relation-, or event-related frames, but rather bear pragmatic value. Through the comparison of examples from English, Brazilian Portuguese and German, we illustrate why the annotation of pragmatic properties is informative on a cross-linguistic level: Frames and constructions associated with a conventionalized pragmatic meaning do not need to coincide in form, but may be linked to each other through their pragmatic meaning.

We begin by explaining why pragmatic frames should be addressed and included in any framenet and constructicon approach (Section 2). We do this by example of tag questions in English which highlights that pragmatic frames need not be linked to specific lexemes. In Section 3, we present examples on greetings and tag questions from the Shared Annotation Task in English, Brazilian Portuguese and German, discussing formal differences and how these could be bridged by introducing pragmatic frames in framenet-like annotation efforts. In Section 4, we sketch out basic aspects (potentially) included in the description of pragmatic frames, assuming that these shared aspects (in terms of family resemblances) motivate

---

[1] In the following, we use capital letters ("FrameNet") for referring to specific projects like, for example, to Berkeley FrameNet; in contrast, "framenet" is reserved for cases where no reference to a specific project is made.

[2] https://www.globalframenet.org/

[3] See http://www.ufjf.br/framenetbr-eng/summer-of-code/

pragmatic frames as a separate group of frames. We close with some suggestions as to the annotation and further empirical investigations on pragmatic frames.

2.   Why pragmatic frames? The case of tag questions in English

The notion of pragmatic frame - including phenomena sometimes also subsumed under the notion of "interactional" or "interactive frame" (Blyth and Koike 2014) - goes back to Goffman's early work on verbal interactions, building on what he has called "interactional frames" (Goffman 1961, 1967, 1974). Moreover, Fillmore's (1977, 1985) early terminological division between scenes and frames - only the latter being evoked by linguistic material - also made room for the existence of frames whose nature is different from that captured by a lexicographic analysis (for a discussion of Fillmore's notion of scene see Ziem 2014a, pp. 188–195).

Therefore, before diving into the kind of phenomena whose analyses motivated the notes in this paper, we must point out that the case for pragmatic frames presented here is restricted in two ways. First, it should not be interpreted as a claim towards the revision of any theory, neither Frame Semantics (Fillmore 1982) nor Frame Analysis (Goffman 1974), since both of them already had room for this type of frames in their frameworks. Second, it should not be taken as embracing every aspect of what falls under the umbrella of pragmatics in linguistics. Most importantly, following the Fillmore tradition, our notion of "pragmatic frames" crucially differs from the one introduced by Rohlfing and colleagues (2016) in that it only relates to pragmatic information conventionally attached to linguistic expressions and *not* to ad hoc inferences or framing activities in individual communicative experiences. Also, we do not intend to address frames as linguistic 'devices' that help explain linguistic phenomena of any kind, such as resolutions of (associative) anaphora (Ziem 2014b). Instead, our main point is that, in a framenet-like annotation setting, such as that provided by the Global FrameNet Shared Annotation Task or the one derived from constructicon-building efforts (Benjamin Lyngfelt et al. 2018), we should also take account of conventionalized pragmatic affordances and requirements that can be associated to the text units being annotated.

One example of such associations can be found in tag questions. Tag questions take the form of short questions mostly attached to a main declarative clause, such as in "You're coming to dinner with us, aren't you?". They do not necessarily require a response; in terms of Searle's speech act theory (1969), their illocutionary force lies elsewhere. Tag questions are said to be multi-functional, depending on the context they may serve as signals for emphasising, hedging, reinsurance, maintenance of intersubjectivity, among others (Columbus 2010; König 2017). Tag questions thus do not denote an entity (of whatever kind), they rather fulfill an interactive function in a communication between at least two parties.

In order to describe the frame-evoking potential of tag questions, single-word LUs cannot function as frame-evoking elements because they alone are not able to account for the meaning of the constructions they occur in (see Torrent et al. 2014 for a discussion of criteria to assign frame meaning to lexical items versus constructions). At first glance, there seems to be a rather simple solution to take account of tag questions within the construction-and-frame approach presented here. The frame-evoking power of the constructions cannot be traced back to single lexical elements but must rather be assigned to the phrase as a whole. In other words, tag questions are multi-word expressions that evoke frames in a holistic rather than a compositional fashion, in that the building blocks of the expressions cannot be considered units carrying frame-semantic information on their own.

Tag questions are multi-word expressions because they do not feature schematic CEs that can be filled in a productive or even semi-productive way (see Clausner and Croft 1997 for different degrees of productivity). Instead, different languages may provide specific inventories of tag questions, very much in parallel to substantive idioms (in the sense of Fillmore et al. 1988, p. 505f.) that take a variety of forms. This inventory must be treated just like LUs, that is, one-word units that evoke a frame. In this view, tag questions are LUs in that they evoke a frame in their own right.

However, it is anything but trivial to specify the frames evoked. In contrast to fully, or partially, schematic constructions, they cannot be said to evoke frames that mirror, at least partially, the valence of a lexical item that might or might not be part of the construct. Rather, it seems that they evoke frames that do not even consist of frame elements (FEs), usually defined as semantic roles that abstract away from the specific semantics of instances. Following Fillmore's proposal (1982, p. 117), it seems as if they do not evoke linguistic but interactional frames. Tag questions, in this regard, are not only substantive idioms but also what Fillmore, Kay and O'Connor (1988, p. 506) call idioms with a pragmatic point. However, the concept of interactional frame is far from being well-explored. From the standpoint of a construction-and-frame analysis, Ohara (2018) points out that a lot of questions still remain unanswered; it is neither clear what interactional frames really are nor, more crucially, how a FrameNet approach may address them; as a matter of fact, so far interactional frames are almost completely missing in FrameNet, the exceptions including the `Attention_getting` frame, as pointed out by Ohara (2018, p. 158). Therefore, our analysis also remains somewhat incomplete. However, aside from Japanese FrameNet, other initiatives, such as the German FrameNet, consider interactional frames highly relevant[4]. Moreover, the Global FrameNet Shared Annotation Task has created an opportunity to the discussion of such frames in a multilingual setting, as we discuss next.

---

[4] For more details, see www.german-framenet.de, last accessed: October 1, 2019.

3. Pragmatic frames in the Shared Annotation Task

The first text to currently be jointly annotated in the Global FrameNet Shared Annotation Task is the most viewed TED talk, given by Sir Ken Robinson with the title "Do schools kill creativity" (2006) which at the time of writing has been viewed more than 64 million times. The close captioning of the 20-minute talk in English contains 267 sentences. These subtitles have been translated to 63 languages by TED community members.

For the annotation, members of the English, Brazilian Portuguese and German annotation teams worked with the 1.7 release of Berkeley FrameNet. While this raises a number of questions as to cross-linguistic applicability of frames and framenets, this decision greatly facilitated the comparison of the annotations. The first thirty annotated and aligned sentences were fed into an evaluation system which is designed to automatically compute a similarity measure between a pair of sentences for machine translation evaluation purposes, based on semantic frames (Czulo et al. 2019).

What stood out in the analysis were a few sentences which, contrary to our intuition, would show a lack of similarity. Most notably this concerned the first two sentences between all three languages, with no frame overlap and no similarity at all. The reason was quickly identified: the first two sentences contained formulae of greetings which had not been annotated at all for English and Brazilian Portuguese, but with lexical frames in German (see Section 3.1). Still, it was clear that the German annotation was not an adequate description of the sentences, as it did not reflect the role of the expression in the sentence of being a greeting formula. Up to now, the FrameNet database does not include a Greeting frame, or any other frame that matches the pragmatic value of the unit under consideration.

Similarly, sentences with tag questions lead the evaluation system to calculate larger differences than anticipated, as they had been annotated again in German, but not in the other two languages. Especially with regard to those, however, Section 3.2 explains why annotating pragmatic frames is desirable and informative here: Tag questions vary in form between these languages, even as regards the lexical material used to form them, but in terms of an evaluation, they should be seen as (pragmatically) equivalent expressions. If pragmatic frames existed for tag questions, an automatic evaluation measure would benefit from more precisely assessing the similarity of two sentences in two languages.

3.1 Greetings[5]

The TED talk does not dive right into the topic but begins with some remarks by the speaker the function of which can at this point roughly be characterized as establishing a connection with the audience of the talk. This is spearheaded by a greeting, with the English and Brazilian Portuguese versions as in (1).

(1)   a. Good morning.
        b. Bom dia.

In the annotation effort, the English (1a) and Brazilian Portuguese (1b) variants remain unannotated. It is only in the case of the German annotation, that the greeting was annotated with frames, given in (2) :

(2)   [Guten$_{\text{Desirability}}$] [Morgen$_{\text{Calendric_unit}}$].
        Good   *morning*

Obviously, however, the frame annotation of the lexemes in itself with the frames Desirability and Calendric_unit does not point to (2) being a greeting. The annotation in (2) was originally provided with the goal of presenting an analysis of the semantic part of the constructional pattern licensing a greeting, much like proposed in (Fillmore et al. 2012). Note, however, that such an approach to (2) does not take us far either; the greeting formula instantiated in (2) does not allow for substantial internal variation, though premodification is possible in specific registers (e.g., *Schönen guten Morgen!* 'Top of the morning!', lit. "Beautiful good morning). Thus, it seems to be more adequate to treat *Guten Morgen* as multi-word unit (MWU; Ruppenhofer et al. 2016, p. 21), similar to other MWUs already included in Berkeley FrameNet, such as *good idea.n* evoking the Desirable_event frame in expressions like *X is a good idea*.

What an adequate semantic-pragmatic representation of the MWUs in (1-2) should include is the meaning of the expressive speech act, that is, the fact that it's a greeting. This situation type includes (a) the involvement of a speaker interacting with an addressee by means of the MWU, (b) time specification of the uttered MWU (roughly: before noon), and (c), by default, the supposition that it is the first encounter of speaker and addressee in a given time span. These specifications come with the frame evoked without materializing themselves as frame elements that are instantiated by parts of the MWU or the other linguistic material surrounding it.

Thus, pragmatic frames substantially differ from semantic frames in that they define situational settings as usage parameters; these settings resemble much more non-linguistic "scenes" (Fillmore 1985) attached to the MWU used than valency-based frames as incorporated in Berkeley FrameNet and the lexicographically oriented initiatives for other languages that derived from it.

Looking at examples (1) and (2), we can state that the internal frame structure for the greeting at hand is the same in all three languages. As a different case, let us look at a construction which is more variable across languages and allows different interpretations in (3):

(3)   a. How are you?
        b. Como   estão?
            How   be.3.PERS
        c. Wie   geht es Ihnen?
            How   go   it   you.3.PERS.DAT

While the English and Brazilian Portuguese versions are only superficially different (with a pro-drop in the Brazilian version), the German version uses a different verbal lexeme: *gehen* 'go'[6]. When taken literally, this would evoke a different frame than the verb *be* in English or Brazilian Portuguese, but this annotation of a 'literal default' meaning would not reflect the pragmatics behind the formula. The annotation of an interactional frame would indicate that there is a greeting with the function to open an interaction. Moreover, if interpreted literally in the given situation and answered with something like *Terrible, my dog just died*, in this kind of interactional scenario, (3a-c) would not be successful.

As Bunt and colleagues (2010, p. 2549) point out, though, assigning a singular function to a linguistic item could run "into the problem that the same linguistic form can often be used to express different communicative functions." In the case of greetings like *How are you*, a literal interpretation besides the function of opening an interaction can easily be imagined, such as a doctor greeting a patient, where the patient is actually expected to answer according to the question. Still, primarily pragmatic items such as greetings may be among the easiest to detect in texts for purposes of annotation, notwithstanding other questions of interpretation. Moreover, as it is already the case for polysemous lexemes in any FrameNet, expressions such as *How are you* could be easily associate to different sets of frames - pragmatic or not.

An answer of how such interpretations could be modelled can be found in the framework of Systemic-Functional Linguistics (Halliday 1973; Halliday and Matthiessen 2004). Distinctions such as between the ideational and the interpersonal function could help model which kind of function is in the foreground and should be guiding the interaction, which types of interactions are expected etc.

3.2 Tag questions

In the annotated sample text, we find three instances of tag questions. (4) exemplifies one of them.

(4)   a.   It's been great, hasn't it?

        b.   Tem   sido   ótimo,
            have.PRES.3SG   *be.PART*   *great*
            não tem?
            no   have.PRES.3SG

        c.   Es war   großartig,
            It   be.PST.3SG great
            nicht wahr?
            not   true

The tag questions in English and Brazilian Portuguese, illustrated in (4a-b), feature finite forms of the auxiliaries *have* and *ter* ('have'), respectively. In contrast, the German tag question is realized in the form of a negated adjective *nicht wahr* (lit. 'not true'). It is obvious that a frame-based annotation of the respective LUs is insufficient to capture the pragmatic function of the tag

questions. LUs such as *have.v* and *ter.v* cannot be said to evoke a frame that refers to any kind of 'assurance' that the speaker wants to express. Moreover, the Brazilian construction can also feature the ver *ser* ('be') in the tag, instead of repeating the auxiliary used in the main clause. Even though the German LU *wahr.a* ('true') points to this direction, it still fails to trigger a specific frame that provides the pragmatically relevant information required.

Another case in point relates to the tag questions exemplified in (5).

(5)   a.   I mean, Sirena last night was a marvel, wasn't she?

        b.   Sirena   ontem   a   noite foi
            Sirena   yesterday at   night
            be.PST.3SG
            uma maravilha, não foi?
            one wonder   no be.PST.3SG

        c.   Sirena   gestern   Abend   war
            Sirena   yesterday evening be.PST.3SG
            wunderbar, nichtwahr?
            marvellous not   true

Again, English and Brazilian Portuguese include the auxiliaries *be.v* and *ser.v* ('to be') whereas the German tag question is equivalent to the one introduced in (4). Just like the auxiliaries in (4), the verbs in the English and Brazilian Portuguese instances cannot be said to evoke a frame that point to the pragmatics of tag questions (Columbus 2010). To be successful, we need an integrated frame-and-construction approach that also accounts for both the clausal form (sub-aux inverted clause, where applicable) underlying tag questions and context requirements to be met. The latter includes not only (a) the existence of a pre-established referent to which the personal pronoun anaphorically refers, be it a person ("haven't *you*") or an entity or any kind of propositionally expressed state of affair ("hasn't it"); (b) also, the tense of the verb included in a tag question must be consistent with the context, more precisely with previous uses of tenses. In the next section, we provide a proposal as to how such an approach may be implemented in practical terms.

4.   Suggestions for a basic structure of pragmatic frames

Conventionalized pragmatic frames are viewed here as situation- or genre-bound concepts specified by a set of conditions defining adequate uses at peculiar occasions. These frames, like greetings and tag questions, help organise interaction between two or more parties rather than relating to conceptual structures representing objects, attributes, relations, states or events. These parties can be individuals or groups with members being humans or ascribed human-likeness (real or imagined entities such as AI machines, fairies, aliens etc.).

Presumably, this commonality of pragmatic frames and the conceptual systematicities resulting therefrom groups these frames in terms of family resemblances (for suggestions on operationalisation see Ziem 2014a, pp.

297–299). Having at this point looked at only two types of pragmatic frames, especially with regard to the variety of meanings that tag questions can express, we expect that central aspects of pragmatic frames may relate to, but are not limited to,

- circumstances such as time, in-/formal type of the occasion licensing the use of the target expression,
- situational presuppositions, including artefacts, such as materials and objects (e.g. water for baptizing), recipient/audience addressed,
- text- and sociolinguistic affordances specific to the type of communication, including, for example, choice of register and text genre,
- further sociolinguistically relevant factors including diatopic and diastratic variation, roles and statuses of the parties involved and how they may evolve during communication, relations to parties outside of the communication situation at hand, face-saving actions of parties involved.

Importantly, pragmatic information of this kind needs to be integrated in a frame description, regardless of the fact that they are not part of the target valence frame since they do not necessarily instantiate semantic roles (FEs). Thus, pragmatic frames differ substantially from semantic frames in that they relate to conditions of appropriate use in specific situational settings. While we expect that the configuration of pragmatic frames vastly differs between cultures[7], or even between communities within a culture, pragmatic frames should, due to their common core structure, be more comparable between each other even across languages than many object-, state-, attribute, relation- or event-related frames.

We also assume that in one way or another, pragmatic frames are always at work during communication, though not necessarily evoked by linguistic items. Most prominently, Goffman (1974) argued that human interaction is in general framed by its embedding situational setting. Such frames, however, seem to be fundamentally different from current FrameNet frames. In terms of frame semantic theory, this is not problematic in principle, as in the early version, Fillmore already pointed out that frames (or, in the old terminology, 'scenes') are linked and co-activate each other e. g. "by virtue of [...] their contexts of occurrence" (Fillmore 1975, p. 124); i. e. unlike often practiced in annotation, there is no reason to believe that a linguistic expression or any other frame-evoking material or circumstance necessarily evoke one and only one frame. As pointed out above in 3.1, Systemic-Functional Linguistic could provide a framework to model how semantic and pragmatic aspects of interactions are composed and thus interact with each other. Currently, however, we miss an integrative approach, combining FrameNet frames with a more general situation-bound and context-sensitive frame theory that addresses semantic, pragmatic and interactional properties of communication on a par.

The practical question arising from this is when to annotate which frame and what these frames should be. The examples discussed here may leave little room for interpretation, but in cases e. g. in which two variants of an expression exist which reflect different levels of formality, the choice may not be straightforward. Annotation will probably depend on the question whether, and to what extent, the lexical-semantic or pragmatic meaning is in the focus of the current research interest. As for the questions of what types of frames we may need, previous work by Bunt and colleagues (2010) on an ISO standard for annotating interaction types in dialogues may be a good starting point. In their proposed taxonomy of functions, they first distinguish between information-transfer functions and action-discussion functions, then specifying various types of requests, suggestions, denials etc. In combination with systemic-functional aspects, the taxonomy could be extended to include further interactional aspects and be reflected in the pragmatic sub-group of frames in framenets in different languages accordingly.

5. Conclusions: pragmatic frames and constructions in the constructicon

In this paper, we made the case for considering pragmatic frames as important components of any frame-based repository such as FrameNet. One reason for this is that pragmatic aspects - just like semantic roles - may well belong to the conventionalized content of linguistic signs. This forces us to extend the description of frames in such a way that it includes not only a well-defined configuration of semantic roles (FEs) but also conditions for using the frame-evoking elements adequately. It still remains an open issue, however, in which way pragmatic information can, and should, be built into a frame definition. One option is to introduce a new category "pragmatic roles"; yet, it is anything but clear how to consistently define such roles in parallel to the well-established notion of semantic roles. Another option is to specify usage requirements in the prose part of a frame definition. Yet another option is to enrich 'traditional' frame-semantic descriptions by pragmatic templates as introduced by Liedtke (2013, 2018).

Not surprisingly, very similar issues arise with reference to construction entries (Cappelle 2017; Finkbeiner 2019). Beyond the pragmatic frames addressed here, there is assumingly a huge variety of other types of both pragmatic frames and pragmatic constructions peculiar to a language. Even though these units challenge standard frame-semantic and constructionist approaches in several ways, we have no general reservation about the integration of these units into the type of constructicon that we have in mind (Ziem and Flick 2019). Without doubt, however, it is an empirically challenging task to identify and describe pragmatic frames and constructions in a comprehensive way.

As a first guess, we consider the following examples, among others, as good candidates for LU or MWU evoking pragmatic frames or construction: Greeting and leave-taking expressions (*Good morning, Dear X, Goodbye, Kind regards*); performative verbs and

---

[7] We use the term with all reservations as to what an 'exact' definition of 'culture' could be.

expressions (*I baptize you*); deictic and multimodal constructions (*so*+ADJ+gesture; Ziem 2017); expressions of preference (*von wegen* 'No way!'); implicatures; text genre-specific constructions (e.g., pro drop in recipes); information structure (*it was the girl who...*). Taking phenomena like this as a benchmark (also for forthcoming efforts in the Global FrameNet Shared Annotation Task), we consider it worthwhile to gradually develop a robust and sophisticated concept of "pragmatic frame" on an empirical basis.

6. Bibliographic References

Blyth, C., & Koike, D. (2014). Interactive frames and grammatical constructions. In S. K. Bourns & L. L. Myers (Eds.), *Perspectives on Linguistic Structure and Context: studies in honor of Knud Lambrecht* (pp. 87–108). Amsterdam ; Philadelphia: John Benjamins Publishing Company.

Bunt, H., Alexandersson, J., Carletta, J., Choe, J.-W., Chengyu Fang, A., Hasida, K., et al. (2010). Towards an ISO standard for dialogue act annotation. In *Seventh conference on International Language Resources and Evaluation (LREC'10)*. La Valette, Malta. https://hal.inria.fr/inria-00544997

Cappelle, B. (2017). What's pragmatics doing outside constructions? In I. Depraetere & R. Salkie (Eds.), *Semantics and Pragmatics: Drawing a Line* (pp. 115–151). Cham: Springer International Publishing. https://doi.org/10.1007/978-3-319-32247-6_8

Clausner, T. C., & Croft, W. (1997). Productivity and Schematicity in Metaphors. *Cognitive Science*, *21*(3), 247–282.

Columbus, G. (2010). "Ah lovely stuff, eh?" - invariant tag meanings and usage across three varieties of English. In S. Th. Gries, S. Wulff, & M. Davies (Eds.), *Corpus-linguistic applications: current studies, new directions* (Vol. 71, pp. 82–105). Brill | Rodopi. https://doi.org/10.1163/9789042028012_007

Czulo, O., Torrent, T. T., Matos, E., Diniz da Costa, A., & Kar, D. (2019). Designing a Frame-Semantic Machine Translation Evaluation Metric. In *Proceedings of The Second Workshop on Human-Informed Translation and Interpreting Technology (HiT-IT 2019)*. Varna, Bulgaria.

Czulo, O., Torrent, T., Willich, A., Ziem, A., & Laviola, A. (submitted). A multilingual approach to the interaction between frames and constructions: towards a joint framework and methodology.

Fillmore, C. J. (1975). An alternative to checklist theories of meaning. In *Annual Meeting of the Berkeley Linguistics Society* (Vol. 1, pp. 123–131).

Fillmore, C. J. (1977). Scenes-and-frames semantics, Linguistic Structures Processing. In A. Zampolli (Ed.), *Fundamental studies in computer science* (pp. 55–88). North Holland Publishing.

Fillmore, C. J. (1982). Frame Semantics. In The Linguistic Society of Korea (Ed.), *Linguistics in the Morning Calm. Selected Papers of SICOL-1981* (pp. 111–137). Seoul: Hanshin.

Fillmore, C. J. (1985). Frames and the semantics of understanding. *Quaderni di Semantica*, *6*(2), 222–254.

Fillmore, C. J., & Baker, C. F. (2010). A Frames Approach to Semantic Analysis. In B. Heine & H. Narrog (Eds.), *The Oxford Handbook of Linguistic Analysis* (pp. 313–339). Oxford: Oxford University Press.

Fillmore, C. J., Kay, P., & O'Connor, M. C. (1988). Regularity and Idiomaticity in Grammatical Constructions: The Case of "Let Alone." *Language*, *64*(3), 501–538.

Finkbeiner, R. (2019). Reflections on the role of pragmatics in Construction Grammar. *Constructions and Frames*, *11*(2), 171–192. https://doi.org/10.1075/cf.00027.fin

Goffman, E. (1961). *Encounters: Two studies in the sociology of interaction*. Indianapolis: Bobbys-Merrils.

Goffman, E. (1967). *Interaction rituals: Essays on face to face behavior*. New York: Anchor.

Goffman, E. (1974). *Frame analysis: An essay on the organization of experience*. Cambridge, MA, USA: Harvard University Press.

Halliday, M. A. K. (1973). *Explorations in the functions of language*. London: Arnold.

Halliday, M. A. K., & Matthiessen, C. M. I. M. (2004). *An introduction to functional grammar* (3 (revised by C.M.I.M. Matthiessen).). London: Arnold.

König, K. (2017). Question tags als Diskursmarker? Ansätze zu einer systematischen Beschreibung von "ne" im gesprochenen Deutsch. In H. Blühdorn, A. Deppermann, H. Helmer, & T. Spranz-Fogasy (Eds.), *Diskursmarker im Deutschen: Reflexionen und Analysen* (pp. 233–258). Göttingen: Verlag für Gesprächsforschung.

Liedtke, F. (2013). Pragmatic templates and free enrichment. In F. Liedtke & C. Schulze (Eds.), *Beyond words: content, context, and inference* (pp. 183–205). Berlin ; Boston: De Gruyter Mouton, Walter De Gruyter GmbH.

Liedtke, F. (2018). Frames, Skripte und pragmatische Templates. In M. Wengeler & A. Ziem (Eds.), *Diskurs, Wissen, Sprache: Linguistische Annäherungen an kulturwissenschaftliche Fragen* (pp. 115–135). Berlin ; Boston: De Gruyter.

Lyngfelt, Benjamin, Borin, L., Ohara, K., & Torrent, T. T. (Eds.). (2018). *Constructicography: Constructicon development across languages*. John Benjamins.

Ohara, K. (2018). The relations between frames and constructions: A proposal from the Japanese

FrameNet constructicon. In Benja Lyngfelt, L. Borin, K. Ohara, & T. T. Torrent (Eds.), *Constructicography: Constructicon development across languages* (pp. 141–163). Amsterdam; Philadelphia: Benjamins.

Rohlfing, K. J., Wrede, B., Vollmer, A.-L., & Oudeyer, P.-Y. (2016). An alternative to mapping a word onto a concept in language acquisition: Pragmatic frames. *Frontiers in Psychology*, *7*, 1–18. https://doi.org/10.3389/fpsyg.2016.00470

Searle, J. R. (1969). *Speech acts : an essay in the philosophy of language*. Cambridge: Univ. Pr.

Torrent, T. T., Lage, L. M., Sampaio, T. F., da Silva Tavares, T., & da Silva Matos, E. E. (2014). Revisiting border conflicts between framenet and construction grammar: Annotation policies for the brazilian portuguese constructicon. *Constructions and Frames*, *6*(1), 34–51. https://doi.org/10.1075/cf.6.1.03tor

Ziem, A. (2014a). *Frames of understanding in text and discourse: Theoretical foundations and descriptive applications*. (C. Schwerin, Trans.). Amsterdam ; Philadelphia: John Benjamins Publishing Company.

Ziem, A. (2014b). Frames and constructions enhance text coherence: The case of DNI resolutions in spoken discourse. *Yearbook of the German Cognitive Linguistics Association*, *2*(1), 3–20.

Ziem, A. (2017). Do we really need a Multimodal Construction Grammar? *Linguistics Vanguard: Special issue "Towards a multimodal construction grammar," 3*(1), 1–9. https://doi.org/10.1515/lingvan-2016-0095

7. Language Resource References

Baker, C. F., & Sato, H. (2003). The framenet data and software. In *Proceedings of the 41st Annual Meeting on Association for Computational Linguistics* (Vol. 2, pp. 161–164). Association for Computational Linguistics.

Borin, L., Dannélls, D., Forsberg, M., Gronostaj, M. T., & Kokkinakis, D. (2010). The past meets the present in Swedish FrameNet++. In *14th EURALEX international congress* (pp. 269–281).

Burchardt, A., Erk, K., Frank, A., Kowalski, A., Pado, S., & Pinkal, M. (2006). The SALSA corpus: a German corpus resource for lexical semantics. In *Proceedings of LREC 2006* (pp. 969–974). Genoa, Italy.

Fillmore, C. J., Lee-Goldman, R. R., & Rhomieux, R. (2012). The FrameNet Constructicon. In H. C. Boas & I. A. Sag (Eds.), *Sign-Based Construction Grammar*. (pp. 309–372). Stanford: CSLI Publications.

Gilardi, L., & Baker, C. F. (2018). Learning to align across languages: Toward multilingual framenet. In *Proceedings of the International FrameNet Workshop* (pp. 13–22).

Ohara, K., Fujii, S., Ohori, T., Suzuki, R., Saito, H., & Ishizaki, S. (2004). The Japanese FrameNet project: an introduction. In *Proceedings of the satellite workshop "Building lexical resources from semantically annotated corpora"* (pp. 9–11). Presented at the Fourth international conference on Language Resources and Evaluation, European Language Resources Association.

Robinson, K. (2006). *Do schools kill creativity?* Presented at the TED - ideas worth spreading. https://www.ted.com/talks/sir_ken_robinson_do_schools_kill_creativity. Accessed 20 February 2020

Ruppenhofer, J., Ellsworth, M., Petruck, M. R. L., Johnson, C. R., Baker, C. F., & Scheffczyk, J. (2016). FrameNet II: Extended Theory and Practice. https://framenet2.icsi.berkeley.edu/docs/r1.7/book.pdf

Subirats Rüggeberg, C., & Petruck, M. (2003). Surprise: Spanish FrameNet! In E. Hajičová, A. Kotěšovcová, & J. Mirovský (Eds.), *Proceedings of the workshop on Frame semantics*. Presented at the XVII International Congress of Linguists, Prague: Matfyzpress.

Torrent, T. T., & Ellsworth, M. (2013). Behind the Labels: Criteria for Defining Analytical Categories in FrameNet Brasil. *Veredas*, *17*, 44–65.

Torrent, T. T., Ellsworth, M., Baker, C. F., & Matos, E. (2018). The Multilingual FrameNet Shared Annotation Task: a Preliminary Report. In T. T. Torrent, L. Borin, & C. F. Baker (Eds.), *Proceedings of the International FrameNet Workshop 2018: Multilingual Framenets and Constructicons*. Paris, France: European Language Resources Association (ELRA).

Ziem, A., & Flick, J. (2019). Constructicography at work: implementation and application of the German Constructicon. In *Yearbook of the German Cognitive Linguistics Association*,

Acknowledgements

Research presented in this paper is funded by CAPES/PRODRAL and DAAD PPP Programs, under the grant numbers 88887.144043/2017-00 and 57390800, respectively.

Proceedings of the International FrameNet Workshop 2020: Towards a Global, Multilingual FrameNet, pages 8–12
Language Resources and Evaluation Conference (LREC 2020), Marseille, 11–16 May 2020
© European Language Resources Association (ELRA), licensed under CC-BY-NC

Finding Corresponding Constructions in English and Japanese in a TED Talk Parallel Corpus using Frames-and-Constructions Analysis

Kyoko Ohara
Keio University/RIKEN
4-1-1 Hiyoshi, Kohoku-ku, Yokohama City 223-8521, Japan
ohara@hc.st.keio.ac.jp

Abstract

This paper reports on an effort to search for corresponding constructions in English and Japanese in a TED Talk parallel corpus, using frames-and-constructions analysis (Ohara, 2019; Ohara and Okubo, 2020; cf. Czulo, 2013, 2017). The purpose of the paper is two-fold: (1) to demonstrate the validity of frames-and-constructions analysis to search for corresponding constructions in typologically unrelated languages; and (2) to assess whether the "Do schools kill creativity?" TED Talk parallel corpus, annotated in various languages for Multilingual FrameNet, is a good starting place for building a multilingual constructicon. The analysis showed that similar to our previous findings involving texts in a Japanese to English bilingual children's book, the TED Talk bilingual transcripts include pairs of constructions that share similar pragmatic functions. While the TED Talk parallel corpus constitutes a good resource for frame semantic annotation in multiple languages, it may not be the ideal place to start aligning constructions among typologically unrelated languages. Finally, this work shows that the proposed method, which focuses on heads of sentences, seems valid for searching for corresponding constructions in transcripts of spoken data, as well as in written data of typologically-unrelated languages.

Keywords: Japanese FrameNet, pragmatic function, multilingual conststructicon

1. Introduction

This paper reports on an effort to find corresponding Japanese and English grammatical constructions in a TED Talk parallel corpus, using the frames-and-constructions analysis method proposed in Ohara (2019) and Ohara and Okubo (2020). The method focuses on heads of sentences in language, where a head is defined as "the most contentful word that most closely denotes the same function as the phrase (or clause) as a whole (cf. Croft, In Preparation: 417)." The purpose of the paper is two-fold: (1) to demonstrate the validity of frames-and-construction analysis as a methodology to search for corresponding constructions in a pair of typologically-unrelated languages such as English and Japanese; and (2) to assess whether the "Do schools kill creativity?" TED Talk parallel corpus, whose sentences have been annotated in frame-semantic terms in various languages, including English, Brazilian Portuguese, French, German, and Japanese for Multilingual FrameNet, is a good starting place to align constructions for building a multilingual/contrastive constructicon.

Our analysis revealed the following:

- There are indeed pairs of sentences that constitute instances of corresponding constructions in English and Japanese that share similar pragmatic functions in the TED Talk bilingual transcripts, similar to our previous findings for texts in a Japanese–English bilingual children's book;
- While the TED Talk parallel corpus constitutes a good resource for frame semantic annotation, it may not be the ideal place to start aligning constructions across typologically-unrelated languages, likely as a result of characteristics of the genre of subtitles;
- The proposed frames-and-constructions analysis method, an approach that focuses on heads of sentences, seems valid to search for corresponding

constructions in transcripts of spoken data, as well as in written data of typologically-unrelated languages.

The organization of the rest of the paper is as follows. Section 2 discusses background to the study. Section 3 presents the hypothesis, method, and the results of the analysis. Section 4 addresses the functional mismatches in the parallel corpus, the validity of the method, and the appropriateness of the corpus as a starting point for aligning constructions in a multilingual constructicon. Finally, Section 5 provides a conclusion and prospects for future work.

2. Related Work

The frames-and-constructions analysis method describes meanings and structures of sentences, focusing on the semantic frames evoked by various linguistic expressions in the sentences. It is grounded in the theories of Frame Semantics and Construction Grammar (Fillmore and Baker, 2010; Fillmore, 2013). Czulo (2013, 2017, elsewhere) proposed this method as a translation model, based on analyses of German and English parallel data[1]. Those works hypothesized that ideally the semantic frame of the translation matches that of the original (the primacy of the frame hypothesis). However, often cases of frame mismatches exist between pairs of source and target sentences and Czulo (2013, 2017) argued that structural divergence can be a cause for frame mismatch, in addition to cultural, typological, and perspectival differences. Czulo also observed that even when a frame mismatch exists because of structural divergence between source and target sentences, the two sentences may share the same pragmatic function. This observation led to the suggestion that the function of a construction may take precedence over exact frame match.

---

[1] Czulo uses the term "constructions-and-frames analysis" in Czulo (2013) but since frame comparison is a crucial step in this method (cf. Section 3.2), I will use the term "frames-and-constructions analysis" in this paper.

Building on Czulo's (2013) work, Ohara (2019) and Ohara & Okubo (2020) examined whether frames-and-constructions analysis is a valid methodology to search for and align comparable constructions between Japanese and English, a pair of typologically unrelated languages. That work analyzed 674 pairs of Japanese and English sentences in a bilingual children's book. They identified the semantic frames evoked by the heads of source and target sentences and found 483 pairs of frame mismatches. Among them, 106 pairs exhibited structural divergences. Among the 106 pairs of structurally divergent sentences, 55 pairs exhibited the same pragmatic functions (cf. Table 1, Section 3.3). In other words, the study found corresponding constructions in Japanese and English based on pragmatic functions, even in cases of structural divergence and frame mismatches. Those results suggested the usefulness of frames-and-constructions analysis for finding comparable constructions across typologically unrelated languages such as Japanese and English, where structural divergence is well-documented.

However, the study that Ohara (2019) and Ohara and Okubo (2020) reported is preliminary; and no study exists that explored the validity of the method in analyzing translation from English to Japanese, spoken language, genres other than narratives, and anything other than children's language. Thus, this paper applies the method to analyze English and Japanese sentences that appear in the "Do schools kill creativity?" TED Talk parallel corpus. Analysts already have annotated this corpus with semantic frames and FEs in various languages for Multilingual FrameNet.

3. Frames-and-Constructions Analysis of TED Talk Parallel Transcripts

This section is divided into three parts that describe the following: (1) hypotheses formed prior to the present analysis; (2) details about the proposed method; and (3) results of the analysis on the TED Talk bilingual transcripts.

3.1 Hypotheses

Prior to the present analysis, we formed three hypotheses about characteristics of the English and Japanese sentences in the TED Talk parallel transcripts. First, the TED Talk "Do schools kill creativity?" is a presentation aimed at persuading its audience. Thus, one hypothesis is that the English original transcript would include many constructions that exhibit pragmatic functions. Second, the Japanese version is a translated version of the English original transcript. Consequently, another hypothesis is that the Japanese translation would contain constructions that exhibit similar pragmatic functions as those in the English original. Finally, a third hypothesis is the likelihood of finding corresponding English and Japanese constructions sharing the same or similar pragmatic functions, in spite of also showing frame mismatch and structural divergence.

3.2 Method

The actual adopted steps of the frames-and-constructions analysis in this study appear below. The analysis concentrated on sentence-level grammatical constructions.

1. Head Identification:
   Identify the head of each of the English and Japanese sentence pairs.
2. Frame Comparison:
   Determine the semantic frames evoked by the heads of the English and Japanese sentence pairs; check for frame mismatch; exclude two kinds of cases from frame mismatch. One kind has to do with cases in which a pair of English and Japanese sentences ultimately evokes the same set of semantic frames through frame integration (integration of frames evoked by words and phrases in a sentence that ultimately leads to an understanding of the whole sentence) within each sentence. The other kind involves cases in which the two frames evoked by the English and Japanese heads are related via any FrameNet frame-to-frame relations (Ruppenhofer et al., 2016).
3. Structural Comparison:
   Identify the structure of each of the English and Japanese sentences; check for English and Japanese structural divergence.
4. Functional Comparison:
   Identify the functions of the English and Japanese constructions.

3.3 Results

We examined 242 English original sentences from the TED Talk. Sometimes one English sentence was translated into Japanese with more than one sentence; at other times, multiple English sentences were translated into one Japanese sentence. We concentrated on analyzing sentence pairs in which the English original sentence is more or less straightforwardly translated into Japanese with one sentence. There were 122 such sentence pairs.

Table 1 summarizes the results of our analysis using the steps described in Section 3.2. The table shows the numbers of sentence pairs that exhibit frame match/mismatch, structural divergence, and functional match in the TED Talk parallel corpus, in comparison with those in a bilingual children's book *Anpanman I* (cf. Section 2).

	TED (E to J)	*Anpanman* (J to E)
1) Sentence Pairs	122	674
2) Frame Match in 1)	75	191
2') Frame Mismatch in 1)	42	483
3) Structural Divergence in 2')	22	106
4) Functional Match in 3)	9	55

Table 1: The numbers of frame match/mismatch, structural divergence, and functional match in TED

There was one sentence pair that ultimately evoke the same set of semantic frames through frame integration. In addition, there were four sentence pairs in which the two frames evoked by the English and Japanese heads are related via a FrameNet frame-to-frame relation (cf. Step 3 above). These are the reasons why the sum of the number of frame match and that of frame mismatch does not equal the total number of sentence pairs in the TED Talk parallel corpus.

Let us describe the results in relation to the three hypotheses in Section 3.1. Our first hypothesis was that the English original transcript would contain many constructions that exhibit pragmatic functions. Indeed, the English version of the talk includes sentence structures that focus either the whole or parts of a sentence, such as pseudo-cleft sentences (1), repetition (2), emphasis (3), and cataphora (4).

(1) Pseudo-cleft:

a. *Actually, <u>what I find is</u> everybody has an interest in education.* (#13)
b. *<u>What we do know is</u>, if you're not prepared to be wrong, you'll never come up with anything original -- if you're not prepared to be wrong.* (#77)

(2) Repetition:

a. *What we do know is, <u>if you're not prepared to be wrong</u>, you'll never come up with anything original -- <u>if you're not prepared to be wrong</u>.* (#77)
b. *Picasso once said this, <u>he said</u> that all children are born artists.* (#84)

(3) Emphasis:

    <u>My contention is that</u> creativity now is as important in education as literacy, and we should treat it with the same status. (#43)

(4) Cataphora:

a. *Picasso once said <u>this</u>, he said that all children are born artists.* (#84)
b. *If you were to visit education, as an alien, and say "What's <u>it</u> for, public education?"* (#141)

Second, we expected to find in the Japanese translation constructions with similar pragmatic functions as those of the English original. The results of the analysis refuted that expectation. Except for the translation of (4a), listed below as (4'a), which uses cataphora to emphasize a quote from Picasso, none of the Japanese translations of the aforementioned English sentences (1-4) has structures that focus the whole or a part of the sentence or emphasize the speaker's claims. This situation contrasts with that of the English original sentences.

(1')

a. *jissai daremo ga   kyôiku ni kanshin ga arundesu*
   actually everybody NOM education DAT interest NOM exist
   literal translation[2]. 'Actually, everybody has an interest in education.'
b. (=(2'a))
   ... machigaeru koto o   osoreteitara kesshite
   make.mistake thing ACC be.afraid   never
   dokusôteki na mono nado omoitsuk   anai
   original   thing etc. come.up.with NEG
   '... if (you are) afraid of making mistakes, (you) will never come up with anything original.'

(3')

   sôzôsei wa shikiji nôryoku to   onaji kurai

---

creativy TOP literacy ability   COM same degree
kyôiku ni   hitsuyô desu
education DAT necessity COP
'Creativity is as necessary to education as literacy.'

(4')

a. (=(2'b))
   *Pikaso wa   katsute <u>**kô**</u>   îmashita*
   Picaso   TOP once   like.this said
   "kodomo wa   mina umarenagara no âtisuto da"
   children TOP all   born   GEN artist COP
   'Picasso once said like this, "children are all born artists."'
b. *moshi eirian ga   kyôiku   genba ni yatteki tara*
   if   alien NOM education site   LOC come COND
   "kô kyôiku tte   nan no   tame ni   aru no?"
   public education CONJ what NOM purpose DAT exist Q
   to   hushigini omou deshô
   QUOTE mysteriously think   would
   'If an alien comes to (an) education site, (s/he) would wonder, "for what purpose does public education exist?"'

The third hypothesis concerned finding English and Japanese constructions that exhibit a structural divergence and frame mismatch, yet have the same pragmatic function. The analysis indeed found instances of such cases. (5) is an example. The heads of the English and Japanese sentences in (5) are *stop* and *surunja arimasen* 'don't!' respectively (Step 1, Section 3.1). The English and Japanese structures are of the `Imperative` construction (cxn) and of `V-surunjanai` cxn respectively (Step 2). The head *stop* in the English sentence evokes the `Activity_stop` frame, while *surunja arimasen* in the Japanese sentence evokes the `Preventing_or_letting` frame (Step 3). Finally, both sentences function to order the addressee to stop an activity (Step 4).

(5) Structural divergence, frame mismatch, and same pragmatic function:

E: *And <u>**stop**</u>*[Activity_stop] *speaking like that.* (#105)
J: *sonna   hanashi kata <u>**surunja arimasen**</u>*[Preventing_or_letting]
   that.way speech   way don't
   'Don't speak like that.'

    E: `Imperative` construction (cxn)
    J: `V-surunjanai` cxn

    E&J: Prohibiting function

4. Discussion

This section discusses functional mismatches in English and Japanese in the parallel transcripts, the validity of the frames-and-constructions analysis method, and the appropriateness of using the TED Talk transcripts for aligning constructions for building a multilingual constructicon.

4.1 Functional mismatches in the TED parallel transcripts

This subsection discusses the results with respect to the second hypothesis in Section 3.1. The second hypothesis in Section 3.1 was that the Japanese translation would contain constructions that exhibit similar pragmatic functions as those in the English original. It turned out that English sentence structures that focus certain of their elements were often NOT translated into Japanese using constructions with similar pragmatic functions.

It may be a consequence of properties of the genre, specifically, of the Japanese transcript. While the English version is an actual transcript of the oral presentation, the Japanese version is primarily a set of subtitles, that is, captions displayed at the bottom of a screen that translate the English transcript. In fact, the sentences in the Japanese version tend to be short and telegraphic, presumably because of the limited space allocated for subtitles and the requirement to be displayed in synch with the audio-visual information in the video clip. Thus, what makes sense is to think of the Japanese transcript as a set of subtitles, something that should be seen and read together with the video clip as part of multimodal information, NOT as a translation. This study has yet to conduct a thorough analysis of the video clip. Some sort of substitute for the pragmatic function to focus a sentence element missing in many of the Japanese sentence structures may be found in the audio-visual information (including speech and gestural information) in the video clip.

4.2 Validity of the Frames-and-Constructions Analysis

Since we were able to found pairs of corresponding constructions in English and Japanese in the TED transcripts, the four steps of the frames-and-constructions analysis proposed in Section 3.2 seem useful in analyzing transcripts of spoken data, in addition to written data. This assessment is legitimate since the concepts embodied in the four steps (i.e., head, sentence structure, semantic frame, and function) are also found in transcripts of spoken data. The proposed four steps particularly emphasize the notion of head. Since the concept is considered universal and since heads can be found in sentences in transcripts of spoken data as well, identifying sentential heads first facilitates accurate linguistic analysis of sentence structures (cf. Croft, In Preparation; Croft et al. 2017).

In this respect, note Lyngfelt et al.'s (2018) proposal concerning alignment of constructions across languages. Based on the analyses of English, Swedish, and Brazilian Portuguese constructions, that work proposed a four-step comparison of constructions (Lyngfelt et al. 2018: 267). The first step is to ask the question "is there a corresponding construction, or set of constructions, in the target language?". While finding corresponding constructions among typologically related languages such as the three languages above may be easy, at least in the case of Japanese and English, identifying corresponding structures is quite difficult. Analyzing a parallel corpus using the frames-and-constructions analysis method, which primarily relies on the concept of head, seems to be a more straightforward way of conducting the analysis.

The proposed four steps of frames-and-constructions analysis predicts that even when frame mismatch and structural divergence are present, if functions are the same, then the two constructions can be considered

corresponding. Pairs of constructions exist in the TED Talk parallel transcripts that share the same pragmatic function while exhibiting frame mismatch and structural divergence. It may thus be possible to hypothesize that the function of a construction takes precedence over exact frame match as Czulo suggests. However, it is beyond the scope of this present paper to test this hypothesis.

4.3 Toward a multilingual constructicon

While the TED Talk parallel corpus is a good resource for frame-semantic annotation in individual languages, it may not be the ideal resource as a starting point to align constructions for building a bilingual constructicon between English and another language, because of the characteristics of the genre of subtitles discussed in Section 4.1. We may indeed be able to find better functional alignment between two translated subtitle transcripts, as opposed to comparing one translation to the original[3]. Applying the frames-and-constructions method to translated subtitles of two or more languages may therefore be a better strategy to build a multilingual constructicon from the parallel corpus.

5. Summary and Future Work

This section summarizes the findings of the work presented here:

- Pairs of constructions in English and Japanese that share similar pragmatic functions exist in the TED Talk bilingual transcripts. This is similar to our findings involving texts in a Japanese to English bilingual children's book. Therefore, the proposed frames-and-constructions analysis method seems valid not only for written language but also for transcripts of spoken data.
- While the TED Talk parallel corpus is a good resource for frame semantic annotation in individual languages, it may not be the ideal place to start aligning constructions across typologically unrelated languages, because of the characteristics of the genre of subtitles.
- The frames-and-constructions analysis method proposed here, namely, the one that focuses on the head of a sentence in each language, seems valid to search for corresponding constructions in typologically-unrelated languages.

As Section 4.2 indicates, the four steps of the present frames-and-constructions analysis predicts that even in the case of frame mismatch, and even when structural divergence exists, if the functions of two constructions in the two different languages are the same, then the two constructions are comparable. Croft (In Preparation) and Croft et al. (2017) argue that syntax is primarily motivated by information packaging, and secondarily by semantics. Therefore how the proposed frames-and-constructions analysis method relates to Croft's claim is worth

---

[3] I would like to thank one of the reviewers for pointing this out to me.

investigating in detail. Of particular interest is how what we have called "pragmatic functions" interacts with Croft's "information packing."

Bibliographical References

Croft, W. (In Preparation). *Morphosyntax: Constructions of the World's Languages*.

Croft, W., Nordquist, D., Looney, K., and Regan, M. (2017). Linguistic typology meets universal dependencies. In Markus Dickinson, et al. editors, Proceedings of the 15th International Workshop on Treebanks and Linguistic Theories (TLT15), pages 63-75. CEUR Workshop Proceedings.

Czulo, O. (2013). Constructions-and-frames analysis of translations: the interplay of syntax and semantics in translations between English and German. Constructions and Frames, 5(2): 143-167.

Czulo, O. (2017). Aspects of a primacy of frame model of translation. In S. Hansen-Schirra, O. Czulo and S. Hofmann (Eds.), *Empirical modelling of translation and interpreting*. Berlin: Language Science Press, pp. 465-490.

Fillmore, C. J. (2013). Berkeley Construction Grammar. In: T. Hoffmann, & G. Trousdale (Eds.), *The Oxford Handbook of Construction Grammar*. Oxford: Oxford University Press, pp. 111–132.

Fillmore, C. J. & Baker, C. F. (2010). A frames approach to semantic analysis. In: B. Heine and H. Narrog (Eds.), *The Oxford Handbook of Linguistic Analysis*. Oxford: Oxford University Press, pp. 313–339.

Lyngfelt, B., Torrent, T.T., Laviola, A., Bäckström, L., Hannesdóttir, A.H., and Matos, E.E.S. (2018). Aligning constructions across languages: a trilingual comparison between English, Swedish, and Brazilian Portuguese. In B. Lyngfelt, L. Borin, K. Ohara, and T.T. Torrent (Eds.), *Constructicography: Constructicon Development across Languages*. Amsterdam: John Benjamins Publishing, pp. 255-302.

Ohara, K. (2019). Frames-and-constructions analyses of Japanese and English Bilingual Children's Book. Paper presented at the Theme Session "Cross-theoretical Perspectives on Frame-based Lexical and Constructional Analyses: Bridging Qualitative and Quantitative Studies" the 15th International Cognitive Linguistics Conference (ICLC 15), Nishinomiya, Japan, August 9.

Ohara, K. and Okubo, Y. (2020). Finding corresponding constructions in a Japanese-English Contrastive children's book using the frames-and-constructions analysis. (In Japanese). Proceedings of NLP2020, pages 921-924, Ibaraki, Japan, March. The Association for Natural Language Processing.

Ruppenhofer, J., Ellsworth, M., Petruck, M., Johnson, C., & Scheffczyk, J. (2016). FrameNet II: Extended theory and practice. Technical report. Berkeley: ICSI.

Language Resource References

Japanese FrameNet.
http://jfn.st.hc.keio.ac.jp
FrameNet.
https://framenet.icsi.berkeley.edu
"Do schools kill creativity?" TED2006, February 2006.
https://www.ted.com/talks/sir_ken_robinson_do_school s_kill_creativity?language=en

Takashi Y. (1991). *Anpanman 1.* Translated by Yuriko Tamaki. Tokyo: Froebel Kan.

Proceedings of the International FrameNet Workshop 2020: Towards a Global, Multilingual FrameNet, pages 13–22
Language Resources and Evaluation Conference (LREC 2020), Marseille, 11–16 May 2020

Towards Reference-Aware FrameNet Annotation

Levi Remijnse[a] and Gosse Minnema[b]

[a]Vrije Universiteit Amsterdam
De Boelelaan 1105, 1081 HV Amsterdam, The Netherlands
l.remijnse@vu.nl
[b]Rijksuniversiteit Groningen
Oude Kijk in 't Jatstraat 26, 9712 EK Groningen, The Netherlands
g.f.minnema@rug.nl

Abstract

In this paper, we introduce the task of using FrameNet to link structured information about real-world events to the conceptual frames used in texts describing these events. We show that frames made relevant by the knowledge of the real-world event can be captured by complementing standard lexicon-driven FrameNet annotations with frame annotations derived through pragmatic inference. We propose a two-layered annotation scheme with a 'strict' FrameNet-compatible lexical layer and a 'loose' layer capturing frames that are inferred from referential data.

1. Introduction

Written narratives can describe a single real-world event in different ways. In particular, an event of great cultural importance often generates a growing portion of written referential texts over time, all displaying various linguistic forms when referring to that same event or components of the event (Vossen et al., 2018a). These linguistic forms activate conceptual representations displaying perspectives, goals and motivations. In order to systematically investigate how the components of a single event are conceptually represented across texts, large-scale resources are needed that, on the one hand, link knowledge about real-world events to event mentions in text, and on the other hand link these mentions to conceptual information of that event. FrameNet can be a useful resource for linking event mentions to conceptual information, given that it provides a rich database of conceptual knowledge about event and situation types, which are linked both to each other and to lexical expressions evoking this conceptual knowledge.

In this paper, we will show how FrameNet annotations can be used as a resource for showing how structured knowledge about real-world events is conceptualized in text. Figure 1 shows an example of how FrameNet can be used to analyze how a single event can be described from different perspectives. While both texts mention the basic fact that a killing took place, the lower text stays close to the facts and provides details about the shooting event itself, whereas the upper text is less detailed and takes a more interpretative perspective by telling us that the event came to be seen as a crime (murder). This is reflected in the frame annotations: both texts evoke KILLING, but only the upper text evokes OFFENSES, whereas the lower one evokes USE_FIREARM.

In this fictitious example, the frames that are expressed by the lexical items in the texts fit well with the conceptual information needed to understand the perspective taken by these texts. However, this is not always true in natural texts, as in many cases, event descriptions are implicit. For example, "John was shot and died" does not contain any particular lexical item expressing a killing event, and would not be annotated with KILLING following FrameNet annotation standards. Yet, the sentence clearly refers to such an event.

In this paper, we will analyze such challenges, and propose a way to more comprehensively annotate the relationship between frames and referential data. In short, we will introduce an *inferred frame layer* of annotation on top of a 'regular' FrameNet annotation layer. In this way, we can annotate event mentions that standard frame annotation would not be able to capture, while preserving a standard FrameNet layer, thus contributing to the global FrameNet effort. We will illustrate the challenges and proposals we discuss with examples in English and Dutch, but we expect them to be relevant cross-linguistically.

Contributions The main contributions of our work are:

- We identify challenges for performing FrameNet annotation guided by referential data (Section 4.);

- We propose a solution in the form of an extra anno-

Figure 1: Fictitious example of the same event described in different ways with different frames

tation layer for pragmatically inferred frames (Section 5.);

- We show the implications of our approach for pragmatics and frame semantics (Section 6.);

- We implement the inferred frame layer in an annotation tool as part of the Dutch FrameNet project[1] – for more details, see Postma et al. (this workshop).

2. Terminology

In order to avoid confusion between concepts from the 'reference world' and the 'frame world', some key terminology that we will rely on throughout this paper is given in Box 1. While these definitions might seem obvious, when linking frame annotations to information about real-world events, it is important to make an explicit distinction between events and frames on one hand and types, instances, and mentions on the other hand. Not doing so could easily cause confusion in an example like (1):

(1)   a. He killed the murderer of JFK, who was assassinated two days earlier.

        b. He shot the murderer of JFK, who had died two days earlier.

        c. He murdered someone yesterday, and did it again today.

In (1a), "killed", "murderer", and "assassinated", all describe the same event type (murder) but refer to two different instances of this event type (the "murderer" and "assassinated" refer to the murder of JFK, "killed" refers to the murder of JFK's killer). They also all evoke the same frame type (KILLING), while each of them is a separate mention of this frame. On the other hand, in (1b), "shot", "murderer" and "died", again refer to two event instances of the type murder,[2] but evoke three different frame types (HIT_TARGET, KILLING, DEATH), introducing a single mention of each of these. Finally, in (1c), "murdered" and "did it again" describe two instances of the murder event type, but only "murdered" is a mention of the KILLING frame type.

3. Background

3.1. FrameNet and conceptual information

FrameNet (Baker et al., 2003; Ruppenhofer et al., 2010a) provides a useful paradigm to analyze how conceptual information is encoded in language. Within this paradigm, *lexical units* (word forms with a specific sense) can *evoke* frame types, which are schematic representations of situations involving participants and other conceptual roles. These semantic roles (*frame elements*, or FEs) are expressed by constituents. Frame mentions are analyzed within clause boundaries. Two typical examples are given in (2):

Frames vs. events

Event type: category of real-world events
Example: murder, election

Event instance: individual event in the real world
Example: the murder of JFK

Frame type: frame entry in the FrameNet database, formally a tuple $\langle T, E, R \rangle$ (T: set of target LUs, E: set of frame elements, R: set of frame-frame relations).
Example: KILLING $= \langle \{\text{kill.v}, \ldots\}, \{\text{Killer}, \ldots\}, \{\langle \text{Inherited\_by}, \text{EXECUTION}\rangle, \ldots\}\rangle$.

Frame mention: expression of a frame type in text, formally a tuple $\langle f, t, e \rangle$ (f: frame type, t: target LU, e: set of (frame element name, frame element span) pairs.
Example: given "He killed JFK", annotate: $\langle \text{KILLING}, \text{killed}, \{\langle \text{Killer}, \text{he}\rangle, \langle \text{Victim}, \text{JFK}\rangle\}\rangle$.

Box 1: Key terminology for our annotation task

(2)   a. COMMERCE_SELL
        [Time Yesterday], [Seller John] ⊙sold [Buyer Mary] [Goods a book].

        b. COMMERCE_BUY
        [Buyer A woman] ⊙bought [Goods a novel] [Place in the shop].

In (2a), "sold" is a lexical unit that evokes COMMERCE_SELL. This frame comes with an inventory of frame elements, some of which are necessary for the reader to process the frame (*core elements*). For COMMERCE_SELL, these are the Buyer, "Mary", the Seller, "John", and the Goods, "a book". Similarly, in (2b), "bought" evokes COMMERCE_BUY, which has the same frame elements: a Buyer, expressed by 'a woman', Goods, expressed by "a novel", and a Seller, which is unexpressed in this sentence.

The overlap of semantic roles between these two frame types indicates that both COMMERCE_SELL and COMMERCE_BUY have a Perspective_on relation with the abstract ('non-lexical') frame type COMMERCE_GOODS-TRANSFER. This relation encodes the fact that both frame types describe the same abstract concept, but from different perspectives: COMMERCE_SELL takes the point of view of the Seller, whereas COMMERCE_BUY takes that of the buyer. In this way, FrameNet provides us with rich information about variation in framing on a conceptual level.

3.2. Reference-driven annotation

Besides representing conceptual knowledge, a point of interest is to capture variations in the way that texts frame components of the real-world event that they refer to. We want to know, for instance, whether the sentences in (2) describe the same event instance, and hence, whether "Mary" in (2a) and "a woman" in (2b) both refer to the same participant of this event instance. In order to annotate texts with this type of information, we need a resource providing structured data about events in the real world and texts describing these events.

---

[1] www.dutchframenet.nl

[2] Note that knowledge of the real-world event is necessary to recognize that "shot" and "died" both describe a murder event: the lexical content of these words does not imply murder (one can be shot without dying, and one can die without having been murdered), but in this context they do refer to (subevents of) murders.

We make use of the *data-to-text* method (Vossen et al., 2018b; Vossen et al., in press) in order to establish such a resource. This method inverts the usual process of annotating data: instead of starting from (unstructured) text and then annotating it with referential information, we start from structured information about real-world event instances and then match these to texts describing these instances. More concretely, we query Wikidata (Vrandečić and Krötzsch, 2014) for a set of event instances belonging to a particular event type. The Wikidata API then returns records of such instances, accompanied by structured data (minimally: the event type, data, location and participants). Wikidata also provides the Wikipedia text pages in various languages, which in turn provide hyperlinks that point to other texts referring to the same event. We aggregate the Wikipedia texts themselves with the texts they point to, to build a corpus of *reference texts* linked to event instances.

Next, we prepare the corpus for manual FrameNet annotation. FrameNet contains a large number of different frame types (1224 in Berkeley FrameNet for English).[3] In order to efficiently annotate large corpora, we restrict the scope of our FrameNet annotations to only include frame types that are known to be relevant for the event types in our dataset. To achieve this, we first automatically annotate the acquired corpus using Open-SESAME, a state-of-the-art frame semantic role labeler (Swayamdipta et al., 2017). Then, by analyzing the frequency distribution of the frame types found in the automatic annotations, we define a list of *typical frames* containing the frame types that are most dominant in texts referring to a particular type of event.[4]

To summarize, utilizing the data-to-text method results in the following data:

- Records of a set of event instances belonging to one event type (e.g. 'murder');

- A corpus of reference texts for each event instance;

- Structured data for each event instance;

- A list of typical frames belonging to the event type.

The next subsection elaborates on the integration of frame annotations and referential annotations.

3.3. Integrating FrameNet in Referential Annotations

The product of the data-to-text method enables the annotator to annotate frame mentions representing the conceptual content of each text, and then link these mentions to structured data about the corresponding event instance. Returning to the examples in (2), we see that on the conceptual (frame) level, "Mary" is the Buyer of COMMERCE_SELL in (2a) and that "a woman" is the Buyer of COMMERCE_BUY in (2b). Next, let us assume that the structured data we

found, tells us that the two sentences refer to the same event instance in the real world. This allows us to make the link to the referential level by annotating "buy" and "sell" as referring to the event instance, and "Mary" and "a woman" as referring to the same participant in that event instance. In integrating these annotations, we find that the two sentences show conceptual variation in framing of the same event instance in the real world.

The typical frames generate expectations about the frame types to be found in the reference texts. Often, these frame types are also conceptually necessary for recognizing the for instance, a text can only be interpreted as describing a murder event if the conceptual content of KILLING is somehow expressed in the text. Hence, in addition to guiding expectations of the most probable frame types to be found in the texts, the typical frames function as a 'checklist' for the annotator to explore to what extent the typical frame types are encoded in the text. Annotating whether or not each typical frame is indeed expressed provides much information about the perspective of a text; for instance, in the example texts discussed in the introduction (Figure 1), OFFENSES is a typical frame for describing murder events, but the fact that only one of the texts expresses this frame type tells us something about the different perspectives of the two texts.

As we will show in Section 4., in some cases, typical frames are expressed in the text, but do not have a target word corresponding to a lexical unit in FrameNet, nor can they be derived through frame-to-frame relations. In such cases, we run into an inherent limitation of FrameNet: FrameNet is, at heart, a lexicographical project; conceptual information is always 'activated' through a direct correspondence between a lexical unit and a frame. This limitation has been noted even from within the field of frame semantics: Fillmore himself has allowed for the possibility that frame types, in some cases, are not evoked by lexical units, but by other linguistic features (Andor, 2010, p. 158). If we want to account for the way in which frame types related to the referential level are activated in corpora, we need to complement the lexical semantic approach of FrameNet with a broader view that takes into account compositional semantics and pragmatics. In Section 4., we motivate this view.

3.4. FrameNet and Inference

The notion of 'inference' is crucial for the annotation approach proposed in this paper: we aim to annotate frame mentions that are not directly evoked by a lexical unit but whose relevance can be inferred from the textual and referential context of an event. Inference in the context of frame semantics has been studied in the literature, but the notion we use in this paper is subtly different. Here, we provide a brief overview of notions of inference found in the FrameNet literature and how our notion differs from it.

Frame-to-frame relations In the FrameNet literature, inference is often connected to frame-to-frame relations. For example, Chang et al. (2002) propose a scheme for modeling *shared inferential structure* between frame types. An example of frame types with shared inferential structure

---

[3]See `https://framenet.icsi.berkeley.edu/fndrupal/current_status`, consulted on 2020-02-20.

[4]This is done by applying TFIDF weighting to frame type frequencies; see Vossen et al. (in press) for a detailed description of this method.

are COMMERCE_BUY and COMMERCE_SELL: both refer to the same type of event in the real world; hence, when one of these frame types is used, it can be inferred that the other frame type is also conceptually 'active'. Different frame-to-frame relations give rise to different kinds of inferences; for example, Sikos and Padó (2018), investigate the Using relation as a source for paraphrases. This allows, for example, for the inference of LABELING ("he ⊙called him a hero") from JUDGEMENT_COMMUNICATION ("he ⊙praised him for being a hero").

For the purposes of this paper, we focus on a different kind of inference: we are interested in frame types whose conceptual content is 'activated' by a text, but cannot be annotated as being evoked by a lexical unit. While, in a subset of such cases, there might be a frame-to-frame relationship between the frame type of interest and other frame types that are evoked in the text, this is not always the case. Moreover, even if such a frame-to-frame relationship is present, this might not be sufficient for licensing the inference. In the example "John was shot and died" (discussed in the introduction), "die" evokes DEATH, which has a Causative relation with KILLING, but this relation alone is not enough to make the inference: the fact that someone died does not imply that this person was also killed. Instead, we can infer that a killing did take place from the textual context ("John was shot").

Cognitive frames   The idea of frames that are present but not evoked by a lexical unit is also known from the literature about cognitive frames,[5] as is evident in the following famous example from Minksy:

(3)   Mary was invited to Jack's party. She wondered if he would like a kite.   (Minsky, 1974)

Here, the lexical unit "party" evokes SOCIAL_EVENT. The second sentence, "she wondered if he would like a kite" gives us reason to think that the party described is of a specific kind: most likely a birthday party. This would suggest the relevance of a frame type such as BIRTHDAY_PARTY (not currently existent): from our cultural knowledge, we know that parties at which gifts are given are typically birthdays or some other type of commemorative event.

However, this notion of inference goes beyond what we are aiming for in this paper. In the above example, it could be guessed what kind of party is at play, but the inference does not follow directly from the text: it could be some other party where, for whatever reason, gifts are given. This means that annotators would have to rely on their cultural knowledge. By contrast, within our framework, world knowledge can play a role in deriving inferred frame types, but their conceptual content should always be fully specified by the linguistic cues in the text. However, unlike in standard FrameNet annotation, these cues are not limited to single lexical items, but can comprise larger constructions.

---

4.   Challenges for Reference-Aware Annotation

In this section, we detail and motivate the main challenges that we see for structured-data-driven frame annotation that cannot be solved within the standard framework of FrameNet. We first motivate the general problem, and then discuss a number of concrete problems that we would like to address. An overview of these problems is shown in Box 2.

Annotation Challenges

Problem: how to link *n* LUs to *m* frame types

Many-to-One
Compositionality: ≥ 2 LUs, ≥ 1 frame type
Complex Verbs: verb components, ≥ 1 frame type(s)

One-to-Many
Frame Overlap: 1 LU, ≥ 2 frame types
Lexical Gaps: out-of-vocab LU, ≥ 1 frame type(s)

Box 2: Overview of the annotation challenges

4.1.   The Coverage Problem

A general issue of FrameNet that has been noted in the literature is that it covers many frame types while only a limited number of number of annotations are available per frame type and per lexical unit (Palmer and Sporleder, 2010; Vossen et al., 2018b). As a logical consequence, when annotating texts with a limited set of frame types, as in our approach, the number of annotations per text would be expected to be small. Indeed, results from the CALOR project for French (Marzinotto et al., 2018), in which a small subset (53 frame types) of all possible FrameNet frame types was annotated, show that the number of sentences with at least one frame mention varied between 21%–34%, depending on the topic of the annotated texts.

One of the texts that we annotated in preliminary annotation experiments, describing the killing of visitors of a Christmas market in Berlin during a terror attack in 2016, is shown in Table 1. Our aim is to show whether each of the referential attributes of the event is expressed in the text, and if so, how it is conceptualized with frame mentions. For this particular text, reasoning from structured data, one would expect at least KILLING to be activated, and possibly also OFFENSES, USE_FIREARM, and/or WEAPONS (depending on whether the event is seen as an offense and whether the authors choose to mention the weapon). Surprisingly, it turns out that none of these frame types is evoked in the text in relation to the event mention of interest; even though "he was ⊙killed in a shootout . . ." contains a KILLING frame mention, this is in relation to a secondary event mentioned in the text (i.e. the killing of the perpetrator of the main murder event described in the text). Moreover, none of the frame types evoked by the lexical units in the text can be linked to the typical frames through a frame-to-frame relation; if this had been the case, we might have been able to indirectly annotate the frame types of interest,

[Wikidata] Q28036573	[Text] "2016 Berlin truck attack"	[Typical Frames]
Event type: *murder*	*On 19 December 2016, a truck was deliberately driven into the*	{ KILLING,
Time: *2019-12-19*	*Christmas market next to the Kaiser Wilhelm Memorial Church*	USE_FIREARM,
Location: *Berlin*	*at Breitscheidplatz in Berlin, leaving 12 people dead and 56 oth-*	OFFENSES,
Participant: *Annis Amri*	*ers injured. […] The perpetrator was Anis Amri, a Tunisian*	WEAPON,
Number_deaths: *12*	*failed asylum seeker. Four days after the attack, he was killed in*	COMMIT_CRIME }
Weapon: *truck*	*a shootout with police near Milan in Italy. […]*	

Table 1: Example output of the data-to-text pipeline.

as discussed in Section 3.4..

However, from a close examination of the text, we find that each of the referential attributes from the structured data is in fact mentioned, but without using any lexical units belonging to one of the typical frames. We argue that the conceptual content of these frame types is still relevant for describing how the event instance is expressed in the text, and that this should be reflected in the annotations. For example, in FrameNet, the definition of KILLING is given as "A *Killer* or *Cause* causes the death of the *Victim*". A 'killing' event is very clearly expressed in the text by "a truck was deliberately driven into the Christmas market … leaving 12 people dead". However, it is difficult to specify which lexical unit(s), if any, evokes this particular frame mention in the standard FrameNet sense.

Work on what has become known as the *implicit semantic role labeling* task (Ruppenhofer et al., 2010b) addresses a related problem: semantic roles are sometimes 'missing' in the sentence of their associated predicate, but are conceptually 'activated' by this predicate and expressed elsewhere in the discourse. In example (4), the Charges role of "cleared" is not explicitly expressed, but can be inferred because "murder" is still active from the previous sentence:

(4)   In a lengthy court case the defendant was tried [Charges for murder]. In the end, he was ⊙cleared. (Ruppenhofer et al., 2010b, p. 107)

The challenges we address in this paper are also related to implicit semantic roles, but in a more abstract way: in our case it is not the fillers of semantic roles, but the frame types defining these semantic roles that are unexpressed and have to be inferred. In the remainder of this section, we will discuss these challenges in more detail. In Section 5., we will propose a solution to these challenges.

4.2. 'Many-to-One' Problems

In the first class of challenges we encountered, at least one frame type is relevant for describing how an event instance is conceptualized, but there is no lexical unit in the text that, under standard FrameNet assumptions, would evoke this frame type. Instead, several items in the text together allow the reader to infer that the frame type is relevant, and give rise to annotating a mention of this frame.

Compositionality   The Compositionality Problem occurs when multiple lexical items, through the composition of their meanings, 'activate' a single frame type. The sentence

in (5) (already briefly discussed above) is a clear example of this:

(5)   KILLING
     [Cause a truck] was deliberately ⊙?driven …
     ⊙?leaving [Victim 12 people] ⊙?dead …

The sentence describes an action ("drive") with the consequence ("leaving") of people dying ("dead"); while none of these is a 'killing word' per se, the sum of these components imply (or even entail) that a killing event took place. We would like to capture in our annotations that (the conceptual content of) KILLING is relevant for this sentence, but standard FrameNet annotation does not allow us to annotate this, since there is no lexical target for KILLING, nor can KILLING be derived through other frame types that are evoked in the text.[6]

Complex Verbs   A special case of the Compositionality Problem is the Complex Verbs Problem, in which the targets that jointly activate a frame type are all part of a complex (prepositional) verb:

(6)   a.   OPERATE_VEHICLE
          … [Vehicle a truck] was deliberately ⊙driven [Goal into the Christmas market] …
     b.   IMPACT
          … [Impactor a truck] was deliberately ⊙?driven ⊙?into [Impactee the Christmas market] …

Since FrameNet lists "drive", but not "drive into", as a lexical unit, the canonical analysis of (6) should be (6a). However, in this sentence, "into" does not simply add a destination to "drive", but modifies the meaning of "drive" so that it expresses not just a driving event, but also a hitting event. Hence, one would like to annotate a mention of IMPACT as well as of OPERATE_VEHICLE.

The Complex Verb Problem is particularly relevant in Dutch, which has many complex verbs that are often discontinuous.[7]

(7)   Toen **reed** een vrachtwagen **op** het publiek **in**
     then drove a   truck   on the crowd   into

---

[6]For example, "dead" evokes DEAD_OR_ALIVE, which is (distantly) related to KILLING, but does not imply its relevance (the fact that someone dies does not imply that someone was killed).

[7]From the Dutch version of the Wikipedia article about the Berlin Christmas market attack (`https://nl.wikipedia.org/wiki/Aanslag_op_kerstmarkt_in_Berlijn_op_19_december_2016`).

'Then, a truck (deliberately) drove into the crowd'

  a. OPERATE_VEHICLE
    [Time toen] ⊙?reed [Vehicle een vrachtwagen]
    [Goal op het publiek in]

  b. IMPACT
    [Time toen] ⊙?reed [Impactor een vrachtwagen]
    [Impactee ⊙?op het publiek] ⊙?in

Here, the verb *inrijden (op)* "(deliberately) drive into" expresses the same two meanings (i.e., driving and hitting) as "drive into" in (6). However, "in" in "inrijden" is arguably 'more part of the verb' than "into" in "drive into"; thus, it is likely that "inrijden" would be a separate lexical unit in the (still to be developed) Dutch FrameNet. Hence, in (6), the correct analysis under standard FrameNet annotation would be to use OPERATE_VEHICLE (because "drive", not "drive into" exists in FrameNet). By contrast, in Dutch FrameNet, "inrijden" would most likely be a lexical unit of IMPACT. Hence, (6) and (7) have an almost identical semantic content but would get very different analyses, where one of the relevant frame types is lost. Ideally, in our annotations we would like to capture both of the two relevant frame types.

4.3. 'One-to-Many'

The second class of challenges that we identify applies in the inverse situation of the 'many-to-one' challenge: these consist of cases with a certain number of relevant frame types, but not enough lexical units to evoke all of these frame types.

Frame Overlap Under the Frame Overlap Problem, a single lexical unit is relevant for more than one frame type. An example is given in (8):

(8) HOSTILE_ENCOUNTER
    [Side 1 he] was killed in a ⊙shootout [Side 2 with police]

In FrameNet, "shootout" is listed as a lexical unit of HOSTILE_ENCOUNTER. However, the lexical semantics of "shootout" clearly involves the use of a firearm, which makes USE_FIREARM conceptually relevant as well. Since USE_FIREARM is part of the typical frames for murder events, we would like our annotations to reflect the fact that the text indeed expresses a USE_FIREARM event. A naive solution would be to add a lexical unit "shootout" to USE_FIREARM so that we could annotate that frame type. This would not work well, since USE_FIREARM, though conceptually relevant, does not fit well with the structure of the sentence: a typical context of USE_FIREARM are sentences like "[Agent she] ⊙fired [Firearm her gun]", with the firearm and the shooter, rather than the participants in a conflict, as core roles.

An even more subtle version of the Frame Overlap Problem arises from the hypothetical example in (9):

(9) OFFENSES
    [Perpetrator He] was convicted for the
    [Offense ⊙murder] of [Victim JFK].

"Murder" is a lexical unit in both OFFENSES and KILLING, and has an almost identical meaning in both of them. Which of the two frame types should be annotated depends on the context: OFFENSES.murder is activated only when there is a governing verb such as 'convict' or 'accuse'; in other contexts KILLING.murder is activated. In (9), we clearly have an OFFENSE context rather than a KILLING context, but this does not mean that the meaning of KILLING is not also active: while the sentence, through a mention of OFFENSES, tells us that someone was convicted of a crime (further specified as the 'murder of JFK'), it also tells us that the murder happened in the first place, which we would like to capture using a mention of KILLING.

Lexical Gaps An extreme case of the Frame Overlap Problem occurs when a particular lexical unit does not exist in FrameNet, but would be a potential target for some frame type. We call this the Lexical Gaps Problem: a single lexical unit is associated with zero frame types in FrameNet, but at least one frame type is relevant for annotation. For example, in (10), "perpetrator" is not listed as a lexical unit for COMMIT_CRIME, but is a very likely target for it, especially because the verb "perpetrate" is listed under that frame type.[8]

(10) COMMIT_CRIME
    The ⊙?perpetrator was [Perpetrator Anis Amri] ...

It is well-known that the FrameNet lexicon is incomplete, especially when annotating out-of-domain corpora (Hartmann et al., 2017). In this sense, the Lexical Gaps problem seems more superficial than the other problems discussed in this section. Yet, the lexical gaps detected by using our method of structured-data-driven annotation require some kind of inference on the part of the annotator. Namely, the list of typical frames guides the annotator in inferring frame types from potential lexical units currently missing in FrameNet.

5. Towards a Workable Solution for Annotating Inferred Frames

In this section, we aim to address the challenges previously explained by proposing an extra annotation layer (next to, not instead of, traditional FrameNet annotation) for capturing *inferred frames* whose conceptual content is expressed in the text without explicitly using one of the frame type's lexical units, but through inference. This layer would allow annotators to use any combination of words in the text as a 'trigger' for any number of frame mentions. While this idea is conceptually simple, some challenges need to be overcome for implementing it in practice: how do we make sure we get enough data? How do we apply the annotations in a consistent way?

5.1. Introducing Inferred Frame Annotation

The overall annotation pipeline that we propose is shown in Figure 2. The process starts with choosing event types

---

[8]For comparison: in KILLING, both "murder" and "murderer" are listed as targets.

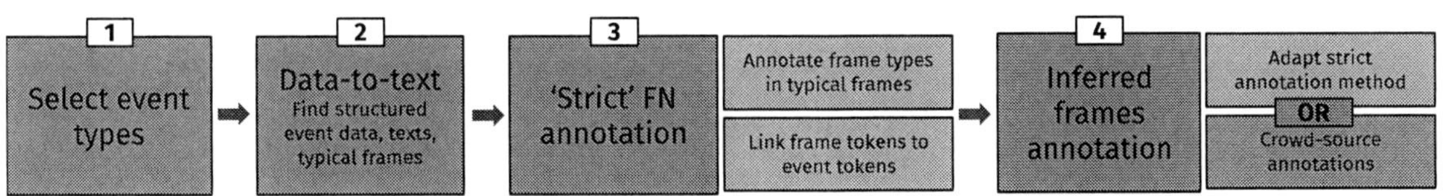

Figure 2: Overall annotation pipeline

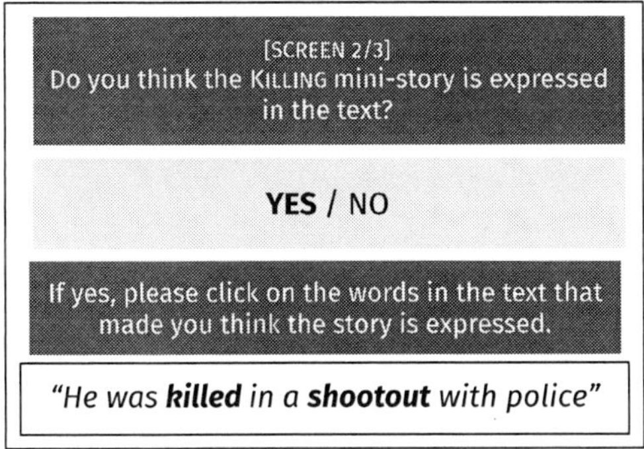

(a) Screen 1: explanation of frame types

(b) Screen 2: selecting target words

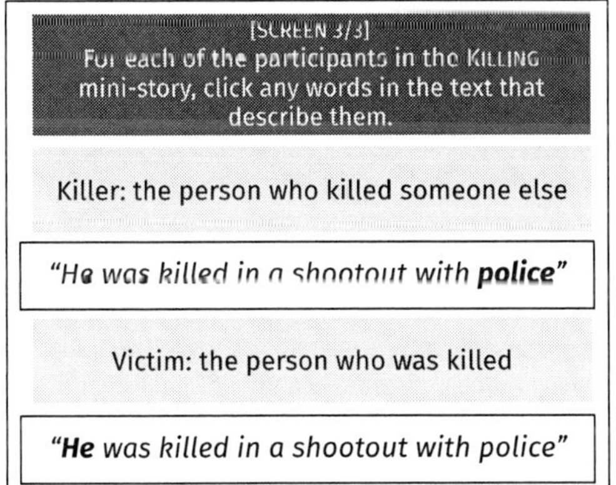

(c) Screen 3: selecting frame elements

Figure 3: Mockup of a crowd-sourcing interface (possible user input marked in bold)

of interest and running the data-to-text pipeline (see Section 3.2.) to obtain linked event data and texts (Steps 1 and 2). Then, 'strict' FrameNet annotation is applied (Step 3): this annotation step will be done following standard FrameNet guidelines, except that (i) only frame types in the typical frames, selected by the data-to-text algorithm, will be taken into consideration and that (ii) frame mentions will be linked to event instances and their attributes in the structured data, much like in the initial example we gave in Figure 1. This step will be done by annotators, who need to be trained in applying FrameNet annotation guidelines. Finally (Step 4), we will annotate the inferred frame layer that we have motivated in this paper.

Annotation on this layer is much 'looser' than the annotation done in step 3. Annotators do not need to respect the FrameNet rule of 'one lexical unit, one frame mention', but are free to annotate any number of frame mentions based on any combination of lexical items in the text. An inherent risk of this type of 'free-style' annotation is that inter-annotator agreement is likely to be lower, simply because the number of possible annotation decisions is much larger and less constrained than under standard FrameNet annotation.

5.2. Annotation Strategies

Currently, we see two possible (not necessarily exclusive) paths to mitigating this risk. The first option involves a *qualitative* approach that aims to make the procedure that annotators follow as consistent as possible. Alternatively, a *quantitative* approach would use crowd-sourcing for gathering as much data for every text as possible, and then comparing and aggregating the annotations from different annotators.

Under the qualitative option, we would integrate annotation of Step 3 and Step 4: the annotators would annotate both layers in the same way, using the same tools. The advantage would be that the annotators are trained in doing FrameNet annotation, which improves the consistency of the annotations. However, due to the looseness of the task, we still expect considerable disagreements between different annotators. Moreover, training and deploying expert annotators is costly and time-consuming.

On the other hand, the quantitative option would 'embrace' the unconstrained nature of the inferred frame layer, and use crowd sourcing to gather as much data as possible. This would mean moving further away from standard FrameNet annotation, given that the annotators would be unfamiliar with FrameNet and its philosophy. Annotations are also likely to be less consistent: different annotators might have different standards for what words are relevant for each frame mention.

However, previous studies have shown that annotation tasks similar to FrameNet annotation, such as PropBank-style semantic role labeling, can be successfully addressed using (partial) crowd sourcing (Wang et al., 2017). Moreover, the task of annotating the inferred frame layer is potentially more suitable for crowd sourcing than standard FrameNet annotation is: since there are no strict guidelines that the annotations need to adhere to, it is not clear how consistent the annotations need to be with one another in order to be acceptable. In fact, provided that enough data points are collected, it might be interesting to get a wide range of possible annotations from different annotators applying slightly different strategies, and then to look for patterns that apply across annotators. After the annotation process, a 'canonical' representation of the annotations could be obtained by filtering out infrequent annotations.[9]

A possible way to present the task to crowd annotators would be as shown in the example in Figure 3. In the first screen, the sentence to be annotated would be shown together with simple explanations of the frame types in the typical frames (which could be called 'mini-stories' for people unfamiliar with FrameNet). Next, for every frame type, the annotators would be asked to indicate if they think the text expresses it, and if so, which words in the sentence contribute to it. Finally, if the frame type is indeed expressed, the same question is asked for all of the (core) frame element.

For implementing the crowd-sourcing task, we propose making use of the Wordrobe gamification platform (Venhuizen et al., 2013). In Wordrobe, annotators get scores based on how consistent they are with other annotators, and are encouraged (e.g. through 'leader boards') to aim for higher scores. This encourages consistency and makes the annotation task more interesting for participants.

6. Discussion

The output of the inferred frame layer forms a scheme displaying a group of n words for each frame mention that, according to the annotator, activates the corresponding frame type. In this section, we will argue that the inferences that led to each of these annotations can be categorized as either 'conventional' (i.e., always apply) or 'situational' (i.e., only apply in a specific context). We expect that most conventional inferences indicate coverage gaps in FrameNet. Once identified, these could be used to enrich the database. On the other hand, we expect the situational inferences to

be pragmatic instead of lexical in nature. In the following subsections, we will elaborate on the potential benefits of categorizing the output in this way.

6.1. Conventional Inferences and FrameNet Coverage

Certain annotations can be categorized as conventional. These annotations could not be performed in traditional FrameNet, but nevertheless seem to show a consistent mapping to the same targets across texts, and therefore might show a lexical coverage problem. These conventional inferences can provide useful insights for enriching or adapting the FrameNet database. The most typical examples of annotations that reveal coverage problems, are the ones related to the Lexical Gaps Problem (see Section 4.3.). When a word that is not yet listed in FrameNet is consistently annotated as activating a particular frame type, this word might be a lexical unit that is still missing in the frame type's inventory and could be added to it. However, because of the 'looseness' of the inferred frame layer, it is also possible that a word is very often annotated with a particular frame type, but does not qualify for being a lexical unit in the standard FrameNet sense.

For instance, "perpetrator" is currently not listed in FrameNet, but is conceptually relevant for OFFENSES, so it is conceivable that many annotators would annotate it as activating this frame type, even though it does not fit well with the structure of OFFENSES (which exclusively lists kinds of offenses such as "murder.n", "robbery.n"). However, the fact that the word is frequently annotated still suggests it should be added to FrameNet. A potential strategy to deal with this is to look for a better fit in frame types directly related to the one that is annotated. In this case, a good fit could be COMMITTING_CRIME (as we argued previously), which is connected to OFFENSES through the Is_used_by relation.

Another type of conventional annotation that provides cues for enriching FrameNet is related to the Frame Overlap Problem (see Section 4.3.): if annotators consistently annotate particular frame types on the inferred frame layer as activated by the same targets, this could be a strong indicator that there exists a relation between these frame types. For instance, if OFFENSES is often annotated for the same lexical items as KILLING, then these frame types are likely to be related.

Finally, the Frame Overlap problem can also provide cues that some lexical units are conceptually related to more than one frame type. Even when one of these frame types clearly fits best (e.g., HOSTILE_ENCOUNTER for "shootout", see example (8)), the conceptual content of another frame type may still be relevant to such a degree that it can be viewed as part of the lexical meaning of the target word. This could be suggested by a large number of annotations of this frame type on the inferred frame layer (e.g., USE_FIREARM for "shootout"). A possible way for encoding this in the lexicon would be to introduce frame-lexical unit relations in FrameNet. Currently, lexical units can only be related to frame types through the 'evoke' relationship, which means

---

[9]This should be done on different levels. For example, in Figure 3b, there should be a mention of KILLING in the final representation only if a majority of annotators answers "yes" (frame level); "shootout" should be kept as a target word for this mention only if a majority of annotators included it in their target span (target level); and "police" should be kept as a mention for the Killer frame element only if a majority of annotators included it (frame element level).

that every lexical unit can be related to only one frame type. However, as we have shown, lexical units can make the conceptual content of more than one frame type relevant without, strictly speaking, evoking all of these frame types. Allowing for secondary frame-lexical unit relations would allow us to model one-to-many mappings without weakening the existing 'evoke' relationship.

6.2. Situational Inferences and Pragmatics

The remainder of the annotations in the inferred frame layer can be categorized as situational. For instance, from the conceptually related linguistic components in sentence (5), KILLING is inferred with the aid of situational knowledge about the incident. This inference differs from the inference leading to BIRTHDAY_PARTY in (3), which is derived from both cultural knowledge and cues that are not conceptually related but frequently co-occur in the context of this frame type.

In the field of Gricean pragmatics, annotations like the one in (5) can be analyzed with respect to the means of inference (entailment, implicature, etc., see Levinson (1983) and Grice (1975)) by which frame mentions are pragmatically derived. Also, one could investigate external factors, such as historical distance and cultural background, underlying these inferences.

Another way in which this type of situational inference is relevant for pragmatics is by exposing discourse relations. This crucially depends on the observation that event instances, after being introduced in the beginning of a text, may be implicated in the remainder of the text. By annotating the referential relationship between the initial event mention and implicated event mentions, we implicitly capture this discourse relation and use it to combine the conceptual content from the frame types they evoke. For example, in the text in Table 1, once the murder event instance has been introduced (by "a truck was deliberately driven into the Christmas market … leaving 12 people dead", which under our approach could be annotated with KILLING), it will be implicitly active in the remainder of the text. This leads words like "perpetrator" (which evokes COMMITTING_CRIME) to be interpreted against the background of this event. Marking the two event mentions as referentially related then allows us to connect their associated frame mentions as well. Given that KILLING is still 'active' in the discourse, we can infer that "perpetrator" refers to a murder, and not to some other crime.

The incidental nature of these inferences makes it hard for researchers to model them in such a way that they can be added to FrameNet. One could wonder if researchers want incidental relations between frame types to be implemented in such a lexicographical project at all. Rather, situationally inferred frames show that even a fully developed version of FrameNet would not allow us to annotate all frame mentions referring to an event instance.

7. Summary

In this paper, we introduced a new use case of FrameNet: using frame annotations for showing how a single event instance in the real world can be conceptualized in text in different ways using frames. We showed that, in some cases (e.g. in the example in Figure 1), this can be done within the standard FrameNet annotation framework. However, in many cases the annotation scheme needs to be extended in order to allow for annotating frame mentions without an explicit lexical target. As a general solution, we proposed adding an *inferred frame* layer that allows arbitrary text spans to serve as a 'trigger' for any number of frame mentions, and suggested two possible ways to annotate the layer: either using a traditional FrameNet annotation process with annotators trained specifically for the task, or using crowd-sourcing. Finally, we show that the output of the inferred frame layer could be used as a basis for pragmatic analysis, and for extending the lexical coverage of FrameNet.

8. Acknowledgements

The research reported in this article was funded by the Dutch National Science organisation (NWO) through the project *Framing situations in the Dutch language.*

9. Bibliographical References

Andor, J. (2010). Discussing frame semantics: The state of the art: An interview with Charles J. Fillmore. *Review of Cognitive Linguistics*, 8(1):157–176.

Baker, C. F., Fillmore, C. J., and Cronin, B. (2003). The structure of the FrameNet database. *International Journal of Lexicography*, 16(3):281–296.

Chang, N., Petruck, M. R. L., and Narayanan, S. (2002). From frames to inference. In *In Proceedings of the First International Workshop on Scalable Natural Language Understanding*.

Fillmore, C. J. (2008). The merging of "frames". In Favretti R. Rossini, editor, *Frames, corpora, and knowledge representation*, pages 2–12. Bologna: Bononia University Press.

Grice, H. P. (1975). Logic and conversation. In Peter Cole et al., editors, *Speech acts*, pages 41–58. Brill, Leiden.

Hartmann, S., Kuznetsov, I., Martin, T., and Gurevych, I. (2017). Out-of-domain FrameNet semantic role labeling. In *Proceedings of the 15th Conference of the European Chapter of the Association for Computational Linguistics: Volume 1, Long Papers*, pages 471–482.

Levinson, S. C. (1983). *Pragmatics*. Cambridge Textbooks in Linguistics. Cambridge University Press.

Marzinotto, G., Auguste, J., Bechet, F., Damnati, G., and Nasr, A. (2018). Semantic frame parsing for information extraction: the CALOR corpus. In *Proceedings of the Eleventh International Conference on Language Resources and Evaluation (LREC 2018)*.

Minsky, M. (1974). A framework for representing knowledge. *MIT-AI Laboratory Memo*, 306.

Palmer, A. and Sporleder, C. (2010). Evaluating FrameNet-style semantic parsing: the role of coverage gaps in FrameNet. In *COLING 2010: Posters*, pages 928–936.

Postma, M., Remijnse, L., Ilievski, F., Fokkens, A., Titarsolej, S., and Vossen, P. (this workshop). Combining conceptual and referential annotation to study variation in framing.

Ruppenhofer, J., Ellsworth, M., Petruck, M. R. L., Johnson, C. R., and Schefczyk, J. (2010a). FrameNet II: Extended theory and practice.

Ruppenhofer, J., Sporleder, C., Morante, R., Baker, C., and Palmer, M. (2010b). SemEval-2010 Task 10: Linking Events and Their Participants in Discourse. In *Proceedings of the 5th International Workshop on Semantic Evaluation*.

Sikos, J. and Padó, S. (2018). Framenet's using relation as a source of concept-based paraphrases. *Constructions and Frames*, 10(1):38–60.

Swayamdipta, S., Thomson, S., Dyer, C., and Smith, N. A. (2017). Frame-semantic parsing with softmax-margin segmental rnns and a syntactic scaffold. *arXiv preprint arXiv:1706.09528*.

Venhuizen, N. J., Basile, V., Evang, K., and Bos, J. (2013). Gamification for word sense labeling. In *Proceedings of the 10th International Conference on Computational Semantics (IWCS 2013) – Short Papers*, pages 397–403.

Vossen, P., Caselli, T., and Cybulska, A. (2018a). How concrete do we get telling stories? *Topics in cognitive science*, 10(3):621–640.

Vossen, P., Ilievski, F., Postma, M., and Segers, R. (2018b). Do not annotate, but validate: a data-to-text method for capturing event data. In *Proceedings of the Eleventh International Conference on Language Resources and Evaluation (LREC-2018)*.

Vossen, P., Ilievski, F., Postma, M., Fokkens, A., G., M., and L., R. (in press). Large-scale cross-lingual language resources for referencing and framing. Paper to be presented at LREC 2020.

Vrandečić, D. and Krötzsch, M. (2014). Wikidata: a free collaborative knowledge base.

Wang, C., Akbik, A., Chiticariu, L., Li, Y., Xia, F., and Xu, A. (2017). CROWD-IN-THE-LOOP: A hybrid approach for annotating semantic roles. In *Proceedings of the 2017 Conference on Empirical Methods in Natural Language Processing*, Copenhagen, Denmark.

10.   Language Resource References

Collin F. Baker. (2015). *FrameNet*. International Computer Science Institute, Berkeley, version 1.7.

Vrandečić, Denny and Krötzsch, Markus. (2014). *Wikidata: a free collaborative knowledge base.*

Proceedings of the International FrameNet Workshop 2020: Towards a Global, Multilingual FrameNet, pages 23–30
Language Resources and Evaluation Conference (LREC 2020), Marseille, 11–16 May 2020
© European Language Resources Association (ELRA), licensed under CC-BY-NC

Frame-Based Annotation of Multimodal Corpora: Tracking (A)Synchronies in Meaning Construction

Frederico Belcavello, Marcelo Viridiano, Alexandre Diniz da Costa, Ely Edison da Silva Matos, Tiago Timponi Torrent
FrameNet Brasil – Federal University of Juiz de Fora
Juiz de Fora, Brazil
{frederico.belcavello, alexandre.costa, ely.matos, tiago.torrent}@ufjf.edu.br
marcelo.viridiano@gmail.com

Abstract

Multimodal aspects of human communication are key in several applications of Natural Language Processing, such as Machine Translation and Natural Language Generation. Despite recent advances in integrating multimodality into Computational Linguistics, the merge between NLP and Computer Vision techniques is still timid, especially when it comes to providing fine-grained accounts for meaning construction. This paper reports on research aiming to determine appropriate methodology and develop a computational tool to annotate multimodal corpora according to a principled structured semantic representation of events, relations and entities: FrameNet. Taking a Brazilian television travel show as corpus, a pilot study was conducted to annotate the frames that are evoked by the audio and the ones that are evoked by visual elements. We also implemented a Multimodal Annotation tool which allows annotators to choose frames and locate frame elements both in the text and in the images, while keeping track of the time span in which those elements are active in each modality. Results suggest that adding a multimodal domain to the linguistic layer of annotation and analysis contributes both to enrich the kind of information that can be tagged in a corpus, and to enhance FrameNet as a model of linguistic cognition.

Keywords: Frame Semantics, Multimodal Annotation, FrameNet

1. Introduction

The FrameNet Brasil Lab has been engaged in developing resources and applications for Tourism (Torrent el al., 2014; Diniz da Costa et al., 2018) using Frames – in the way they were defined by Fillmore (1982) – as structured representations of interrelated concepts. Frames are, then, the pivot structures for Frame Semantics, in which words are understood relative to the broader conceptual scenes they evoke (Fillmore, 1977). As the computational implementation of Frame Semantics, FrameNet has been developed as a lexicographic database that describes the words in a language against a computational representation of linguistic cognition based on frames, their frame elements (FEs) and the relations between them. The analysis is attested by the annotation of sentences representing how lexical units (LUs) instantiate the frames they evoke. FrameNet projects have been started producing databases in many languages, such as Brazilian Portuguese.[1]

In order to make FrameNet Brasil able to conduct multimodal analysis, we outlined the hypothesis that similarly to the way in which words in a sentence evoke frames and organize their elements in the syntactic locality accompanying them, visual elements in video may, then, (i) evoke frames and organize their elements on the screen or (ii) work complementarily with the frame evocation patterns of the sentences narrated simultaneously to their appearance on screen, providing different profiling and perspective options for meaning construction.

To test the hypothesis, we designed a pilot experiment for which we selected a Brazilian television travel show critically acclaimed as an excellent example of good practices in audiovisual composition. The TV format

chosen also configures a novel experimental setting for research on integrated image and text comprehension, since, in this corpus, text is not a direct description of the image sequence, but correlates to it indirectly in a myriad of ways.

The methodology defined was to:

1. annotate the audio transcript using the FrameNet Brasil Annotation WebTool (Matos and Torrent, 2018), that allows for the creation of frames and relations between them, as well as for the annotation of sentences and full texts;
2. considering audio as the controlling modality in this corpus, annotate the frames evoked by visual objects or entities that are grounded on or related to the auditory guidance;
3. analyze synchronies and asynchronies between the annotations.

To accomplish the steps (ii) and (iii) we developed a Multimodal Annotation Module for the FrameNet Brasil Webtool.

The results achieved so far suggest that, at least for this TV format but maybe also for others, a fine grained semantic annotation tackling the (a)synchronous correlations that take place in a multimodal setting may provide data that is key to the development of research in Computational Linguistics and Machine Learning whose focus lies on the integration of computer vision and natural language processing and generation. Moreover, multimodal annotation may also enrich the development of FrameNets, to the extent that correlations found between modalities can attest the modeling choices made by those building frame-based resources.

---

[1] See https://www.globalframenet.org/partners.

2. Computational Processing of Multimodal Communication

Multimodal analyses have been growing in importance within several approaches to both Cognitive Linguistics and Natural Language Understanding, changing the scenario depicted by McKevitt (2003), according to whom little progress had been made in integrating the areas of Natural Language Processing (NLP) and Vision Processing (VP), although there had been much success in developing theories, models and systems in each of these areas separately.

Aksoy et al. (2017) present a review of the state of art on linking natural language and vision, highlighting that the related literature mostly focuses on generating descriptions of static scenes or object concepts. They, then, offer an unsupervised framework which is able to link continuous visual features to textual descriptions of videos of long manipulation activities. The results show interesting capacity of semantic scene understanding, although the linguistic material is limited to automatically generated text descriptions.

Sun et al. (2019), on the other hand, report the development of a joint model for video and language representation learning, VideoBERT, in which the text processed is captured from the original audio of the videos that integrate the corpus. Therefore, this model is capable of learn bidirectional joint distributions over sequences of visual and linguistic inputs. Although it is shown that the model learns high-level semantic features, it should be pointed out that the genre of videos selected – cooking instructions or recipe demonstrations – offers a very straightforward correlation between visual and auditory content, when compared with many other TV, audiovisual or cinematography genres.

Turner (2018) explains that multimodality is traditionally expressed in three different forms of communication and meaning construction: auditory, visual and text. Steen et al. (2018) highlight that multimodal corpora have been annotated for correlations involving mainly gesture communication and text data, and that computational infrastructure for dealing with large multimodal corpora has been under development. Both Turner and Steen lead an effort on this direction through the collaborative works of The International Distributed Little Red Hen Lab™[2], in terms of establishing tools and methodology for analyzing large multimodal corpora, mostly exploring correlations between spoken and gesture communication.

FrameNet Brasil, then, aims to establish an approach complementary to these works, since it is based on the establishment of fine-grained frame-based relations between the auditory and visual modalities, which is not restricted to human gestures. Moreover, it builds on Cohn's (2016) systematization of the semantic investigation in multimodal data, according to the grammaticality of the modalities involved. It was used as a reference to evaluate the relation expressed by audio and video in the selected corpus. This aspect will be discussed next.

3. Multimodal Grammars

Based on Jackendoff's (2002) parallel architecture of language, Cohn (2016) focuses on how grammar and meaning coalesce in multimodal interactions, extending beyond the semantic taxonomies typically discussed within the domain of text–image relations. He thus classifies the relations between text and image in visual narratives, evaluating the presence or absence of grammar structuring each of the modalities and also the presence or absence of semantic dominance by one of the modalities.

The first step of this method for analyzing multimodal interactions would be to determine if one of the modalities controls the other in terms of meaning, that is, if there is a semantic dominance according to which one of the modalities plays a preponderant role in determining the meaning expressed by the media. If the answer is yes, there will be a relation of assertiveness or dominance. If the answer is no, the relation will be of co-assertiveness or co-dominance.

Cohn's model considers that there is assertiveness (or co-assertiveness) when both modalities have grammar - in the case of text modality, the grammar is expressed in terms of syntax; in the case of image, what counts as grammar is the narrative. The dominance (or co-dominance) will occur when one of the modalities has grammar and the other doesn't.

In our study we consider that, throughout the TV show, audio plays a controlling role in establishing meaning, although there are significant visual sequences in the form of video clips that express a linear narrative.

Although Cohn's (2016) model offers a coherent framework to approach multimodal data, the author does not incorporate any sort of fine-grained semantics into his model. Nonetheless, he recognizes the importance of using one for adequately tackling the interrelations and interactions between modalities and its components.

Given the lack of research incorporating fine-grained models of semantic cognition into multimodal analyses, the research presented in this paper aims to tackle the issue of meaning construction in multimodal settings, specifically on what concerns the interaction between audio (verbal expression transcribed into text) and video (not necessarily gesture communication), based on a principled structured model of human semantic cognition: FrameNet. Such a model is presented next.

4. FrameNet and Frame-Based Semantic Representation

Frames have a long history in both AI (Minsky, 1975) and linguistics (Fillmore, 1982) as structured representations of interrelated concepts. In Frame Semantics, words are

---

[2] See http://www.redhenlab.org

understood relative to the broader conceptual scenes they evoke (Fillmore, 1977). Hence, the expression *child-safe beach*, for example, is understood only in the context of a scene in which an Asset (the child) is exposed to some potentially Harmful_event (a strong sea current, for example).

This theoretical insight is the basis for lexicographic resources such as Berkeley FrameNet and its sister projects in other languages. Currently, there are FrameNet projects for several languages besides English, including Chinese, French, German, Italian, Japanese, Korean, Spanish, Swedish and Brazilian Portuguese. These frame-based resources have been applied to different Natural Language Understanding problems, such as conversational Artificial Inteligence (Vanzo et al. 2019) and paraphrase generation (Callison-Burch and Van Durme 2018).

4.1 Frame-to-Frame and Frame Element-to-Frame Relations

All framenets are composed of frames and their associated roles in a network of typed relations such as inheritance, perspective and subframe. The `Risk_scenario` frame alluded to above, for example, is an umbrella frame for several more specific perspectivized frames such as `Being_at_risk` (in which the Asset is exposed to a risky situation) and `Run_risk` (in which a Protagonist puts an Asset at risk voluntarily). Each perspective may be evoked by different words or by one same lexeme with different syntactic instantiation patterns.

`Being_at_risk`, for example, is evoked by adjectives such as unsafe.a and nouns such as risk.n in constructions like X is at risk. On the other hand, `Run_risk` is evoked by verbs such as risk.v and also by risk.n, but in a different construction: Y has put X at risk (Fillmore and Atkins 1992). The database structure also features annotated sentences, which attest the use of a given word in the target frame.

On top of the frame-to-frame relations traditionally used in most if not every FrameNet, FrameNet Brasil also developed other types of relations aimed at enriching the database structure. One of these relations links FEs to the frames licensing the lexical items that typically instantiate those elements. Hence, the FE Tourist, in the `Touring` frame, for instance, is linked via and FE-to-frame relation to the `People_by_leisure_activity` frame. Another relation connects core FEs to non-core FEs in the same frame when the latter can act as metonymic substitutes for the first (see Gamonal, 2017)

Another group of relations developed by FrameNet Brasil holds between LUs and is inspired by qualia roles, based on Pustejovsky's (1995) categorization. From the four original qualia types – agentive, constitutive, formal and telic – FrameNet Brasil has developed frame-mediated ternary relations in which a given LU is linked to another LU via a subtype of quale elaborated on by a frame. Those relations will be discussed next.

4.2 Frame Mediated Ternary Qualia Relations

Although frame-to-frame and frame element-to-frame relations already provide a fine-grained semantic representation, they are unable to capture differences in the semantics of a group of lexical units within one same frame. Such differences are relevant for the semantic representation of (multimodal) texts, as the pilot analysis in this paper will demonstrate.[3]

The Generative Lexicon Theory (GLT) (Pustejovsky, 1995) arises as an approach to lexical semantics focusing on the combinatorial and denotational properties of words, as well as on peculiar aspects of the lexicon such as polysemy and type coercion. The advance of the theory is due to a dissatisfaction of many theoretical and computational linguists with the characterization of the lexicon as a closed and static set of syntactic, morphological and semantic traits.

Qualia roles emerged as characteristics or different possible context predication modes of a lexical item. Pustejovsky and Jezek (2016) argue that qualia roles "indicate a single aspect of a word's meaning, defined on the basis of the relation between the concept expressed by the word and another concept that the word evokes". There are four main qualia roles:

1. The Formal quale is the relation that distinguishes an entity within a larger domain. Like a taxonomic categorization, it includes characteristics like orientation, shape, dimensions, color, position, size etc.
2. The Constitutive quale is established between an object and its constituents and the material involved in its production.
3. The Telic quale is associated with the purpose or function of the entity. We can expand this role to a persistent and prototypical property (function, purpose or action) of the entity (object, place or person).
4. The Agentive quale refers to the factors that are involved in the origin or "coming into existence" of an entity. Characteristics included in this relation are the creator, the artifact, the natural type and a causal chain.

Figure 1 exemplifies these qualia roles for the word pizza.n.

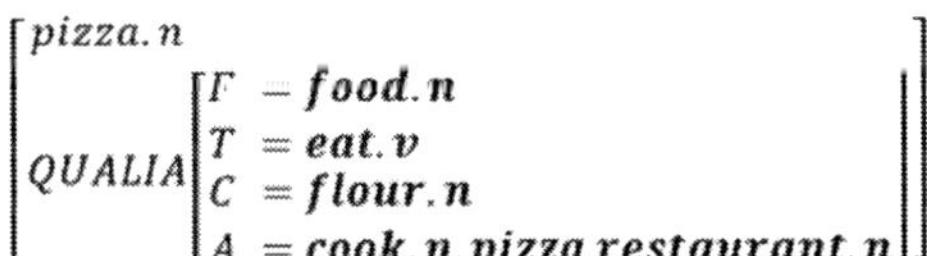

Fig. 1. Qualia roles for pizza.n

In Figure 1, we see that food.n is represented as formal_of pizza.n, being a more general category to which pizza belongs. The word eat.v is telic_of pizza.n since the latter is made to be eaten. Because it is an ingredient used in it, flour.n is constitutive_of pizza.n, while cook.n and pizza restaurant.n are agentive_of pizza.n, because they represent the person who causes the pizza to come into existence, and the place that prototypically sells it, respectively. Through qualia roles, a semantic relation is established between two words, providing a specific word with semantic features.

One recurrent problem of working with qualia is that the four relations just presented above are too generic. This has led to the proposal of long lists of subtypes for each relation (Lenci et al. 2000). However, instead of incorporating another list of relations to the FN-Br database, we use frames in this same database as mediators of ternary qualia relations to address both the lack of direct links between LUs in the framenet model and the poor specificity of qualia relations. In this innovative type of ternary relation, two LUs, 1 and 2, are linked to each other via a given quale using the background structure of frames as a way to make the quale role denser in terms of semantic information. For each quale, a set of frames was chosen from the FN-Br database based on the aspects of such quale they specify. LU1 would be related to an FE of the background frame, whereas LU2 would be related to another FE of the same frame. The frame would specify the semantics of the relation. The relations are represented in a directional fashion, that is, they are to be interpreted as unidirectional, although it is possible to create inverse relations.

Type	LU1	Relation	LU2
agentive	pizza.n	created_by	cook.n
agentive	pizza.n	created_by	pizza restaurant.n
constitutive	pizza.n	is_made_of	flour.n
formal	pizza.n	instance_of	food.n
telic	pizza.n	meant_to	eat.v

Fig. 2. Ternary qualia relations for pizza.n in the FrameNet Brasil database

Figure 2 provides an example of this implementation. In the FrameNet Brasil database the LU pizza.n has relation with five other LUs via qualia. The LU pizza.n has an Agentive relation (created_by) with pizza restaurant.n and cook.n. This relation is mediated by the Cooking_creation frame, which relates pizza.n to the FE Produced_food and pizza restaurant.n and cook.n to the FE Cook.[4] The LU pizza.n has also a Constitutive relation (is_made_of) with the LU flour.n, which is mediated by the Ingredients frame, pizza.n being related to the FE Product and flour.n to the FE Material. The Formal relation (instance_of) is established via the Exemplar frame, pizza.n being related to the FE Instance and food.n to the FE Type. Finally, the Telic relation (meant_to) establishes that pizza.n is related to the FE Tool, i.e. the object or process that has been designed specifically to achieve a purpose, in the Tool_purpose frame. As for eat.v, it is related to the FE Purpose in the same frame.

Figure 3 presents a diagram which details the ternary relations described for pizza.n .

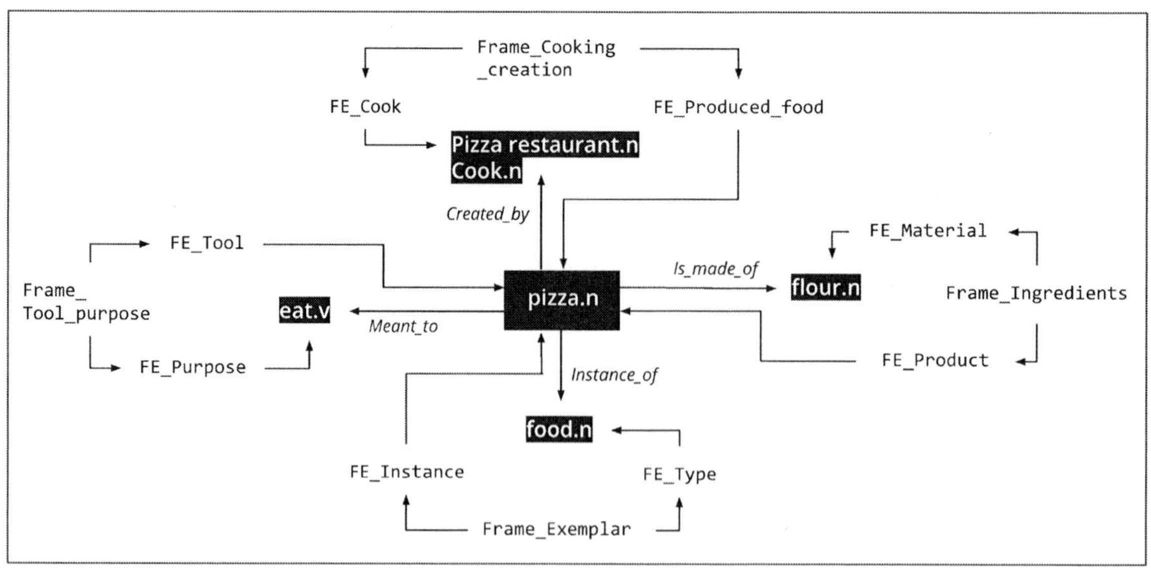

Fig. 3. Diagram of the ternary qualia relations for *pizza.n*

---

[4] Because we also implement metonymy relations between FEs, the peripheral FE Place can stand for the core FE Cook in the Cooking_creation frame.

As a general policy, only core – and core unexpressed – FEs can be recruited as ternary qualia mediators. The reason behind this policy relates to the very distinction between core and non-core FEs in FrameNet methodology: only core FEs are absolutely frame-specific, hence, they are the only ones that actually differentiate one frame from another.

The other policy refers to the degree of generality of frames recruited as mediators for the ternary qualia relations. Frames should be as general as possible, provided that they do not conflict with or overgeneralize the quale. For example, there are two more general frames in the inheritance chain leading to the `Tool_purpose` frame in the FrameNet Brasil database: `Inherent_purpose` and `Relation`. The `Relation` frame overgeneralizes the Telic quale, since it states that two Entities are related via a Relation_type. Because no constraints are posited for the Relation_type, it could actually refer to any type of qualia.

On the other hand, `Inherent_purpose` and `Tool_purpose` differ in terms of the nature of the LU1. In the former, it is a natural entity or phenomenon, while, in the latter, it is created by a living being. Such a difference relates to Pustejovsky's (2001) discussion on the difference between natural and functional types, and, therefore, the `Tool_purpose` frame should be used as the mediator for the Telic relation between some manmade item and its intended purpose, while the `Inherent_purpose` frame should be used for the Telic relation between a natural entity and the purpose that may be imposed to it in some context.

Given the possibilities enabled by the language model just described, as pointed out before, the hypothesis being investigated in this work is that, similarly to the way in which words in a sentence evoke frames and organize their elements in the syntactic locality accompanying them, video scenes may also either (i) evoke frames and organize their elements on the screen, or (ii) complement the frame evocation patterns of the sentences they are attached to, providing different profiling and perspective options for meaning construction, while also exploring alternative connections between concepts in the FrameNet Brasil model. To test the validity of this hypothesis and, therefore, the potential relevance of the project, an exploratory corpus study was conducted and is described in the next section.

5. Exploratory corpus study and annotation tool

FrameNet Brasil has been building a fine-grained semantic infrastructure and developing resources and applications for the Tourism domain (Torrent et al., 2014; Diniz da Costa et al. 2018). Therefore, this exploratory study reported in this paper refers to the same such domain.

5.1 The Corpus

The corpus is composed by the first season of the Brazilian television travel show "Pedro pelo Mundo" (Pedro around the world). There are 10 episodes, of 23 minutes each. In each episode we see the host exploring a city, region or country, highlighting its cultural and socioeconomic aspects. The TV format combines voice-over sequences, short interviews and video clip sequences in a well-integrated script that offers rich composition of audio and video. For each episode, the audio transcription generates approximately 200 sentences, which means 2000 sentences for the entire season. Following the FrameNet Brasil full-text annotation average of 6.1 annotation sets per sentence, the annotation of the whole textual part of the corpus should yield, when complete, about 12,200 lexical annotation sets.

5.2 Annotation Method

In the first step for the analysis conducted in the study, one annotator manually annotated the audio transcript of one random episode of the first season, using the FrameNet Brasil Web Annotation Tool (Matos and Torrent, 2018) – an open source database management and annotation tool that allows for the creation of frames and relations between them – and following FrameNet's guidelines for full-text annotation. An example of the sort of annotation carried out in this project is shown in Figure 4.

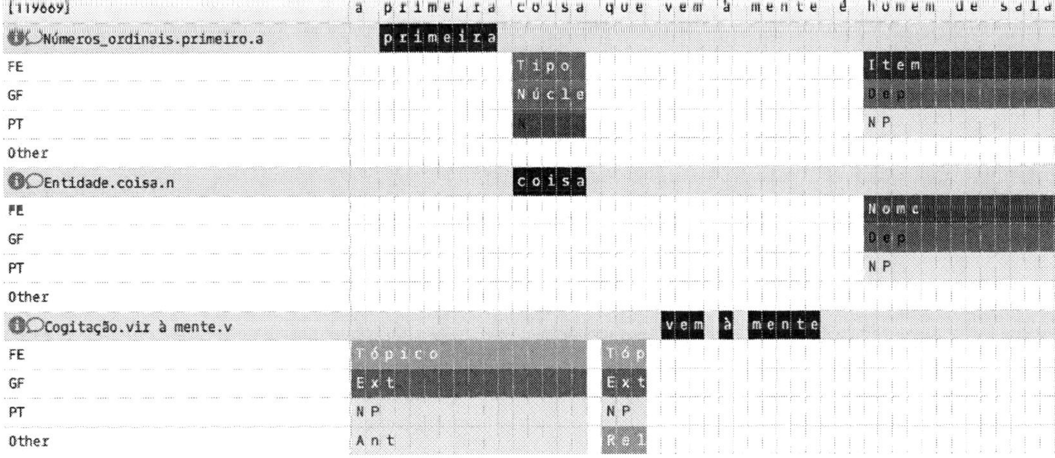

Fig. 4. Example of a sentence annotated for frames in the FN-Br WebTool

LEXICAL UNIT	AUDIO FRAME	AUDIO TIME	VIDEO FRAME	VIDEO TIME	SYNC
quando *(when)*	Temp_collocation	32.03 to 32.08	-	-	async
pensa *(think)*	Cogitation	32.18 to 32.29	-	-	async
primeira *(first)*	Ordinal_numbers	33.20 to 34.02	-	-	async
coisa *(thing)*	Entity	34.03 to 34.11	-	-	async
vem à mente *(come to mind)*	Cogitation	34.14 to 35.02	-	-	async
homem *(man)*	People	35.03 to 35.14	People_by_origin	36.12 to 37.12	async
saia *(skirt)*	Clothing	35.17 to 35.29	Clothing	36.12 to 37.12	async
whisky	Food	36.00 to 36.10	Food	35.02 to 36.12	sync
escocês *(Scottish)*	Origin	36.11 to 36.23	-	-	async
gaita de fole *(bagpipe)*	Noise_makers	36.24 to 37.23	Noise_makers	36.12 to 37.12	sync

Table 1. Audio (text) and video annotation comparison.

After the annotation of the audio transcript has been carried out, the same annotator annotated the video superimposed in the episodes for the same categories. Next, we contrasted the annotations, searching for matching frames while also considering the synchronicity or asynchronicity of the frames instantiated in both. The time stamps associated to the audio transcripts and the video were taken as the correlational unit between the two modalities.

5.3 Sample Annotation Discussion

In the remainder of this section, we present and discuss the data obtained from the multimodal annotation of one sentence in the corpus, transcribed in (1).

(1) Quando a gente pensa na Escócia, a primeira coisa que vem à mente é homem de saia, whisky escocês e gaita de fole.
'When we think of Scotland, the first thing that comes to mind is man in skirt, Scottish whisky and bagpipe'.

The full annotation of (1) yielded ten lexical annotation sets, while the annotation of the video it is superimposed to generated four visual annotation sets. Table 1 presents these data and how they synchronize – or not.

The six lines in white present frames found only in the audio. Because the annotation is audio-oriented, we did not annotate the frames that were present only in the video for this pilot study, although we plan to include them in the near future. The four lines highlighted in grey show the matches between frames annotated for both text/audio and video, although there is asynchrony in two of them and an indirect match in one of those two. The asynchrony is due to the fact that although evoked by both text/audio and video, the occurrences do not coincide in terms of time. In both cases the text/audio evocation occurs before the elements appear visually on screen.

The indirect correspondence between the frames People, annotated for text/audio, and People_by_origin, annotated for the video is more interesting though. Although the latter inherits the first, this seems to be only one of the correspondences between them.

The LU evoking the People_by_origin frame is homem.n *'man'*. This LU does not bring any information on the origin of the person, therefore, the frame evoked is the most general of the People family of frames in FrameNet Brasil. Nonetheless, in the video annotation, the annotator chose the People_by_origin frame, which is evoked by the Object 7, as shown in Figure 5. The reason behind this choice is the fact that the man depicted in the video right after the audio mentions homem de saia *'man in* skirt' is wearing a kilt and playing a bagpipe, which are a typical clothing and musical instrument of Scotland, respectively. This combination of factors makes it very likely to infer that what we see is a Scottish person. Therefore, it makes possible to the annotator to choose the People_by_origin frame instead of the People frame.

The first question that arises from this sample annotation is how such a reasoning could be captured by some non-human tagger. Moreover, one could wonder whether this kind of annotation is supported by the FrameNet Brasil language model. Ternary qualia relations provide the answer to both of them (see Figure 6).

First, a subtype of the formal quale, mediated by the Type frame connects the LUs kilt.n and saia.n *'skirt'* in FrameNet Brasil. Second, a subtype of the constitutive quale mediated by the Idiosyncrasy frame connects the LU kilt.n, instantiating the FE Idiosyncrasy to the LU escocês.n *'Scot'*, instantiating the FE Entity in this frame. Finally, the LU escocês.n evokes the People_by_origin frame, which is precisely the one evoked by the Object 7 in Figure 5.

Figure 6 presents a summary of the connections between the multimodal elements annotated for (1), which can be found in FrameNet Brasil enriched language model.

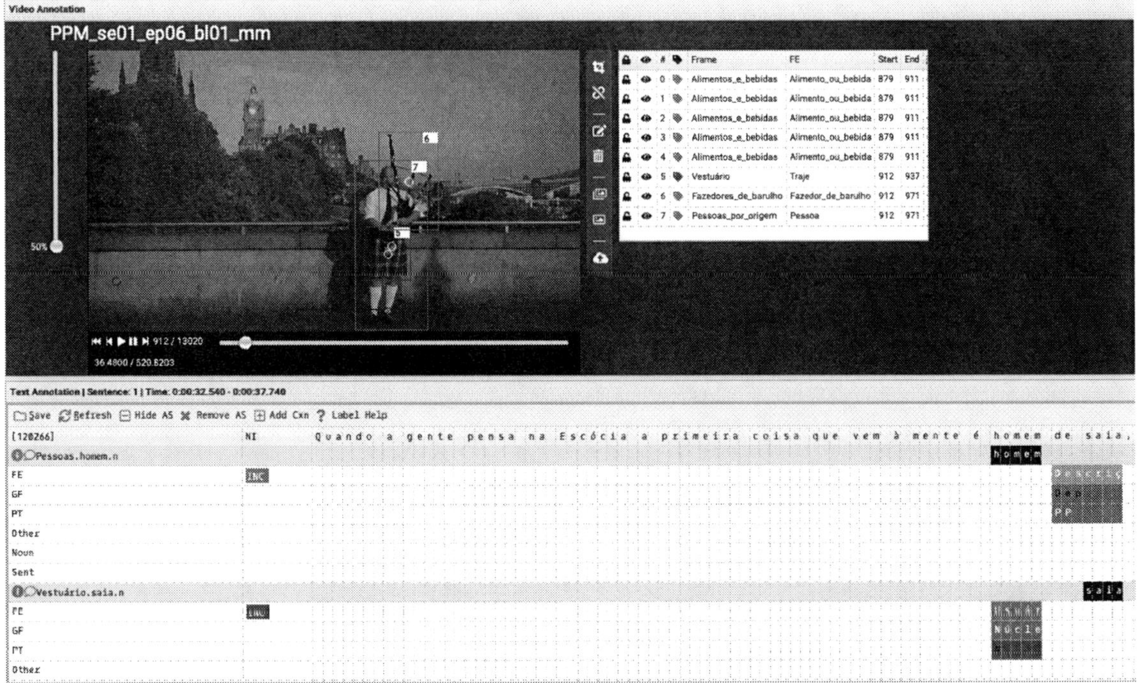

Fig. 5. Screenshot of the FN-Br Webtool Multimodal Annotation Module

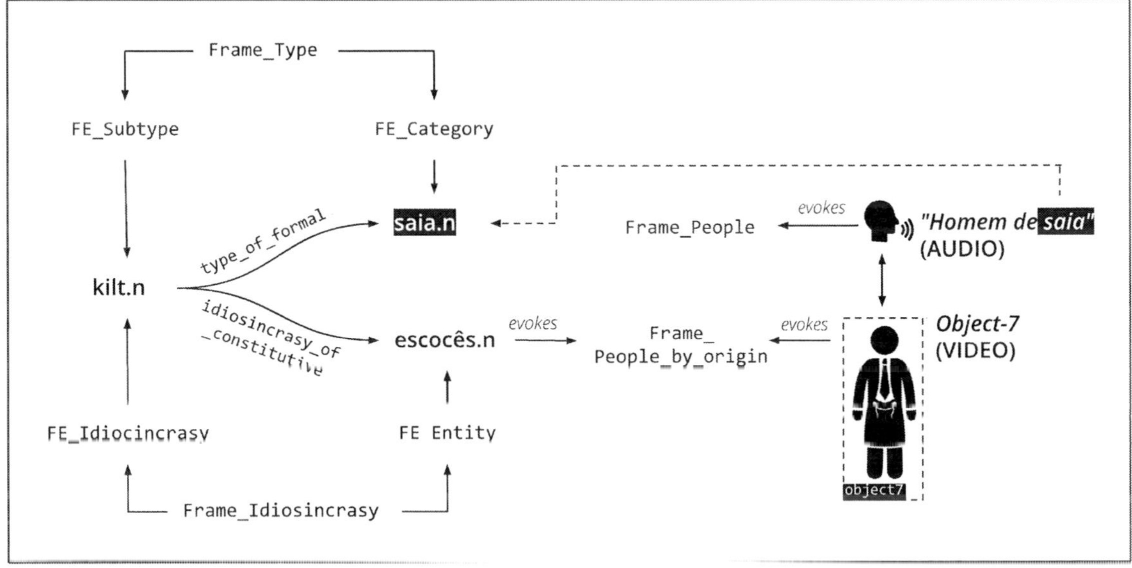

Fig. 6. Summary of connections

6. Conclusions

In this paper, we presented a tool and annotation scheme for fine-grained annotation of multimodal corpora. Such a tool controls for the synchronicity between different media types and allows for cross-modality annotation, yielding, as an annotation product, material that can shed light on the role of multimodality in language comprehension. This new annotation module was projected to run combined with the original FN-Br WebTool, which could annotate only text. The combination of both modules is crucial to multimodal annotation, since timing has demonstrated to be a key issue in measuring frame correlations across different media. Thus, the Multimodal Module allows annotators to choose frames and locate frame elements both in the text and in the images, while keeping track of the time span in which those elements are active in the video and in the audio.

There are several text annotation tools and several video and/or image annotation tools. However, they do not control for the synchronicity between different media types nor allow for cross-modality annotation. Also, none of them are frame-based and, therefore, none of them yield, as an annotation product, material that can shed light on the role of multimodality in language comprehension.

Future work includes the creation of a gold standard multimodal annotated corpus that may be used in Machine Learning applications such as Automatic Visual Semantic Role Labeling and video indexing.

7. Acknowledgements

The FrameNet Brasil Computational Linguistics Lab is funded by the CAPES PROBRAL (grant # 88887.144043/2017-00) and the CAPES STINT (grant # 99999.009910/2014-00) programs. Mr. Belcavello's PhD research is funded by the CAPES PDSE program (grant # 88881.362052/2019-01). Mr. Diniz da Costa's PhD research was funded by the CAPES PROBRAL program (grant # 88887.185051/2018-00).

8. Bibliographical References

Aksoy, E. E., Ovchinnikova, E., Orhan, A., Yang, Y., & Asfour, T. (2017). Unsupervised linking of visual features to textual descriptions in long manipulation activities. *IEEE Robotics and Automation Letters*, *2*(3), 1397-1404.

Callison-Burch, C., & Van Durme, B. (2018). *Large-Scale Paraphrasing for Natural Language Understanding*. Johns Hopkins University Baltimore United States.

Cohn, N. (2016). A multimodal parallel architecture: A cognitive framework for multimodal interactions. *Cognition*, *146*, 304-323.

Diniz da Costa, A., Gamonal, M. A., Paiva, V. M. R. L., Marção, N. D., Peron-Corrêa, S. R., de Almeida, V. G., ... & Torrent, T. T. (2018). FrameNet-Based Modeling of the Domains of Tourism and Sports for the Development of a Personal Travel Assistant Application. In *Proceedings of the Eleventh International Conference on Language Resources and Evaluation* (pp. 6-12).

Fillmore, C. J. (1977). The case for case reopened. *Syntax and semantics*, *8*(1977), 59-82.

Fillmore, C. J. (1982). Frame semantics. IN: Linguistic society of Korea (org). *Linguistics in the morning calm.* (1982) pp. 111-137. Hanshin Publishing Co., Seoul.

Fillmore, C. J., & Atkins, B. T. (1992). Toward a frame-based lexicon: The semantics of RISK and its neighbors. *Frames, fields, and contrasts: New essays in semantic and lexical organization*, *103*, 75-102.

Gamonal, M. A. (2017). *Modelagem Linguístico-Computacional de Metonímias na Base de Conhecimento Multilíngue (m.knob) da FrameNet Brasil.* Ph.D. Dissertation in Linguistics. Universidade Federal de Juiz de Fora. Juiz de Fora.

Jackendoff, R., & Jackendoff, R. S. (2002). *Foundations of language: Brain, meaning, grammar, evolution.* Oxford University Press, USA.

Lenci, A., Busa, F., Ruimy, N., Gola, E., Monachini, M., Calzolari, N. and Zampolli, A. (2000). *Simple Linguistic Specifications, Deliverable D2, 1.* Istituto di Linguistica Computazionale Antonio Zampolli, Pisa, Italy.

Matos, E. E. S., Torrent, T. T. (2018) *FN-Br WebTool: FrameNet Brasil Web Annotation Tool.* INPI Registration Number BR512018051603-3

McKevitt, P. (2003, January). MultiModal semantic representation. In *First Working Meeting of the SIGSEM Working Group on the Representation of MultiModal Semantic Information* (pp. 1-16).

Minsky, M. (1975). A Framework for Representing Knowledge: In Winston, PH (eds.), The Psychology of Computer Vision, 211–277.

Pustejovsky, J. (1995). *The Generative Lexicon.* Cambridge, USA, MIT Press.

Pustejovsky, J. (2001). Type construction and the logic of concepts. In: P. Bouillon and F. Busa. *The language of word meaning* (pp. 91–123). Cambridge University Press, New York, USA.

Pustejovsky, J. & Ježek, E. (2016). Qualia Structure. In: _____. *Integrating Generative Lexicon and Lexical Semantic Resources* (pp. 11–55). Tutorial at The Language Resources and Evaluation Conference (LREC 2016), Protoroz, Slovenia.

Steen, F. F., Hougaard, A., Joo, J., Olza, I., Cánovas, C. P., Pleshakova, A., ... & Turner, M. (2018). Toward an infrastructure for data-driven multimodal communication research. *Linguistics Vanguard*, *4*(1).

Sun, C., Myers, A., Vondrick, C., Murphy, K., & Schmid, C. (2019). Videobert: A joint model for video and language representation learning. arXiv preprint arXiv:1904.01766.

Torrent, T., Salomão, M. M., Campos, F., Braga, R., Matos, E., Gamonal, M., ... & Peron, S. (2014, August). Copa 2014 FrameNet Brasil: a frame-based trilingual electronic dictionary for the Football World Cup. In *Proceedings of COLING 2014, the 25th International Conference on Computational Linguistics: System Demonstrations* (pp. 10-14).

Turner, M. (2018). The Role of Creativity in Multimodal Construction Grammar. *Zeitschrift für Anglistik und Amerikanistik*, *66*(3), 357-370.

Vanzo, A., Bastianelli, E., & Lemon, O. (2019). Hierarchical multi-task natural language understanding for cross-domain conversational ai: HERMIT NLU. *arXiv preprint arXiv:1910.00912.*

Proceedings of the International FrameNet Workshop 2020: Towards a Global, Multilingual FrameNet, pages 31–40
Language Resources and Evaluation Conference (LREC 2020), Marseille, 11–16 May 2020

Combining Conceptual and Referential Annotation to Study Variation in Framing

Marten Postma, Levi Remijnse, Filip Ilievski, Antske Fokkens, Sam Titarsolej, Piek Vossen

Vrije Universiteit Amsterdam

De Boelelaan 1105, 1081 HV Amsterdam, The Netherlands

{m.c.postma,l.remijnse,antske.fokkens,piek.vossen}@vu.nl

ilievski@isi.edu, s.titarsolej@gmail.com

Abstract

We introduce an annotation tool whose purpose is to gain insights into variation of framing by combining FrameNet annotation with referential annotation. English FrameNet enables researchers to study variation in framing at the conceptual level as well through its packaging in language. We enrich FrameNet annotations in two ways. First, we introduce the referential aspect. Secondly, we annotate on complete texts to encode connections between mentions. As a result, we can analyze the variation of framing for one particular event across multiple mentions and (cross-lingual) documents. We can examine how an event is framed over time and how core frame elements are expressed throughout a complete text. The data model starts with a representation of an event type. Each event type has many incidents linked to it, and each incident has several reference texts describing it as well as structured data about the incident. The user can apply two types of annotations: 1) mappings from expressions to frames and frame elements, 2) reference relations from mentions to events and participants of the structured data.

Keywords: FrameNet, reference, annotation tool

1. Introduction

We construct narratives to describe events in the world around us. The language that we use in those narratives forms a lens that filters the actual components of those events, e.g., their time, location, and participants, according to our perspectives. This way, narratives function not only as structured collections of informative references to the event, but also as collections of conceptual representations of that same event. For instance, texts describing the attack on the World Trade Center express their references in various linguistic forms: '9/11', 'September 11 attacks', 'the 2001 attacks' (all of which are timestamps with different specificity), 'a series of four coordinated terrorist attacks' (focus on the organizational aspect), 'destruction of the towers in America' (focus on the damaging aspect), etc. This set of references is a small share of all the various references in a growing portion of written texts. With multiple texts written in different languages about a single real-world event, one could analyze variation of framing of an event by combining the conceptual and referential information. To perform such an analysis, we need both semantic resources to describe this conceptual information, and information about the components of the real-world event.

English FrameNet (Ruppenhofer et al., 2006) brought conceptual framing research to a computational setting. The English lexicon made it possible to gain insight into the relationship between lexical items and the semantic frames that they evoke. English FrameNet has also motivated researchers to create FrameNets in other languages such as in Japanese (Ohara et al., 2004), German (Burchardt et al., 2009), Swedish (Heppin and Gronostaj, 2012), Brazilian Portuguese (Laviola et al., 2017), Spanish (Subirats and Sato, 2003), French (Djemaa et al., 2016), Hebrew (Hayoun and Elhadad, 2016), and Latvian (Gruzitis et al., 2018). Multiple annotation efforts resulted in many corpora and also served as training, development, and test data to train

FrameNet-based Semantic Role Labelers.

The majority of the described efforts have mainly investigated frame annotations at the sentence level, as already observed by Fillmore, evidenced by the following quote: "since FrameNet has been working mainly on single sentences and has done nothing (yet) on connections within whole texts, the FrameNet database has nothing direct to offer." (Andor, 2010, p.168)

We aim at combining FrameNet annotations with referential annotations in order to analyze framing variation in texts describing an event. For this we need to extend FrameNet annotations to the discourse level. Following the data-to-text method described in Vossen et al. (2018), we make use of the data acquisition platform described in Vossen et al. (2020) to enable this type of research, for which we require:

1. a referential representation of an incident, i.e., an event instance such as *the 2012 Slovenian presidential election*, with structured information about the location, time, and participants of the incident. 2. each incident to be tagged with one or more event types, e.g., *election*. This makes it possible to generalize over incidents of the same type to learn which frames are typical. 3. different texts that make reference to the same incident, possibly written in multiple languages with varying document creation times and from different sources, which provides us with insights into cross-lingual differences, source perspectives and the impact of historical distance to the incident time (Cybulska and Vossen, 2011). 4. an environment for efficient and consistent FrameNet and reference annotation to (given) structured data. This makes it possible to consider the framing of the incident throughout all texts that make reference to it as a discourse unit.

In this paper, we introduce an annotation tool in which both structured data about an incident and many reference texts describing that one incident are simultaneously presented to the user. This interface enables both FrameNet-based annotations as well as referential linking to the incident that the reference texts make reference to. The analysis of conceptual and referential framing enriches research into variation in framing beyond the level of sentences and across different types of reference texts and languages.

This paper is structured as follows. In Section 2., we introduce English FrameNet and the related work on frame annotation, followed by a discussion on combining conceptual and referential annotation in Section 3. We introduce the annotation tool in Section 4. Finally, we discuss the possibilities of the tool and future plans in Section 5., and conclude the paper in Section 6.

2. Background

This section introduces the theoretical notions and implementations of FrameNet. Subsection 2.1. describes the relevant terminology and basic principles of frame semantics. In Subsection 2.2., we provide a brief overview of currently available frame annotation tools.

2.1. FrameNet

Frame semantics is a theory of linguistic meaning that assumes that the meaning of words is (partially) activated through the *frames* that they evoke (Ruppenhofer et al., 2006). A frame is a schematic representation of a concept, which is triggered by a lexical unit. This lexical unit is the sense of an expression in spoken or written discourse. For the purpose of this paper, we model these conceptual relationships using RDF, as displayed in Figure 1. In this figure, the expression 'kidnapped' is disambiguated to a lexical unit via the *ontolex:sense* relationship (McCrae et al., 2017). The lexical unit evokes the frame **Kidnapping** via the *ontolex:evokes* relationship.[1]

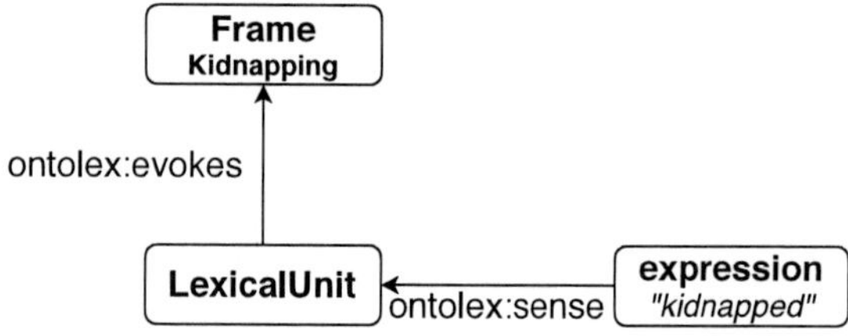

Figure 1: RDF modeling for conceptual relationships. The expression *kidnapped* expresses one of its senses as a lexical unit. This lexical unit evokes the **Kidnapping** frame.

Each frame is further associated with a characteristic set of *frame elements* that apply to the syntactic realization of the phrases dominated by the frame. We refer to Example (1).

(1) **Kidnapping**
     [PERPETRATOR Two men] ⊙kidnapped [VICTIM the children] [TIME yesterday].

In this example, 'kidnapped' evokes **Kidnapping**, which consists of several frame elements. 'Two men' expresses

the PERPETRATOR frame element and 'the children' expresses the VICTIM frame element. These frame elements are called *core* frame elements, i.e., they need to be overtly specified in order for the reader to process the frame. Other types of frame elements, like 'yesterday', are *peripheral*, meaning that they modify the frame.

When a core frame element is not present in the predicate scope, it is annotated as a *Null Instantiation*, which we paraphrase as being *unexpressed*. In Subsection 3.1., we will elaborate on the phenomenon of unexpressed core frame elements and how we propose to treat them. Frames are situated in semantic space through *frame-to-frame relations*. In these relations, one frame is the more abstract superframe, and the other is the less abstract subframe. One of the relations through which **Kidnapping** is situated has an inheritance frame-to-frame relationship with **Committing_crime**, which is a conceptually corresponding yet less specific superframe . In Subsection 3.1., we will show how frame-to-frame relations are used in FrameNet to explore variation in framing.

2.2. FrameNet annotation tools

To the best of our knowledge, there are four publicly accessible and popular FrameNet annotation tools.

Annotation for English FrameNet (Ruppenhofer et al., 2006) is based on four layers. The *target* is the target word that will be tagged with a frame label. Each constituent of the *target* is a candidate for frame element annotation. Each constituent is labeled with a grammatical function and a phrase type. Grammatical functions are syntactic relations that a constituent fulfills with respect to the target word, e.g., *object* in the case of a verbal target word. Phrase types indicate the syntactic category of the constituent, e.g., *noun phrase* in the case of the constituent 'the man'. English FrameNet annotates one sentence at a time, in which one target word is labeled with a frame and its frame elements. An annotator first labels a target word with a frame label. Consequently, the grammatical function and the phrase type of each of the constituents of the target word are shown, which can be corrected manually. The annotation guidelines are built upon the values of the grammatical function and the phrase type of a constituent, i.e., these notions guide the annotator in deciding which frame element to apply. In the online demo of the annotation tool, the grammatical functions and the phrase types are not shown to avoid visual clutter.

The Global FrameNet Project (Torrent et al., 2018) builds upon the annotation setup of English FrameNet. The core novelty lies in moving to a multilingual setting. The aim is to gain insight into how different languages frame translations of the same texts. This is accomplished by enriching the annotation by allowing annotators to specify why a certain annotation was not possible based on the existing frames, e.g., *too specific* or *too general*.

WebAnno (Eckart de Castilho et al., 2016) is a generic web-based annotation tool for semantic and syntactic structures, of which FrameNet annotation is one of the options. The main emphasis of the tool is on the relation between syntactic and semantic structures, which drives the annotation effort. The tool offers the possibility of introducing con-

---

[1]We chose to not use the OntoLex (McCrae et al., 2017) relationship *ontolex:reference* since it might lead to confusion in distinguishing between conceptual and referential relationships.

straint rules in order to speed up annotation.

Salto (Burchardt et al., 2006) is a multi-level annotation tool, which can be used to annotate FrameNet information. The annotation starts with a syntactic analysis of a sentence. After determining the target word and labeling it with a frame, the constituents can be tagged with a frame element by means of drag and drop functionality.

All four described annotation tools provide the functionality to annotate FrameNet information. All of them start with a syntactic analysis of the sentence and annotate FrameNet information on top of that analysis. They differ in what syntactic information is used and how this drives the annotations.

The annotation tool described in this paper differs from the existing annotation tools. The main difference stems from the choice of the central element in the tool. Whereas most existing tools use a sentence as the central element, our tool makes use of an incident, i.e., an event, as the primary unit. For each event, the user is shown both structured data and texts that all make reference to the same incident. The purpose of the annotation effort is to make it possible to annotate mentions conceptually by linking to FrameNet, and referentially towards the structured data.

3. Variation in Framing of Reference

In this section, we discuss variation in framing at the referential level. In Subsection 3.1., the means of variation in framing within the FrameNet paradigm is discussed, as well as the merits of adding the referential level. In Subsection 3.2., we introduce a data model to facilitate referential annotations as well as the main data resource used. In Subsection 3.3., we propose to add a relationship between an expression and a frame in order to make the connection between the referent of an expression and its evoked frame explicit.

3.1. Variation of framing in FrameNet

Within FrameNet, variation in framing can be observed by measuring the degree to which different subframes stand in a similar frame-to-frame relation to a superframe. See a classic example below.

(2) a. **Commerce_sell**
[TIME Yesterday,] [SELLER John] ⊙sold [BUYER Mary] [GOODS a book].

b. **Commerce_buy**
[BUYER A woman] ⊙bought [GOODS a novel] [PLACE in the shop].

In (2a), 'sold' evokes **Commerce_sell**, with 'Mary' labeled as the Buyer. In (2b), 'bought' evokes **Commerce_buy**, with 'a woman' labeled as the BUYER. Both frames are related to the abstract frame **Commerce_goods_transfer** and show a different perspective on this event. This way, variation in framing is measured on a conceptual level, comparing different variants of subframes related to one abstract superframe.

In capturing variation in framing at a conceptual level, the annotation provides no knowledge concerning the referential level of the text. For instance, we lack insight as to whether the two predicates in (2) refer to the same event in the real world, which would entail that 'Mary' and 'a woman' refer to the same referent. The current tool aims to implement structured data about the event, enabling the annotator to annotate on both the conceptual and the referential level. This allows us to investigate variation in a broader sense: not just the framing of abstract concepts, but also with respect to the referent.

In addition to variation in subframes belonging to a superframe, variation in framing can be observed when measuring the extent to which core frame elements are expressed. According to FrameNet, core frame elements are necessary components of a frame (Ruppenhofer et al., 2006). Yet, core frame elements often remain unexpressed in a sentence. FrameNet distinguishes between unexpressed core frame elements that are left out due to syntactic constraints or allowances (e.g., passivization, imperatives, pro-drop) and core frame elements that are left out due to anaphoric reasons: they are already given as part of the surrounding context of the sentence. See the examples below, taken from the FrameNet database (Ruppenhofer et al., 2006).

(3) **Change_of_leadership**

a. [NEW_LEADER Khan himself] was ⊙elected [ROLE a Congress party MP for Rampur].

b. Also [TIME on July 13] [SELECTOR the congress] ⊙elected [NEW_LEADER Gorbarev] [FUNCTION to head a commission [...]]

In both sentences in (3), the verb evokes **Change_of_leadership**. One of the core frame elements of this frame is SELECTOR: the person or group 'responsible for a change in leadership' (FrameNet lexical database; (Ruppenhofer et al., 2006)). In (3a), the SELECTOR is unexpressed, which can be assigned to the syntax, since passivized constructions allow speakers to leave out the agent. However, (3b) shows an active syntax, while the SELECTOR remains unexpressed. Moreover, **Change_of_leadership** contains more core frame elements that are unexpressed in (3), such as, for instance, OLD_LEADER, OLD_ORDER, and BODY. These core frame elements are regarded as part of the contextual knowledge and not considered sufficiently relevant to express.

The current categorization of unexpressed core frame elements in FrameNet is syntax-driven, meaning that these frame elements are analyzed within sentence boundaries. When their absence is assumed to be bounded by sentence-external words or phrases, this information is not further specified. The downside of this approach is that we do not gain insight into the way that these core frame elements are linguistically encoded in the full discourse or if they are encoded at all. Certain approaches address this problem by going beyond the predicate scope in annotating unexpressed core frame elements. For instance, in SemEval-2010 Task 10: Linking Events and Their Participants in Discourse (Ruppenhofer et al., 2010), unexpressed core frame elements were annotated outside of the scope of the predicate in order to gain insight into the referents of these unexpressed roles. A small number of texts from a work of Arthur Conan Doyle were annotated. There were three participating systems. The results showed that this is a very challenging task for Natural Language Processing systems. Building upon the insights gained from SemEval-2010 Task 10, we consider the text as a cohesive narrative structure and allow for annotation of core frame elements throughout the full text. We hypothesize that frames and frame elements are evoked either directly or indirectly throughout the discourse in relation to the minimally required referential level. The tool, therefore, allows for annotation of frame and frame element relations at both the subword level, e.g., compounds, as well as across sentences. Being able to annotate frames and (core) frame elements throughout the text also allows us to analyze how different sources frame the same situation differently and to explore the underlying factors of unexpression and other differences. We discuss the implementation of this adaptation in Section 4. and its function in Subsection 5.1.

3.2. Data model & main data resource

To facilitate the combination of conceptual and referential annotation, we make use of a data model in which an incident is the central element.

Let R be a registry of real-world incidents, i.e., event instances. Let R_i be a real-world incident and let $R_i \in R$. Each R_i contains structured data about the real-world incident, e.g., the period or time when the event happened, its location, and information about which participants played a role and in which capacity. Let E_t be an event type, which is a categorization of a real-world incident. Finally, there are reference texts, which are descriptions of real-world incidents (R_i), e.g., a news article describing what happened. Each R_i can have multiple reference texts.

The main data resource used in the annotation tool is Wikidata (Vrandečić and Krötzsch, 2014). We represent a Wikidata item, i.e., a description of an event instance, as an incident. Wikidata provides structured data about the incident, such as the time, location, and participants. Also, a Wikidata item lists Wikipedia pages in multiple languages that make reference to that specific Wikidata item, which we represent as the reference texts. Finally, each Wikidata item is tagged with one or multiple *instance of* (Property P31) relationships, which indicate the event type(s) of the Wikidata item.

3.3. The connection between a frame and a referent of an expression

English FrameNet (Ruppenhofer et al., 2006) uses the *evoke* relationship to relate lexical units to frames. However, the evoke relationship does not provide information about the relationship between the event that an expression refers to and the evoked frame. In our approach, we make this information explicit in our annotation. We clarify the distinction through the examples in Table 1.

Table 1 provides examples that highlight the relationship between the evoked frames and the instances that the expressions refer to. All examples originate from the English Wikipedia page describing the *2006 Hezbollah cross-border raid* (Wikidata identifier Q2026122), in which Hezbollah conducted a raid on Israeli territory in 2006. During the raid, Hezbollah kidnapped Israeli soldiers. In Sentence 1, the target word 'kidnapped' evokes **Kidnapping** and also refers to the event in which Israeli soldiers were kidnapped that is an instance of a *kidnapping* event. Similarly, the noun 'attack' in Sentence 3 evokes **Attack**, and the event it refers to is an instance of the evoked frame. On the contrary, the noun 'kidnappers' in Sentence 2 evokes **Kidnapping**, but it refers to Hezbollah, which means that the instance that the expression refers to is not an instance of the evoked frame but an instance of the concept *person*. These role-designating nouns typically serve as a frame element of the verb they are governed by. Finally, the verb 'can' in Sentence 4 evokes **Possibility**, but it is unclear what it refers to. There is no clear relationship between the evoked frame and what the target word refers to.

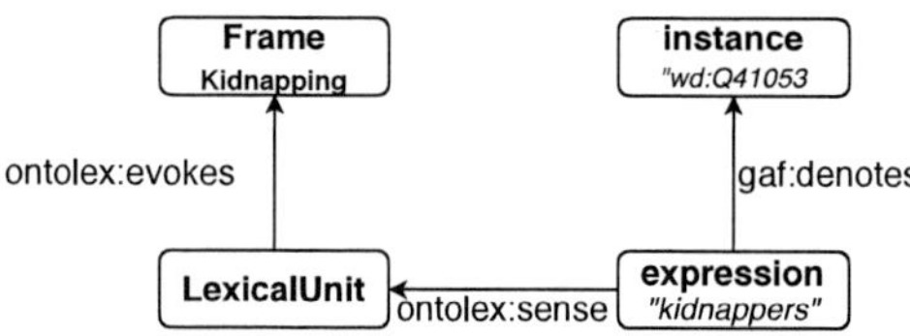

Figure 2: RDF modeling for conceptual and referential relationships without the dfn:isOfFrame relationship. The expression 'kidnappers' refers to the Wikidata item Q41053 (*Hezbollah*) and evokes the **Kidnapping** frame. Since *Hezbollah* is not an instance of kidnapping, no *rdf:type* relationship is assigned.

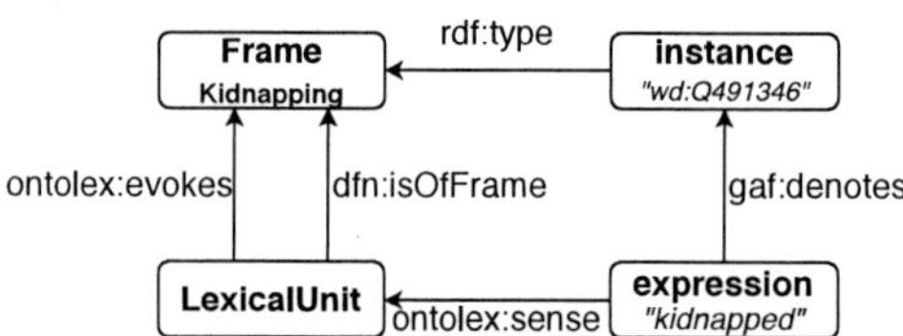

Figure 3: RDF modeling for conceptual and referential relationships with the dfn:isOfFrame relationship. The expression 'kidnapped' refers to the Wikidata item Q491346 (*kidnapping of Kim Dae-jung*) and evokes the **Kidnapping** frame. Since *kidnapping of Kim Dae-jung* is an instance of kidnapping, the *rdf:type* relationship is assigned and hence also the dfn:isOfFrame relationship.

We extend the conceptual RDF relationships with referential ones, for which we use Figures 2 and 3 for clarification purposes. For all target words in Table 1, it is the case that they evoke a frame. For most examples (all except Sentence 4), there is a referential link, which we model via the *gaf:denotes* relationship as part of the GAF framework (Fokkens et al., 2014). In the case that the referent that the expressions refer to is an instance of the evoked frame, we create an *instance of* relationship, for which we use the *rdf:type* relationship, between the incident and the evoked frame (see Figure 3). We make this relationship explicit by establishing a *http://rdf.cltl.nl/dfn/isOfFrame* link between the *LexicalUnit* and the *Frame*. In cases where the referent is not an instance of the evoked frame, the *rdf:type* and *http://rdf.cltl.nl/dfn/isOfFrame* relationship are absent (see Figure 2).

ID	Sentence	POS	Evokes	Refers to	Relation frame to incident
1	Six Western tourists were **kidnapped** by Al-Faran on 4 July 1995.	verb	**Kidnapping**	the kidnapping as part of Wikidata item Q2026122	the referent is an instance of the frame.
2	In December 1995, the **kidnappers** left a note that they were no longer holding the men hostage.	noun	**Kidnapping**	Hezbollah	the referent is not an instance of the frame
3	Top Hezbollah official Ghaleb Awali was assassinated in a car bomb **attack** in the Dahiya in Beirut in July 2004	noun	**Attack**	the car bombing as part of Wikidata item Q2026122	the referent is an instance of the frame.
4	Israel **can** get to Hezbollah anywhere in Lebanon	verb	**Possibility**	-	there is no referential relation

Table 1: Examples sentences taken from the English Wikipedia page describing the *2006 Hezbollah cross-border raid* (Wikidata identifier Q2026122). The first column indicates the example sentence identifier, the second shows the example sentence, the third provides the part of speech tag of the target word, the fourth which frame the target word evokes, the fifth column provides information about what the target word refers to, and the last column indicates the relationship between the evoked frame and its referent.

4. Data-to-text Annotation Tool

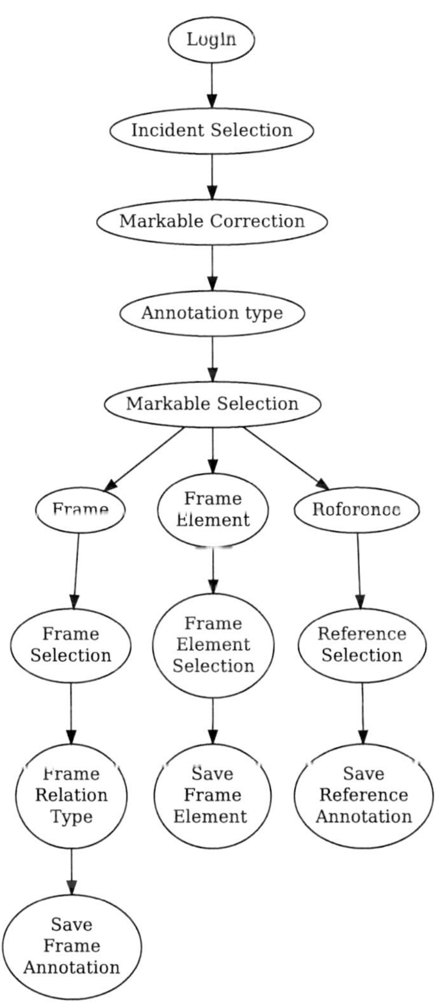

Figure 4: Annotation workflow

In this section, we introduce the annotation tool, for which we present the workflow in Figure 4. The tool starts from data that is aggregated through the MWEP platform described in Vossen et al. (2020). It contains structured data on incidents of a specific type, e.g., *murders, elections, sports events*, etc. paired with reference texts linked to the specific incidents.

After the login, the annotator first selects an event type, after which a list of incidents is given. Next, the annotator can select a specific incident from the list, after which the structured data is shown with all the reference texts.

The user first has the option to correct the tokenization in the texts to ensure that multi-words and compounds are correctly represented. After deciding on the markables, three types of annotation types can be chosen: *Frame, Frame Element*, or *Reference*. With *Frame* and *Frame Element*, the user can annotate predicates with their corresponding frames and frame elements. In contrast, *Reference* is used to link textual mentions to the structured data of the incident. This enables coreferential mentions, i.e., linked to the same incident, to obtain different frame annotations, which forms the basis for analyzing variation

The front-end of the tool makes use of Bootstrap CSS[2] and jQuery[3], and the server-side operations are handled by Node.js[4].

In Subsection 4.1., we introduce the resources used in the tool. The Subsections 4.2., 4.3., 4.4., 4.5., 4.6., 4.7., and 4.8. explain the main components of the annotation tool

4.1. Resources

In this subsection, we introduce the resources used in the annotation tool, i.e., the lexicon and the data.

lexicon We make use of the canonical version 1.7 of FrameNet (Fillmore and Baker, 2010; Ruppenhofer et al., 2006). All annotations make use of a Resource Description Framework (RDF) of FrameNet, for which the two most common resources are Framester (Gangemi et al., 2016)

---

[2]https://getbootstrap.com/docs/3.4/css/
[3]https://jquery.com/
[4]https://nodejs.org/en/

and PreMOn (Corcoglioniti et al., 2016). We chose to use PreMOn since the project was more active.[5]

data acquisition We have developed a data architecture (Vossen et al., 2020) to obtain and represent the data according to the data model as presented in Subsection 3.2., for which we primarily make use of Wikidata (Vrandečić and Krötzsch, 2014).

preprocessing spaCy[6] is used for sentence splitting, tokenization, and part of speech tagging, for which models in English, Dutch, and Italian are used. The preprocessing is stored in the NLP Annotation Format (NAF) (Fokkens et al., 2014), a stand-off, multilayered annotation schema for representing linguistic annotations.[7] We retrained Open-SESAME (Swayamdipta et al., 2017) to tag the reference texts with FrameNet frames.[8]

4.2. Login

A unique session identifier is created for each annotator for each annotation session. Each annotation will then be accompanied by this session identifier and the timestamp of the annotation, which allows analyses per annotation session and per annotator. No annotations are removed. Automatically generated annotations are represented in the same way using identifiers and timestamps.

4.3. Incident Selection

The user will first have to choose a specific data release, e.g., *version 1.0*. From this data release, an event type is chosen, e.g., *murder* (Wikidata identifier *Q132821*). From the available incidents that belong to the chosen event type, one incident is selected.

After clicking on *Load Incident*, the user is presented with the structured data about the incident, e.g., the location, time, and participants. Also, all available reference texts that make reference to the selected incident are shown, possibly in multiple languages.

The existing annotations for each reference text are highlighted. The user can observe the difference between manual and automatic annotations, which is designed such that the user can focus more on validating than on full-text annotation.

4.4. Markable Correction

Linguistic phenomena in which there is a many-to-many relationship between a token and a concept are a crucial problem for language technology (Sag et al., 2002). Idioms, phrasal verbs, and compounds are cases in which this occurs. In at least two phenomena, i.e., idioms and phrasal verbs, multiple tokens combined refer to one concept or semantic unit (Lexicon of Linguistics, 2020b; Quirk, 2010). In contrast, compounds consist of one token, but they can evoke multiple frames and frame element relations.

In this step of the annotation process, the user can correct the automatic tokenization by indicating which combination of tokens serve as phrasal verbs or idioms. Also, the user can decompose compounds into separate components. For cases in which multiple tokens should be merged, the user clicks on the tokens that are part of the construction and indicates whether they belong to the category of phrasal verbs or idioms. We follow English FrameNet in assigning the part of speech tag *V* to phrasal verbs and *idio* for idioms. If the user now clicks on one of the tokens of a construction, all tokens that belong to it are selected. It is no longer possible to annotate parts of the construction as predicates or frame elements. Also, any annotation on the level of the individual parts of the construction is deprecated and will no longer be used nor rendered in the tool.

Annotators are also asked to detect *endocentric* compounds, i.e., compounds consisting of a grammatical head and a modifier (Lexicon of Linguistics, 2020a), which make it possible to annotate components of the compounds with frames and frame elements. After clicking on the detected endocentric compound, the user is asked to indicate the components of the compound as well as which component serves as the frame-evoking unit. For each component, the user needs to indicate the lemma and the part of speech according to the Universal Dependencies version 2 (Nivre et al., 2017) part of speech tagset. After specifying a compound, the user can now click on the separate components of the compound and can no longer click on the compound as a whole. Also, any previous annotation of the compound as a whole is ignored and will no longer be rendered.

4.5. Annotation Type

The next step involves deciding which type of annotation to perform. There are three options: *Frame* (see Subsection 4.6.), *Frame Element* (see Subsection 4.7.), and *Reference* (see Subsection 4.8.). For each annotation, this is the first step. Note that our tool does not assume that there is already a FrameNet lexicon beforehand.

4.6. Frame

The goal of the *Frame* annotation type is to annotate predicates with FrameNet frames as well as to indicate the *Frame Relation Type*. After selecting a markable, the user clicks to observe a dropdown list in which all FrameNet frames are divided into four groups: 1. **Typical frames** this category contains the frames that are typically expected given the type of the selected incident, e.g., **Killing** and **Offenses** for the event type *murder*. 2. **candidate frames for lemma and part of speech**: the candidate frames given the lemma and part of speech of the markable are shown here. 3. **candidate frames for lemma**: the candidate frames given the lemma of the markable are shown here. 4. **other** all other FrameNet frames are shown here.

When a user selects a frame from the dropdown list, more information about the frame is shown in the right panel.

Also, the user has to indicate the *Frame Relation type* (see Subsection 3.3.). In the case that the incident to which the expression refers is an instance of the evoked frame, the user selects *isOfFrame*. Otherwise, the user selects *evoke*.

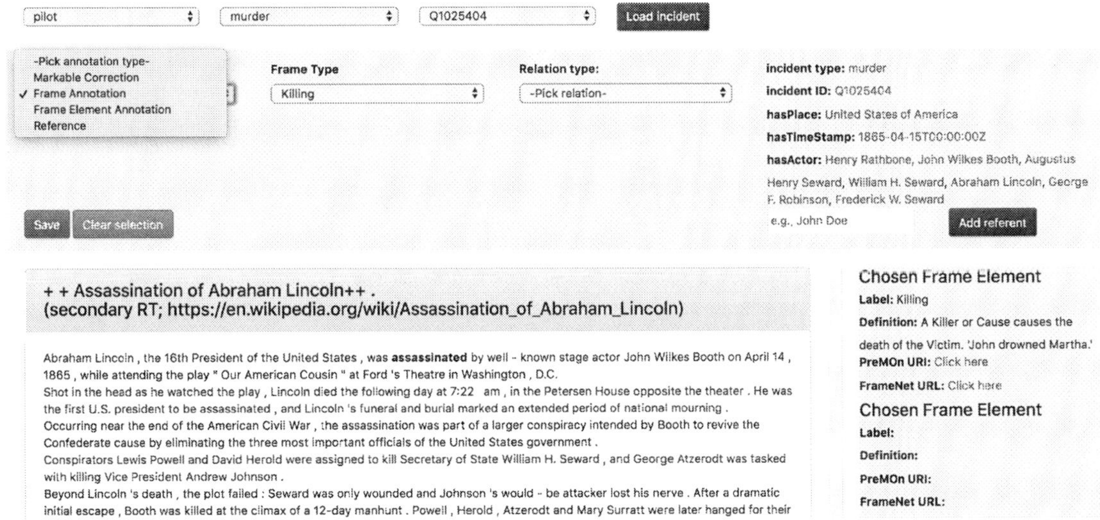

Figure 5: Snapshot of the data-to-text annotation tool.

After clicking *Save*, the annotation is added to the corresponding NAF file of the reference text using the PreMOn URI identifier for the frame.

Finally, we allow the user to click multiple predicates at once and annotate a batch of predicates with the same frame label and frame relation type.

4.7. Frame Element

The goal of the *Frame Element* Annotation Type is first to indicate which frame elements are found in the predicate scope. If core frame elements are not found in the scope of the predicate, the user is asked to try to annotate them in the context surrounding the predicate.

Given that a user has previously annotated a predicate with a frame label, the user can now also annotate frame elements for this predicate. The user clicks on the markable and selects the frame element from a dropdown list. After annotating at least one frame element for a frame, e.g., KILLER for **Killing**, a table is shown in the right panel of the tool, of which an example is shown in Table 2.

Frame Element	Type	Annotated	Expressed
KILLER	Core	true	true
VICTIM	Core	false	false
CAUSE	Core	false	false
MEANS	Core	false	false
INSTRUMENT	Core	false	false

Table 2: Frame Element Annotation

Table 2 presents the information shown to the user during the frame element annotation phase. The user can keep track of all frame element annotations for an active frame. The annotator is asked to attempt to find evidence for each core frame element in the predicate scope. If the frame element is unexpressed, the user is asked to look for evidence of the frame element in the surrounding context, e.g., the VICTIM is mentioned in the sentence before the target sentence. Only after all core frame elements have been annotated, the user is able to switch to a different Annotation Type.

After clicking *Save*, the annotation is added to the corresponding NAF file of the reference text using the PreMOn URI identifier for the frame element.

4.8. Reference

Alongside the reference texts, the user is shown structured data about the main incident, as shown in the top right corner of Figure 5. The structured data table consists of five pieces of information. The *event type* of the incident is shown, which we obtain from the Wikidata *instance of* relationship (Property P31) as well as the Wikidata item identifier. Also, we categorize the properties of a Wikidata item into three classes and model them using the Simple-Event-Model (SEM (Van Hage et al., 2011)). Locations are mapped to sem:hasPlace, temporal expressions to sem:hasTimeStamp, and participants to sem:hasActor.

The user clicks on some tokens and then indicates, by clicking on a link in the structured table, that the markable refers to the reference, e.g., 'The kidnapper' refers to Hezbollah (Wikidata item Q41053) which is expressed in RDF using a gaf:denotes relation.

The annotator can also modify the structured data table. He or she can add and remove values to sem:hasPlace, sem:hasTimeStamp, and sem:hasActor, provided that the user provides Wikidata items as values.

5. Discussion

In this section, we elaborate on the ways in which the current tool supports us in providing frame annotations of texts referring to a real-world event. In Subsection 5.1., we discuss the extent to which the tool in its current state directs the annotator. In Subsection 5.2., we present future plans for the tool to capture inferred frames.

ID	Sentence	Evokes	Frame Element
1	*The Tunisian man* who prosecutors say **perpetrated** last month's terrorist attack [...]	**Committing_crime**	PERPETRATOR
2	*he* **ploughed** a truck into a crowded Christmas market	**Impact**	AGENT
3	*Amri* **carried out** the attack	**Intentionally_act**	AGENT
4	*he* **hijacked** a truck	**Piracy**	PERPETRATOR
5	*he* [...] **shot** its Polish driver	**Hit_target**	AGENT
6	*he* [...] **drove** it into the crowded market	**Operate_vehicle**	DRIVER

Table 3: Example sentences taken from reference texts referencing *Anis Amri* (Wikidata identifier Q28052669), the agent of the *2016 Berlin Attack* (Wikidata identifier Q28036573). The first column indicates the identifier, the second column shows the example sentence with the reference to Anis Amri in italics and the frame-evoking predicate in bold, the value of the third column is the evoked frame, and the last column shows which frame element the reference to Anis Amri expresses.

5.1. Functionality

The current annotation tool enables the annotator to perform two parallel annotations. In choosing Frame or Frame Element as the Annotation Type, the annotator traditionally performs frame annotations. In addition, he or she can select the Reference Annotation Type to mark words that refer to the structured data. These parallel annotations can be performed on the same expression in the text, which means that this expression is annotated as both contributing to a specific frame and simultaneously referencing a component of the real-world event. The resulting annotation scheme displays which words refer to the structured data as well as how these words frame the data. In other words, variation in framing across texts can be measured concerning a fixed real-world referent. For instance, all sentences in Table 3 make reference to the 2016 Berlin attack. In these sentences, *Anis Amri* is being referred to by the expressions 'The Tunisian man', 'he', and 'Amri'. However, these expressions belong to different predicates, each evoking a different frame. Hence, each expression is labeled with a different frame element, which provides insight into how the referent is framed.

A second function of the tool is to annotate unexpressed core frame elements beyond the scope of the predicate. Given the assumption that frames construct a cohesive narrative in referring to a main event, we expect these core frame elements to occur somewhere in the reference text to support the reader's understanding of the narrative. If no evidence is found for a core frame element, this raises questions about its retrievability: whether it is inferred from world knowledge or expressed in other reference texts. Example 4 highlights this functionality.

(4) **Change_of_leadership**

    a. [ROLE Presidential] ⊙elections were held [LOCATION in Slovakia] [TIME in March 2019].

    b. [OLD_LEADER Incumbent President Andrej Kiska] did not run for a second term.

The sentences in (4) form the onset of a text referring to the presidential election of Slovakia in 2019. Assuming that the user first annotates Example (4a), 'elections' is marked as a predicate evoking **Change_of_leadership**, which contains many core frame elements, which are ROLE, BODY, FUNCTION, NEW_LEADER, OLD_LEADER, OLD_ORDER, and SELECTOR. Example (4a) contains annotations for three frame elements, which are Role, Location, and Time. Role is the only core frame element with an annotation in Example (4a) out of the many core frame elements. No evidence is found for the other core frame elements. The next step for the user is to find mentions of these unexpressed core frame elements. Evidence for the specific old leader of the election, i.e., core frame element OLD_LEADER, is found in Example (4b). The annotator continues to look for evidence for the remaining core frame elements.

Finally, we provide the annotator with a list of typical frames. The list consists of frames that are relevant for the perception of the event, e.g., **Offenses** and **Use_firearm** for a *murder* event. Some of those typical frames are even necessarily evoked, e.g., **Killing** in the case of a *murder* event. The main rational to use this list is to restrict the annotations to the most important mentions of the event, based on the assumption that only a subset of frames is used to describe an event of a specific type. Moreover, if the obligatory typical frames are not found in a text, this then leads to questions about evocation through inference.

5.2. Desired functions

During preliminary annotation experiments with the tool, we found that a substantial portion of the frames indicated by the typical frames are not derived from reference texts. For instance, **Killing** is not evoked by lexical units in a reference text of a murder event. We argue that the necessary frames are still activated in the text, but that they are derived through pragmatic inference rather than lexical evocation. These inferences are derived from linguistic cues that are not marked as lexical units within FrameNet. Hence, these are different inferences than the ones discussed by Chang et al. (2002), who use the notion of inference in FrameNet for a frame that is inevitably processed during the evocation of another frame, e.g. **Commerce_buy** is always activated with the evocation of **Commerce_sell** and vice versa. These inferences are actually based on a frame that is evoked by a lexical unit. Also, most inferences we detected could not be derived by any current frame-to-frame relations. See the sentence in (5), which refers to the *2016 Berlin Attack* (Wikidata identifier Q28036573).

(5) **Killing**

[$_{\text{CAUSE}}$ a truck] was $_{\odot?}$deliberately $_{\odot?}$driven into the Christmas market, $_{\odot?}$leaving [$_{\text{VICTIM}}$ 12 people] $_{\odot?}$dead

Although the words in (5) separately do not evoke **Killing**, the sum of the components 'driven', 'leaving', and 'dead' activate this frame by means of entailment. Moreover, 'deliberately' acts as a cue from which **Offenses** could be derived. The way these frames are activated can only be traced by complementing the lexical semantic analysis of frame semantics with a pragmatic analysis in terms of inference. If the annotator is guided in pointing out the linguistic cues, the different ways in which frames are inferred from these cues can be schematized. The data can then be analyzed with respect to their pragmatic type, e.g., entailment, implicature (Levinson, 1983); and the possible factors that account for the inference e.g., historical distance of the publication or genre conventions.

One of the next steps in the development of the annotation tool is to implement an *inferred frame layer* for the annotator that allows him or her to mark linguistic cues from which a frame is pragmatically derived, on top of the traditional FrameNet annotation module. After targeting words as lexical units, this inferred frame layer will ask the annotator to mark *n* linguistic cues in the text that might derive any of the remaining unannotated typical frames. We refer to Remijnse and Minnema (2020) for a detailed description of this proposal.

6. Conclusion

In this paper, we introduced an annotation tool in which annotations can be made to both the conceptual and referential level. For an event type, the tool delivers a collection of incidents, each accompanied with structured data and reference texts in different languages. The annotator can mark targets in the texts to frame-annotate and mark the same targets to annotate referential relations to the structured data. From the output of this annotation process, patterns of variation in framing can be extracted concerning reference to a single referent.

7. Acknowledgements

The research reported in this article was funded by the Dutch National Science organisation (NWO) through the project *Framing situations in the Dutch language*.

8. Bibliographical References

Andor, J. (2010). Discussing Frame Semantics: The State of the Art: An Interview with Charles J. Fillmore. *Review of Cognitive Linguistics. Published under the auspices of the Spanish Cognitive Linguistics Association*, 8(1):157–176.

Burchardt, A., Erk, K., Frank, A., Kowalski, A., Pado, S., and Pinkal, M. (2006). SALTO-A Versatile Multi-Level Annotation Tool. In *Proceedings of the 5th International Conference on Language Resources and Evaluation (LREC 2006)*.

Chang, N., Petruck, M. R. L., and Narayanan, S. (2002). From Frames to Inference. In *Proceedings of the First International Workshop on Scalable Natural Language Understanding*.

Corcoglioniti, F., Rospocher, M., Aprosio, A. P., and Tonelli, S. (2016). PreMOn: a Lemon Extension for Exposing Predicate Models as Linked Data. In *Proceedings of the Tenth International Conference on Language Resources and Evaluation (LREC'16)*, pages 877–884, Portorož, Slovenia, May. European Language Resources Association (ELRA).

Cybulska, A. and Vossen, P. (2011). Historical Event Extraction from Text. In *Proceedings of the 5th ACL-HLT Workshop on Language Technology for Cultural Heritage, Social Sciences, and Humanities*.

Eckart de Castilho, R., Mújdricza-Maydt, É., Yimam, S. M., Hartmann, S., Gurevych, I., Frank, A., and Biemann, C. (2016). A Web-based Tool for the Integrated Annotation of Semantic and Syntactic Structures. In *Proceedings of the Workshop on Language Technology Resources and Tools for Digital Humanities (LT4DH)*.

Fillmore, C. J. and Baker, C. (2010). A Frames Approach to Semantic Analysis. In *The Oxford handbook of linguistic analysis*. Oxford University Press.

Fokkens, A., Soroa, A., Beloki, Z., Ockeloen, N., Rigau, G., Van Hage, W. R., and Vossen, P. (2014). NAF and GAF: Linking Linguistic Annotations. In *Proceedings 10th Joint ISO-ACL SIGSEM Workshop on Interoperable Semantic Annotation*.

Gangemi, A., Alam, M., Asprino, L., Presutti, V., and Recupero, D. R. (2016). Framester: A Wide Coverage Linguistic Linked Data Hub. In *European Knowledge Acquisition Workshop*.

Levinson, S. C. (1983). *Pragmatics*. Cambridge Textbooks in Linguistics. Cambridge University Press.

Lexicon of Linguistics. (2020a). Exocentric compound.
```
https://lexicon.hum.uu.nl/?lemma=
Endocentric+compound&lemmacode=778&
lemma=Endocentric+compound&lemmacode=
778.
```

Lexicon of Linguistics. (2020b). Idiom.
```
https://
lexicon.hum.uu.nl/?lemma=Endocentric+
compound&lemmacode=778&lemma=
Endocentric+compound&lemmacode=778.
```

McCrae, J. P., Bosque-Gil, J., Gracia, J., Buitelaar, P., and Cimiano, P. (2017). The Ontolex-Lemon model: development and applications. In *Proceedings of eLex 2017 conference*.

Nivre, J., Agić, Ž., Ahrenberg, L., Aranzabe, M. J., Asahara, M., Atutxa, A., Ballesteros, M., Bauer, J., Bengoetxea, K., Bhat, R. A., Bick, E., Bosco, C., Bouma, G., Bowman, S., Candito, M., Cebiroğlu Eryiğit, G., Celano, G. G. A., Chalub, F., Choi, J., Çöltekin, Ç., Connor, M., Davidson, E., de Marneffe, M.-C., de Paiva, V., Diaz de Ilarraza, A., Dobrovoljc, K., Dozat, T., Droganova, K., Dwivedi, P., Eli, M., Erjavec, T., Farkas, R., Foster, J., Freitas, C., Gajdošová, K., Galbraith, D., Garcia, M., Ginter, F., Goenaga, I., Gojenola, K., Gökırmak, M., Goldberg, Y., Gómez Guinovart, X., Gonzáles Saavedra, B., Grioni, M., Grūzītis, N., Guillaume, B., Habash, N., Hajič, J., Hà Mỹ, L., Haug, D., Hladká, B., Hohle, P., Ion, R., Irimia, E., Johannsen, A., Jørgensen, F., Kaşıkara, H., Kanayama, H., Kanerva, J., Kotsyba, N., Krek, S., Laippala, V., Lê H`ông, P., Lenci, A., Ljubešić, N., Lyashevskaya, O., Lynn, T., Makazhanov, A., Manning, C., Mărănduc, C., Mareček, D., Martínez Alonso, H., Martins, A., Mašek, J., Matsumoto, Y., McDonald, R., Missilä, A., Mititelu, V., Miyao, Y., Montemagni, S., More, A., Mori, S., Moskalevskyi, B., Muischnek, K., Mustafina, N., Müürisep, K., Nguy˜ên Thị, L., Nguy˜ên Thị Minh, H., Nikolaev, V., Nurmi, H., Ojala, S., Osenova, P., Øvrelid, L., Pascual, E., Passarotti, M., Perez, C.-A., Perrier, G., Petrov, S., Piitulainen, J., Plank, B., Popel, M., Pretkalniņa, L., Prokopidis, P., Puolakainen, T., Pyysalo, S., Rademaker, A., Ramasamy, L., Real, L., Rituma, L., Rosa, R., Saleh, S., Sanguinetti, M., Saulīte, B., Schuster, S., Seddah, D., Seeker, W., Seraji, M., Shakurova, L., Shen, M., Sichinava, D., Silveira, N., Simi, M., Simionescu, R., Simkó, K., Šimková, M., Simov, K., Smith, A., Suhr, A., Sulubacak, U., Szántó, Z., Taji, D., Tanaka, T., Tsarfaty, R., Tyers, F., Uematsu, S., Uria, L., van Noord, G., Varga, V., Vincze, V., Washington, J. N., Žabokrtský, Z., Zeldes, A., Zeman, D., and Zhu, H. (2017). Universal Dependencies 2.0. LINDAT/CLARIN digital library at the Institute of Formal and Applied Linguistics (ÚFAL), Faculty of Mathematics and Physics, Charles University.

Quirk, R. (2010). *A Comprehensive Grammar of the English Language*. Pearson Education India.

Remijnse, L. and Minnema, G. (2020). Towards Reference-Aware FrameNet Annotation. In *The International FrameNet Workshop 2020*.

Ruppenhofer, J., Ellsworth, M., Schwarzer-Petruck, M., Johnson, C. R., and Scheffczyk, J. (2006). *FrameNet II: Extended theory and practice*. FrameNet Project.

Ruppenhofer, J., Sporleder, C., Morante, R., Baker, C., and Palmer, M. (2010). SemEval-2010 Task 10: Linking Events and Their Participants in Discourse. In *Proceedings of the 5th International Workshop on Semantic Evaluation*.

Sag, I. A., Baldwin, T., Bond, F., Copestake, A., and Flickinger, D. (2002). Multiword Expressions: A Pain in the Neck for NLP. In *Computational Linguistics and Intelligent Text Processing*.

Swayamdipta, S., Thomson, S., Dyer, C., and Smith, N. A. (2017). Frame-Semantic Parsing with Softmax-Margin Segmental RNNs and a Syntactic Scaffold. *arXiv preprint arXiv:1706.09528*.

Torrent, T. T., Ellsworth, M., Baker, C., and Matos, E. (2018). The Multilingual FrameNet Shared Annotation Task: a preliminary report. In *Proceedings of the 11th International Conference on Language Resources and Evaluation (LREC 2018)*.

Van Hage, W. R., Malaisé, V., Segers, R., Hollink, L., and Schreiber, G. (2011). Design and use of the Simple Event Model (SEM). *Web Semantics: Science, Services and Agents on the World Wide Web*, 9(2):128–136.

Vossen, P., Ilievski, F., Postma, M., and Roxane, S. (2018). Don't Annotate, but Validate: a Data-to-Text Method for Capturing Event Data. In *11th edition of the Language Resources and Evaluation Conference (LREC 2018)*.

Vossen, P., Ilievski, F., Postma, M., Fokkens, A., G., M., and L., R. (2020). Large-scale Cross-lingual Language Resources for Referencing and Framing. In *12th Edition of the Language Resources and Evaluation Conference (LREC 2020)*.

Vrandečić, D. and Krötzsch, M. (2014). Wikidata: a Free Collaborative Knowledge Base. *Communications of the ACM*, 57(10):78–85.

9.   Language Resource References

Burchardt, A., Erk, K., Frank, A., Kowalski, A., Padó, S., and Pinkal, M. (2009). FrameNet for the Semantic Analysis of German: Annotation, Representation and Automation. *Multilingual FrameNets in Computational Lexicography: methods and applications*, 200:209–244.

Djemaa, M., Candito, M., Muller, P., and Vieu, L. (2016). Corpus Annotation Within the French FrameNet: a Domain-by-domain Methodology. In *The 10th International Conference on Language Resources and Evaluation (LREC 2016)*.

Gruzitis, N., Nespore-Berzkalne, G., and Saulite, B. (2018). Creation of Latvian FrameNet based on Universal Dependencies. In *Proceedings of the International FrameNet Workshop*.

Hayoun, A. and Elhadad, M. (2016). The Hebrew FrameNet Project. In *Proceedings of the 10th International Conference on Language Resources and Evaluation (LREC 2016)*.

Heppin, K. F. and Gronostaj, M. T. (2012). The Rocky Road towards a Swedish FrameNet-Creating SweFN. In *The 8th international conference on Language Resources and Evaluation (LREC 2012)*.

Laviola, A., Lage, L., Marção, N., Tavares, T., Almeida, V., Matos, E., and Torrent, T. (2017). The Brazilian Portuguese Constructicon: Modeling Constructional Inheritance, Frame Evocation and Constraints in FrameNet Brasil. In *2017 AAAI Spring Symposium Series*.

Ohara, K. H., Fujii, S., Ohori, T., Suzuki, R., Saito, H., and Ishizaki, S. (2004). The Japanese Framenet Project: An Introduction. In *Proceedings of LREC-04 Satellite Workshop "Building Lexical Resources from Semantically Annotated Corpora"(LREC 2004)*.

Ruppenhofer, J., Ellsworth, M., Schwarzer-Petruck, M., Johnson, C. R., and Scheffczyk, J. (2006). *FrameNet II: Extended theory and practice*. FrameNet Project.

Subirats, C. and Sato, H. (2003). Surprise! Spanish FrameNet. In *Proceedings of the Workshop on Frame Semantics at the XVII. International Congress of Linguists*.

Proceedings of the International FrameNet Workshop 2020: Towards a Global, Multilingual FrameNet, pages 41–47
Language Resources and Evaluation Conference (LREC 2020), Marseille, 11–16 May 2020
© European Language Resources Association (ELRA), licensed under CC-BY-NC

FrameNet Annotations Alignment using Attention-based Machine Translation

Gabriel Marzinotto
Orange Labs,
22300 Lannion, France
gabriel.marzinotto @orange.com

Abstract

This paper presents an approach to project FrameNet annotations into other languages using attention-based neural machine translation (NMT) models. The idea is to use a NMT encoder-decoder attention matrix to propose a word-to-word correspondence between the source and the target languages. We combine this word alignment along with a set of simple rules to securely project the FrameNet annotations into the target language. We successfully implemented, evaluated and analyzed this technique on the English-to-French configuration. First, we analyze the obtained corpus quantitatively and qualitatively. Then, we use existing FrameNet corpora to assert the quality of the translation. Finally, we trained a BERT-based FrameNet parser using the projected annotations and compared it to a BERT baseline. Results show modest performance gains in the French language, giving evidence to support that our approach could help to propagate FrameNet data-set on other languages. Moreover, this label projection approach can be extended to other sequence tagging tasks with minor modifications.

Keywords: FrameNet, Machine Translation, Cross-lingual Annotation Transfer, Cross-lingual FrameNet Parsing

1. Introduction

Frame Semantics (Fillmore, 1976) and the FrameNet (Fillmore, 2006) dictionary constitute a valuable resource and a very successful semantic representation scheme, widely adopted and adapted for many NLP applications. For many years a lot of works have studied the adaptability of FrameNet into other languages, showing that many frames are entirely cross-lingual (Gilardi and Baker, 2018). At the same time, FrameNet adaptations for more than 15 languages have been arising. Among these languages, we count Chinese, Danish, Dutch, Finnish, Portuguese, French, German, Hebrew, Hindi, Japanese, Korean, Latvian and Spanish.

Most of these projects use either human translation (*e.g.* Finish (Pedersen et al., 2018) and Danish (Lindén et al., 2017)) while others use semi-automatic alignments (Hayoun and Elhadad, 2016). Also, projects focus on translating the lexical units using bilingual alignments and they tend to deliver a set of annotated examples that is significantly smaller than FrameNet.

More recently, we have seen an initiative to build a multilingual FrameNet lexicon (Gilardi and Baker, 2018), or at least to add relations between similar frames across different languages. Their approach is also based on lexical unit translation using bilingual dictionaries. The objective is to give some guidelines to counter the small divergences we experience today, which are due to the separated evolution of each project.

In this paper, we propose a slightly different example-driven approach to bootstrap FrameNet corpora in new languages using Neural Machine Translation. The main idea is to translate entire annotated sentences instead of lexical units. Then, using neural attention models one can align and project the semantic annotations from the source language (English) into the target language. This allows building a synthetic FrameNet corpus with exemplar sentences. A similar approach have already been studied using Hidden Markov Models (Annesi and Basili, 2010) yielding good results in the English-Italian pair. The advances in NMT allow revisiting this technique using attention models.

Using some post-processing, one can find some of the lexical units that could trigger a frame by looking into the trigger's alignment. Even though this approach is limited to the lexical units for which we have an English sentence example, it allows us to introduce the full sentence in the translation process. This yields a context-aware translation of the lexical units, instead of a one by one word comparison using a dictionary and human experts annotation. We believe both approaches are complementary. This NMT approach can bootstrap a FrameNet lexicon with annotated examples, which can be improved and completed by human experts.

In this paper, we detail the methodology to perform translation and alignment on the English-to-French setting. We give metrics to evaluate this translated corpus and we introduce extrinsic evaluation approach that use the synthetic data-set to train and test automatic FrameNet parsers.

2. Translating and Aligning

Our objective is to automatically produce French translations for both FrameNet and SemEval-07 annotations and provide a methodology that can be extended to other languages for which suitable translation models are available. A sentence and its translation do not necessarily evoke the same Frames. (Torrent et al., 2018) studies this phenomenon by looking at sentences from the Multi-lingual FrameNet corpus and comparing the frames evoked in the English sentences and the Portuguese translations. They show that, in many cases, the frames evoked on each language differ due to different lexicalization and constructional strategies. Normally, this would imply that FrameNet projections are extremely complex if not unfeasible. We argue that this frame mismatch is widely observed in human translation, but much rare in machine translations (MT). We show this using an example from (Torrent et al., 2018), comparing an English sentence with the Portuguese human translation (HT) and machine translation (MT):

- **EN:** *We have a huge vested interest in it, partly because it's education that's meant to take us into this future that we can't grasp.*

- **PT-HT:** *Nos interessamos tanto por ela em parte porque é da educação o papel de nos conduzir a esse futuro misterioso.*

- **PT-MT:** *Temos um grande interesse, em parte porque é a educação que nos leva a esse futuro que não podemos compreender.*

In Table 1, we list the frames and the lexical units evoked by each sentence. We observe that MT usually does not modify the constructional strategy and is closer to word-by-word translation than the HT sentences. Even though MT sentences may be less sounding, the frames observed in the source and target language tend to be similar. This ensures that the cross-lingual projections can be done, but show that there may be a domain mismatch between natural language and machine translated sentences.

Frame	EN	PT-HT	PT-MT
Size	huge.a	—	grande.a
Stimulus_focus	interest.n	interessar.v	interesse.n
Degree	—	tanto.adv	—
Degree	partly.adv	em parte.adv	em parte.adv
Causation	because.c	porque.c	porque.c
Education	education.n	educação.n	educação.n
Purpose	mean.v	—	—
Performers_roles	—	papel.n	—
Bringing	take.v	conduzir.v	levar.v
Goal	into.prep	—	—
Temporal_colloc	future.n	futuro.n	futuro.n
Certainty	—	misterioso.a	—
Capability	can.v	—	poder.v
Grasp	grasp.v	—	compreender.v

Table 1: Frames and LUs from an English sentence and its Portuguese human (HT) and machine (MT) translations

2.1. Machine Translation Model

To translate the English FrameNet corpus into French we used a state-of-the-art Neural Machine Translation (NMT) algorithm from (Ott et al., 2018) using publicly available pre-trained models from *Fairseq*[1]. This NMT model uses sequence-to-sequence transformers with a total of 222M parameters, it uses a Moses tokenizer, a Word-Piece representation optimized for NMT (Sennrich et al., 2016) and a beam search decoding strategy with a depth of 5. The model achieves state-of-the-art performance on the *newstest2014* test set from *WMT'14* obtaining 43.2 BLEU score on the English-to-French pair.

The most important property of this model is the encoder-decoder attention mechanism (Luong et al., 2015), which is essential for our label alignment strategy. Encoder-decoder attention allows the target-language decoder to look into relevant word-piece information from the source-language encoder. More precisely, for each output word-piece, there is a soft-max distribution vector across the input word-pieces. This distribution shows in which parts of the input the model focus to yield the given output word-piece.

---

[1]The model is transformer.wmt14.en-fr to be found at `https://pytorch.org/hub/pytorch_fairseq_translation/`

This attention matrix can be used as an indicator of a *soft-alignment* between the word pieces from the input to the output. A simplified example of such an attention matrix is shown in Figure 1. This example is developed in detail in the following subsection.

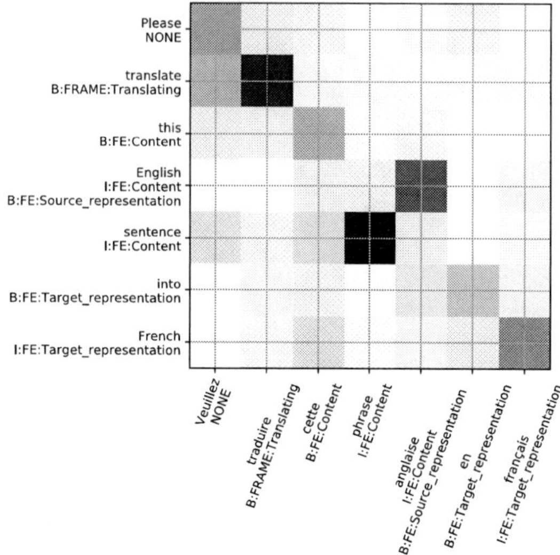

Figure 1: Post Processed Attention Matrix from the NMT

When we look into the raw attention matrix from the NMT we observe that the decoder's attention is distributed between different parts of the input (Ghader and Monz, 2017) and not only on the word-alignment equivalent. For this reason, attention-based alignment is not straightforward. Moreover, in many cases translation inserts tokens that do not have an equivalent. *e.g.* the following sentence and its translation:

"United States helps Australia stop the fire"
"Les États-Unis aident l'Australie à arrêter les incendies"

We observe that the translation adds the definite article for both *"United States"* and *"Australia"* and it also adds a preposition *"à"* to the lexical unit *"stop.v"*. Such word insertions, that are due to some language specific structures, often produce misleading attention vectors. This is the case for the preposition *"à"*, which introduces the goal argument of the verb *"arrêter"*(to stop). Since predicting the word *"à"* depends on both the verb *"aider"* and the role of *"stop"* as the goal, the attention vector for *"à"* is distributed among these two verbs, even though *"à"* is not a viable translation for any of them.

2.2. FrameNet Label Alignment

To generate a translation for the SemEval-07 corpus we translate each sentence using the NMT model described above (2.1.). For each sentence, we recover the attention matrix and apply the following post-processing steps:

Re-establish tokenization: Since the NMT model uses word-piece representations, the first step is to project the attention matrix into a full-word form. To do this, we perform sub-matrix sums on the sets of rows (and columns)

that correspond to the same input (and output) words.

Part-of-Speech (POS) weighting: To avoid alignment mismatches as those described above (2.1.), we perform POS and dependency parsing on both the input and the output sentences using spaCy[2]. SpaCy has close to state-of-the-art performance on these tasks. We use the POS to post-process the attention matrix applying two simple rules. First, we mask structural POS such as `"PUNCT"`, `"DET"`, `"INTJ"`, `"SYM"`, `"X"`, `"AUX"`, `"PART"`. We do this because the attention vectors for these POS are hard to align due to their structural nature (see 2.2.). Second, we encourage the alignment between words with the same POS. To do this, we multiply by 10 the attention matrix entry (i, j) if the input and output words $(w_i\ w_j)$ have the same POS. Finally, we normalize the matrix by columns, *e.g.* we divide each entry (i, j) by the sum of the values in column j. This allows interpreting each matrix entry as the percentage of attention the word w_j pays to the input w_i.

Label Projection: To project annotations from the English FrameNet into the French translation we flattened the FrameNet annotations over the English word tokens. Then, we paired each output word to the input word with the highest attention score and propagated the input labels into the matching output token, as shown in Figure 1. Since the model is not equally confident in every translation, we score each label projection with the value of the attention coefficient between the input and the output word.

Confidence Threshold: To decide which labels project and which reject, we apply a threshold on the confidence score. The choice of the threshold is not straightforward. If it is too low, it introduces alignment mismatches, which can be seen as frame and frame element insertions. On the other hand, a high value will only project a few annotations. We chose the threshold that maximizes the harmonic mean between the the number of annotations projected and the amount of duplicated projections. This step is explained with more detail in Section 2.3..

frame element Completing: To ensure homogeneity in the spans of the frame elements, we used the syntactic dependency parsing to complete the spans of the frame elements applying two simple rules. First, if a determinant or a preposition is attached to a frame element through its syntactic parent, it inherits the label of that parent. Second, for words masked during the POS weighing process (*e.g.* for being either `"PUNCT"`, `"DET"`, `"INTJ"`, `"SYM"`, `"X"`, `"AUX"` or `"PART"`), we assign them a frame element label if words that precede and follow are part of the same frame element. This allows us to merge potential frame element segments, that got split during the alignments.

This sequence of steps is language independent and fairly easy to implement. However, this does not mean the corpora translation process is flawless. In the next sub-section we study the quality of the generated corpus.

2.3. Generated Corpus Analysis

In this subsection, we explore the translated corpus and establish some comparison with the original corpus.

---

[2]spaCy website: `https://spacy.io/`

First, we evaluate the projection using deletion and insertion metrics. To do so, we assign an id to each annotation (frame or frame element) of the SemEval-07 corpus. Then, we use these ids to evaluate the French translation by counting how many ids were lost (deletions) and how many ids got duplicated (insertions). This is a rough metric, somewhat similar to standard precision/recall evaluations. However, it does not imply that annotations are aligned to the right words in the target language. We only measure if the algorithm finds suitable candidates to project the annotations. We use this metric because more precise evaluations require skilled human annotators/validators. This evaluation is strongly tied to the confidence threshold selected during the alignment (see 2.2.). In Figure 2 we observe the deletion/insertion trade-off of the projection computed using different values of the confidence threshold. This trade-off achieves a maximal F1 score of 85.5%. At this point, the insertion metric is 90.1%, meaning that there are no more than 10% of false insertions, while the deletion metric is 81.4%. meaning that we project about 81% of the annotations and delete 19%. These alignment performances show that there is still room for improvement, either via better NMT models or through more complex post-processing strategies. However, in this paper, we settled at this 85.5% F1 and we evaluate how useful this simple approach can be.

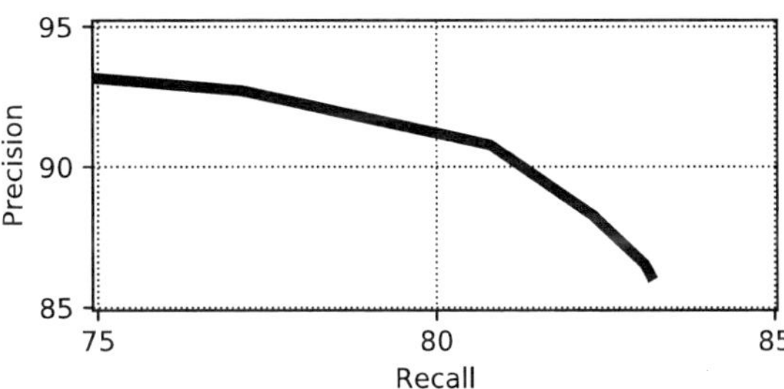

Figure 2: Insertion Deletion Trade-off of the label projection

After this evaluation, we look into more detail which parts of the projection were problematic. In Figure 3, we show the distribution of frames that introduced the highest amount of errors during the translation. Whenever the French column is larger(smaller) that the English column it means that the frame got inserted(deleted) several times.

We observe that frames such as `Existence`, `Quantity`, `Attributed_information`, `Capability` and `Partitive` suffer several deletions. Many times, these deletions are due to alignment constrains (see 2.2.) such as not projecting labels from auxiliary verbs. *e.g.* The frame `Existence` in the expression *"There was a time..."* translates into *"Il fut un temps..."*, here the auxiliary verb *"fut"* was masked. Also, for the frame `Quantity` in the sentence *" Brazil helped several countries..."* which translates into *"Le Bresil a aidé plusieurs pays ..."* the word *"plusieurs"* is a determinant which gets masked. Some of these errors could be fixed by introducing more language specific projection rules. As for the others, changes in the constructional strategies make label projection very difficult and error-prone.

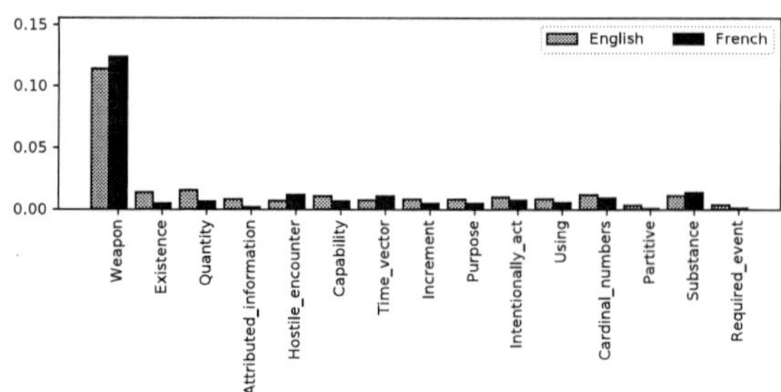

Figure 3: Distribution of the frames with the highest number of projection errors. Whenever the French column is larger(smaller) than the English column it means that the Frame got inserted(deleted) several times.

On the other hand, frames such as `Weapon`, `Hostile_encounter`, `Time_vector` and `Substance` suffered insertions. These insertions were mostly due to lexical units with prepositional or adverbial POS. As we discussed previously, the attention vectors for these words are hard to align and in some cases, they get projected twice.

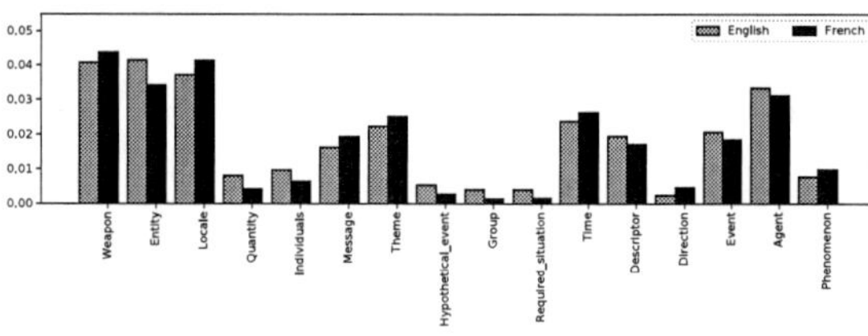

Figure 4: Distribution of the frame elements with the highest number of projection errors

When we repeat the same analysis on the frame element translation we observe that many frame elements projection errors are the proliferation of a frame error. This is expected since we filter frame elements without a trigger. There are a few exceptions for this rule, such as time, agent and theme, which are quite generic frame elements. They can get deleted due to translation errors or due to low confidence scores. For an example of a translation error, consider the sentence "... *due to the urgency, its development was fast* ..." that gets translated into "... *face à l'urgence, le development a été rapide...*". Even though it is an acceptable translation, in the English sentence, the word *"its"* is an agent frame element. When we look into the translation, there is no match for this word (it was deleted). Maybe, a more accurate translation would add a pronoun *"leur"* as in "... *face à l'urgence, leur development a été rapide...*". This sort of error does not seem dangerous, as the final sentence is still fully annotated.

Beam Search: an interesting aspect of this approach is that we can use NMT along with beam search decoding to extract several translation candidates for any sentence. This is particularly useful when building FrameNet dictionaries, as it allows us to generate translations with different lexical triggers taking into account the sentence's context. On the other hand, this technique can also be used to do data aug-

mentation on the target language. We did not explore this option in our paper, and we have left it for future work.

3. `biGRU+BERT` Semantic Parser

We propose a `biGRU+BERT` model architecture, inspired from state-of-the-art models in Semantic Role Labeling (He et al., 2017) and FrameNet parsing (Yang and Mitchell, 2017; Marzinotto et al., 2018b; Marzinotto et al., 2019). Our architecture, uses 2 layers of bidirectional `GRU` stacked on top of a pre-trained *'bert-base-multilingual-cased'* model from Huggingface[3]. A diagram of our model architecture is shown in figure 5. To encode semantic labels into flat structures we use a `BIO` encoding scheme. To ensure that output sequences respect these `BIO` constrains we implement an A* decoding strategy similar to the one proposed by (He et al., 2017).

To deal with sentences containing multiple lexical units we have built training samples containing only one trigger. More precisely a sentence containing N triggers provides N training samples. The downside of this approach is that during prediction time, parsing a sentence with N triggers requires N model applications. At decoding time every pair of { sentence, trigger } is processed by the network to output a probability distribution on the frames and FE for each word. Then, we apply a *coherence filter* to these probabilities to make sure that the predicted frame elements are compatible with the predicted frame by filtering the extraneous frame elements. This *coherence filter* chose the frame with the highest probability on the trigger and uses it as the predicted frame (represented as the label assigned by the tagger to the trigger). Then, given that frame, the *coherence filter* masks all the frame element labels that are incompatible with the selected Frame.

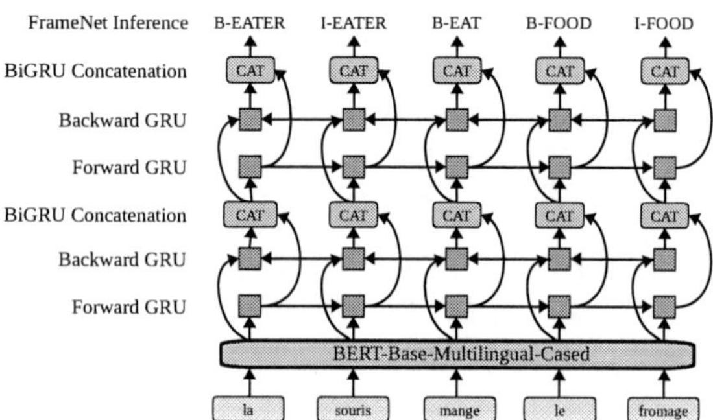

Figure 5: `biGRU` Model Diagram

4. FrameNet Parsing Experiments

4.1. Data

In our experiments we use 4 FrameNet corpora:

SemEval07-EN: A corpus of full-text annotations from FrameNet project used for the shared task 19 from `SemEval-07` (Baker et al., 2007). This corpus consists of annotated journals and it contains 720 different Frames.

---

[3]`https://huggingface.co/transformers/`

	Lang	Data Source	Nb. Diff. Frames	Nb. Diff. LU	Nb. Diff. FE	Nb. Diff. Words	Nb. Sentences w/LU	Nb. Annot. LU	Avg. Nb. Annot. per LU
SemEval-07	EN	Journals	720	3,197	754	14,150	4,020	24,770	7.7
ASFALDA	FR	Journals	121	782	140	33,955	13,154	16,167	20.7
CALOR	FR	Encyclopedias	53	145	148	72,127	22,603	31,440	215.4

Table 2: Summary and statistics about the existing FrameNet corpora. Columns from left to right: (1) Language. (2) Source of the non-annotated data. (3) Number of different frames annotated at least one time. (4) Number of different LU annotated at least one time. (5) Number of different FE annotated at least one time. (6) Number of sentences containing at least one annotated LU. (7) Total number of LU instances annotated. (8) Average number of annotations per LU.

SemEval07-FR: This corpus is the translation of SemEval07-EN into French following the methodology described in Section 2.2.

ASFALDA French FrameNet: is the first French FrameNet project (Djemaa et al., 2016) which outlines and produces a FrameNet equivalent for the French language. This corpus gathers experts frame annotations on sections of the journal *Le Monde*, it contains 121 different frames that focus on four notional domains: commercial transactions, cognitive positions, causality, and verbal communication. ASFALDA tries as much as possible to align with the English FrameNet structure; however, it also introduces new frames whenever the differences in both languages do not allow conciliation.

CALOR: is a publicly available corpus(Marzinotto et al., 2018a) of French encyclopedic documents human-annotated using FrameNet semantics. This corpus was designed from the perspective of Information Extraction tasks. Like ASFALDA, CALOR uses a *partial parsing* policy, in which annotations are limited to a small subset of frames from FrameNet. The CALOR corpus contains 53 different frames selected as the most representative and frequent within the annotated documents. Despite the small number of Frames, CALOR is the corpus with the largest set of annotated lexical units.
Table 2 summarizes relevant statistics on each corpus.

4.2. Evaluation setting

We run experiments using the standard Train, Validation, and Test of each corpus. For the SemEval07-FR corpus, these subsets are equivalent to the ones from SemEval07-EN. To evaluate our models we use 2 of the main sub-tasks of FrameNet parsing:

- **Frame Identification:** Consists in selecting the frames evoked by each of the lexical units in the sentence. One frame per lexical unit. Here, we use the gold annotated lexical units, and we do not try to infer them from raw text.

- **Argument Identification:** Consists in finding the spans of words that correspond to semantic roles and assigning them the correct frame element labels from the selected Frame.

Since the set of lexical units on each corpus is different, and since this difference is due to arbitrary choices about what should be annotated in the *partial annotations* schemes from CALOR and ASFALDA we consider that all the lexical unit instances are known and given as input to our model. For the same reasons, we discard lexical unit annotations that refer to the frame OTHER, which is an artifact to handle frames out of the scope of the *partial annotation*. In this setting, each lexical unit triggers a frame from the frame dictionary of the given corpus.
We score our models using:

- **Frame Identification:** Accuracy on the frame classification Task with gold lexical units. FrameNet official evaluation scripts use the frame hierarchy to introduce a matching metric that gives partial credit when predicting related frames (*e.g.*, a more generic Frame). Since this hierarchy is no available on each corpus, we evaluate using exact frame matching and we do not exploit any of the frame-frame relations proposed in FrameNet.

- **Argument Identification:** Precision, Recall, and F1 or the frame element detection. This metric can be computed either using the gold or the predicted Frames. In the official evaluation scripts, the token span of the hypothesis must be the same as in the reference for a frame element to be correct (Hard Spans or H-Spans). We have loosened this constraint to introduce a new variant of the evaluation metrics. Instead of demanding exact span match, we use a weighted correctness score proportional to the overlap ratio between the gold (S_{ref}) and predicted (S_{hyp}) spans (W-Spans) computed using equation 1.

$$W_{span}(S_{ref}, S_{hyp}) = \frac{|S_{ref} \cap S_{hyp}|}{|S_{ref} \cup S_{hyp}|} \qquad (1)$$

5. Bi-lingual Semantic Parsing Experiments

Recent works (Pires et al., 2019) have shown that BERT language models pre-trained on multilingual corpora have a fairly good performance in a zero-shot cross-lingual transfer setting. More precisely, if we fine-tune a multi-lingual BERT using task-specific annotations from a monolingual corpus and then evaluate the model in a different language, the system will be able to generalize to the new language, up to some extent.

	Test: ASFALDA		Test: CALOR	
	Frame Id.	Arg Id. pred frames	Frame Id.	Arg Id. pred frames
TRAINING CORPUS	ACC	F1-W	ACC	F1-W
CALOR	-	-	98.8	67.8
ASFALDA	73.3	52.6	-	-
SemEval-07-EN	42.2	**19.7**	77.5	30.5
SemEval-07-FR	**73.3**	19.1	**78.1**	**31.0**
SemEval-07-EN+FR	**74.8**	**20.9**	**79.4**	**32.4**

Table 3: Performance of a `biGRU+BERT` on the Gold French FrameNet corpora using different training data-sets

In this experiment, we harness this zero-shot generalization property to evaluate the quality and the relevance of our corpus translation strategy extrinsically.

	Frame Id.	Argument Id. w/pred frames		
	ACC	P	R	F1
SemEval-07-EN	85.3	49.6	40.3	44.5
SemEval-07-FR	80.8	29.8	15.4	20.3
CALOR	77.5	37.3	25.7	30.5
ASFALDA	42.2	24.5	16.4	19.7

Table 4: Performance of a `biGRU+BERT` model trained on the `SemEval-07-EN` corpus and tested on other corpora

	Frame Id.	Argument Id. w/pred frames		
	ACC	P	R	F1
SemEval-07-FR	80.5	38.5	26.0	31.1
SemEval-07-EN	82.8	37.3	23.3	28.7
CALOR	78.1	37.7	26.3	31.0
ASFALDA	73.3	38.6	15.8	19.1

Table 5: Performance of a `biGRU+BERT` model trained on the `SemEval-07-FR` projected corpus

First, we train a model on the `SemEval-07-EN` corpus and test in on all the available corpora to establish a zero-shot baseline performance. We train the model for 40 epochs and we used two validation sets, one from `SemEval-07-EN` and the other form `SemEval-07-FR`. This way, we retained the best performing model for each validation set and language. We observed that the validation error stops decreasing earlier on the French corpus than on the English one. This could be expected due to the monolingual training configuration. However, we did not observe significant over-fitting or catastrophic forgetting on the French language when doing supplementary iterations. After training, we used the best English model to produce inferences on the `SemEval-07-EN` test and the best French model to produce inferences on the 3 French corpora. We evaluate using precision, recall and F-score on Weighted Spans (see Section 4.2.). The results for this experiment are shown in Table 4. We observe that transfer learning and the language similarities between English and French can bootstrap a low-performance baseline for French. The system is surprisingly good at detecting

Frames. However, it has very low performance on the full FrameNet parsing Task, showing a particularly low recall.

In the following step, we train a model using the projected `SemEval-07-FR` corpus. The performance of this model is given in Table 5. We observe that the French model trained on the synthetic data-set achieves slightly better performance than the English model baseline. It is better at the Frame Identification step, and it is slightly better in terms of Argument Identification as well. Moreover, the French model is capable of generalizing back to the English language, showing close performances between `SemEval-07-EN` and `SemEval-07-FR`. The fact that it is easier to generalize toward English can be interpreted in several ways. One possibility is that the French FrameNet parsing task is more difficult than its English equivalent since FrameNet was designed for English or because French is a more verbose language. Another possibility is that due to the alignment errors, the `SemEval-07-FR` test data-set flaws would be penalizing good predictions.

In Table 3 we present the scores for the hand-annotated French data-set for different configurations varying the training corpus. We observe that even though the French model trained on the synthetic data-set achieves slightly better performances than the English baseline, we are still far from the state-of-the-art performances on each corpus obtained through training a FrameNet parser on hand-annotated French data-sets. However, part of this performance gap is due to the differences in the number of Frames. A `SemEval-07` model handles 720 different frames and 3197 different lexical units, therefore it is much more prone to choosing a wrong frame than a `CALOR` model, which handles only 53 Frames. Another reason for this performance gap may be the domain changes, `CALOR` and `ASFALDA` contain natural language sentences instead of translated sentences. Moreover, previous experiments on the `CALOR` corpus from (Marzinotto et al., 2019) have shown that even within the same data source, domain changes yield around 10% F1 performance drop on the Argument Identification Task. Finally, we trained a model combining both `SemEval-07-EN` and `SemEval-07-FR` and obtained small gains on the French corpora, showing that the translated data adds some supplementary information to the model.

6. Conclusion

This paper presented a simple method to project FrameNet annotations into other languages using attention-based neural machine translation (NMT) models. We tested our approach on the English-to-French configuration showing that 90% of the labels can be easily projected without introducing much noise. We performed an in-depth analysis of the French corpus obtained through translation and we showed the most common projection errors. Then, we use existing French FrameNet corpora to assert the quality of the translation. We trained a BERT-based FrameNet parser using the projected annotations and compared it to a BERT baseline showing modest gains on French. All these results support that our approach could help to propagate FrameNet dataset on other languages where sufficiently developed NMT models exist. Moreover, this label projection approach can be extended to other sequence tagging tasks with minor modifications.

7. Bibliographical References

Annesi, P. and Basili, R. (2010). Cross-lingual alignment of framenet annotations through hidden markov models. In Alexander Gelbukh, editor, *Computational Linguistics and Intelligent Text Processing*, pages 12–25, Berlin, Heidelberg. Springer Berlin Heidelberg.

Baker, C., Ellsworth, M., and Erk, K. (2007). Semeval'07 task 19: Frame semantic structure extraction. In *Proceedings of the 4th International Workshop on Semantic Evaluations*, SemEval '07, pages 99–104, Stroudsburg, PA, USA. Association for Computational Linguistics.

Djemaa, M., Candito, M., Muller, P., and Vieu, L. (2016). Corpus annotation within the french framenet: methodology and results. *Proceedings of the Tenth International Conference on Language Resources and Evaluation (LREC)*, X:3794–3801.

Fillmore, C. J. e. a. (1976). Frame semantics and the nature of language. In *Annals of the New York Academy of Sciences: Conference on the origin and development of language and speech*, pages 20–32.

Fillmore, C. J. e. a. (2006). Frame semantics. *Cognitive linguistics: Basic readings*, 34:373–400.

Ghader, H. and Monz, C. (2017). What does attention in neural machine translation pay attention to? *CoRR*, abs/1710.03348.

Gilardi, L. and Baker, C. (2018). Learning to align across languages: Toward multilingual framenet. In *Proceedings of the International FrameNet Workshop*, pages 13–22.

Hayoun, A. and Elhadad, M. (2016). The hebrew framenet project. In *LREC*.

He, L., Lee, K., Lewis, M., and Zettlemoyer, L. (2017). Deep semantic role labeling: What works and what's next. In *Proceedings of the Annual Meeting of the Association for Computational Linguistics*.

Lindén, K., Haltia, H., Luukkonen, J., Laine, A. O., Roivainen, H., and Väisänen, N. (2017). Finnfn 1.0: The finnish frame semantic database. *Nordic Journal of Linguistics*, 40(3):287–311.

Luong, M.-T., Pham, H., and Manning, C. D. (2015). Effective approaches to attention-based neural machine translation. *arXiv preprint arXiv:1508.04025*.

Marzinotto, G., Auguste, J., Bechet, F., Damnati, G., and Nasr, A. (2018a). Semantic Frame Parsing for Information Extraction : the CALOR corpus. In *LREC2018*, Miyazaki, Japan, May.

Marzinotto, G., Béchet, F., Damnati, G., and Nasr, A. (2018b). Sources of Complexity in Semantic Frame Parsing for Information Extraction. In *International FrameNet Workshop 2018*, Miyazaki, Japan, May.

Marzinotto, G., Damnati, G., Béchet, F., and Favre, B. (2019). Robust semantic parsing with adversarial learning for domain generalization. In *Proc. of NAACL*.

Ott, M., Edunov, S., Grangier, D., and Auli, M. (2018). Scaling neural machine translation. *CoRR*, abs/1806.00187.

Pedersen, B. S., Nimb, S., Søgaard, A., Hartmann, M., and Olsen, S. (2018). A danish framenet lexicon and an annotated corpus used for training and evaluating a semantic frame classifier. In *Proceedings of the Eleventh International Conference on Language Resources and Evaluation (LREC 2018)*.

Pires, T., Schlinger, E., and Garrette, D. (2019). How multilingual is multilingual bert? *CoRR*, abs/1906.01502.

Sennrich, R., Haddow, B., and Birch, A. (2016). Neural machine translation of rare words with subword units. In *Proceedings of the 54th Annual Meeting of the Association for Computational Linguistics (Volume 1: Long Papers)*, pages 1715–1725, Berlin, Germany, August. Association for Computational Linguistics.

Torrent, T. T., Ellsworth, M., Baker, C., and Matos, E. (2018). The multilingual framenet shared annotation task: a preliminary report. In *Proceedings of the Eleventh International Conference on Language Resources and Evaluation*, pages 62–68.

Yang, B. and Mitchell, T. (2017). A joint sequential and relational model for frame-semantic parsing. In *Proceedings of the 2017 Conference on Empirical Methods in Natural Language Processing*, pages 1247–1256. Association for Computational Linguistics.

Proceedings of the International FrameNet Workshop 2020: Towards a Global, Multilingual FrameNet, pages 48–55
Language Resources and Evaluation Conference (LREC 2020), Marseille, 11–16 May 2020
© European Language Resources Association (ELRA), licensed under CC-BY-NC

Greek within the Global FrameNet Initiative: Challenges and Conclusions so far

Voula Giouli[1,2], Vera Pilitsidou[1], Hephaestion Christopoulos[1]
[1]National and Kapodistrian University of Athens, [2]Institute for Language & Speech Processing, ATHENA RC
Address 1, Dragatsaniou 4, 105 59 Athens, Greece
Address 2, Artemidos 6 & Epidavrou, Maroussi, Greece
voula@athenarc.gr, verapilitsidou@gmail.com, hchristo@turkmas.uoa.gr

Abstract
Large coverage lexical resources that bear deep linguistic information have always been considered useful for many natural language processing (NLP) applications including Machine Translation (MT). In this respect, Frame-based resources have been developed for many languages following Frame Semantics and the Berkeley FrameNet project. However, to a great extent, all those efforts have been kept fragmented. Consequentially, the Global FrameNet initiative has been conceived of as a joint effort to bring together FrameNets in different languages. The proposed paper is aimed at describing ongoing work towards developing the Greek (EL) counterpart of the Global FrameNet and our efforts to contribute to the Shared Annotation Task. In the paper, we will elaborate on the annotation methodology employed, the current status and progress made so far, as well as the problems raised during annotation.

Keywords: frame semantics, FrameNet, corpus annotation, lexical resource, Greek

1. Introduction

Over the last decades, a number of frame-based lexical resources have been developed based on the Berkeley FrameNet project (Baker et al., 1998) for languages other than English. In this context, the challenge has always been the alignment of frames across languages. In this paper, we describe on-going work carried out in the framework of preparing the Greek component of the Global FrameNet (FrameNet-EL). The purpose of our work is two-fold: (a) participation in the Multi-lingual FrameNet shared task, and (b) the development of language resources, i.e., a general-purpose lexical resource and an annotated corpus that will be applicable for a number of applications. The paper is organized as follows: In section (2), we provide the background and objectives of our work; our corpus data is described in section (3). The methodology adopted towards developing the language resources is presented in section (4), whereas, some preliminary results as well as issues and problematic cases that we faced throughout the various stages of our work so far are presented in section (5). Finally, our conclusions and prospects for future research are outlined in section (6).

2. Background and Objectives

According to Charles J. Fillmore's Frame Semantics (Fillmore, 1977, 1982, 1985), there is continuity between language and experience (Petruck, 1996). In this context, words gain their meaning in a semantic frame which can be an event or a relation. The term "semantic frame" or "frame" refers to any system of meanings which are connected in a way that, to understand any one of these meanings, we must be able to understand the whole structure to which it belongs (Fillmore, 1982: 111). Fillmore calls the elements of such a structure "Frame Elements" (FEs) and the words that evoke the semantic frames "Lexical Units" of the frame (LUs).

FrameNet, the lexical database for the English language for general purposes (Baker et al., 1998), was developed at the University of Berkeley in California based on the aforementioned theory. Over the years, a number of frame-based language resources have been developed for various languages (FrameNet Brazil (Salomão, 2009), Spanish FrameNet (Subirats, 2009) and Japanese FrameNet (Ohara, 2009), and the Swedish FrameNet++ (Ahlberg et al., 2014), inter alia). In this context, the Global FrameNet project (Torrent et al., 2018) has evolved, in order to examine, for example, to what extent the semantic frames developed for English are appropriate for other languages, whether some frames are universal and whether there are certain semantic domains in which frames tend to vary more across languages, or whether there are regular patterns of differences based on language families, regional groupings, etc.

As far as Modern Greek (MG) is concerned, there has been previous work in language for specific purposes and in language for general purposes – yet these studies remain fragmented and limited in scope. In fact, an initial attempt to build a frame semantics lexical resource for MG is reported in Gotsoulia et al. (2007). However, this initial work was conceived of as the preliminary phase of a pilot project for the development of the basic infrastructure and design of the actual resource. Later, Dalpanagioti (2012) followed a frame-driven approach to the bilingual lexicographic process for creating a bilingual lexical database of motion verbs for EL and EN. Another attempt was made by Pilitsidou (2018), who used the FrameNet and Frame Semantics approach to create a domain-specific bilingual terminological database in EL and EN for the financial domain based on corpus evidence; the outcome of this work is a bilingual lexical resource in electronic format consisting of financial terms (LUs) of EL and EN, which are described and defined through the semantic frames that they evoke and the semantic relations, as well as a fully annotated corpus in various levels.

This paper reports on our ongoing participation in the Shared Annotation Task and the contribution to the overall objectives collaborating with teams from other languages towards developing a database of alignments of frames and FEs across languages. Therefore, the paper is aimed at describing the progress made so far as well as the various issues and challenges we faced while working on the EL component of the Global FrameNet project. Effort has also been made to detect and categorize the differences spotted between the MG and English language. In the long run, our objective is to create a frame-based lexical resource for the MG language and to integrate it into existing semantic lexica.

From another perspective, one of our objectives is to examine whether the alignment of a Greek FrameNet with similar resources is feasible and whether the aligned lexica can be utilized for the translation process. Through the efforts for the creation of FN in other languages, the fact that frames are to an extent universal can be proven. As the lexical resource FrameNet can be machine-readable, it has the potential to be a very useful approach for assisting translation. In fact, FN's semantic organization makes it cross-lingual, as different societies are highly likely to recognize the same types of events (Tantos et. al., 2015: 168). A database like FN offers a very useful tool for distinguishing subtle, yet crucial, differentiations in meaning, in a way that differs from other lexical resources, thus rendering it a very promising tool for the translation process.

3. Corpus Description

According to the global guidelines, annotation at this stage was performed on the transcribed TED Talk "Do schools kill creativity?" (Robinson 2006) and the subtitles provided for a number of languages; we report here on the annotation of the Greek counterpart of the TED talk. The EL corpus comprises 251 sentences and 3012 tokens. We pre-processed the raw text at various levels of linguistic analysis (Part-of-Speech tagging and lemmatization, syntactic annotation) using UDPipe annotation platform (Straka & Starková, 2017).

4. Annotation Methodology

The task of annotation was viewed as a two-stage procedure: (a) creation of the LUs (or lexical annotation), and (b) annotation of the corpus using the LUs already created and extending or modifying them where needed. Both tasks, that is, LU creation and corpus annotation, were performed by two annotators via the dedicated MLFN WebTool (Matos & Torrent, 2016). Blind annotation of FEs, GFs and PTs was performed separately by each annotator. At planned intervals, comparisons of the annotated data revealed discrepancies which were extensively discussed and resolved so as to reach a shared understanding of the task at hand and produce an initial version of the annotated text that has been thoroughly checked for mistakes or inconsistencies. At this stage, difficult or ambiguous cases were identified and accounted for. A step-by-step description of the procedure followed is provided below.

4.1. LU Creation

The LUs to be annotated in the corpus were initially created in order to make the annotation process easier; in this respect, the approach we adopted was purely lexicographic in the sense that we first extracted all the lemmas from the EL text and then assigned them a frame

on the basis of their semantics. As expected, this agnostic procedure yielded different LUs for polysemous lemmas. In these cases, word sense discrimination was aided by existing reference works (monolingual and bilingual dictionaries) and corpus evidence in order to decide about the number (and types) of senses. At the next stage, selection of the appropriate frame each LU evokes was challenging. Following the global guidelines provided by the shared task organizers (Torrent el al, 2018), we adopted the frames as defined in the 1.7 release of the Berkeley FrameNet data (BFN 1.7). Since we were not allowed to make any changes, we tried to identify the frame each LU evokes through extensive search in the BFN 1.7 in order to locate the most appropriate one taking also into account its best translational equivalent(s) in English.

In case no translational equivalent of a Greek LU in English has been created yet in the BFN 1.7, the selection of the appropriate frame was performed by annotators using the following decision tree:

- Firstly, option (A) was to search in the BFN 1.7 data for a morphologically related LU that belonged to a different grammatical category (Part-of-Speech) – yet, it retained the meaning of the word to be annotated. In case an LU was spotted, we adopted the frame assigned to it. For example, the LU *αλήθεια.n* (truth) was created under the frame Correctness, based on the adjective *αληθής.a* and its translational equivalent *true.a*.
- If search (A) failed, we proceeded to option (B), that is, we checked if we could locate a synonymous word. In case a synonym was found in the BFN 1.7 data, we adopted its frame, as in the case of the adjective *ταλαντούχος.a* (talented); since its translational equivalent *talented.a* was not listed in the BNF 1.7, its synonymous word *skilled.a* led us adopt the frame Expertise.
- In both cases, (A) and (B), we also checked that the frame selected was a perfect fit, that is, it was actually evoked by the meaning of the LU, in that the latter (a) matches the underlying meaning of the frame and (b) features at least its core FEs.
- If both (A) and (B) failed, then we tried option (C), which entailed searching the list of existing frames and trying to identify a frame that would be the nearest match. In this case, we were expected to report the reason the frame was not considered as a perfect fit by selecting the most appropriate one from a list provided in the annotation tool: (a) different perspective, (b) different causative alternation, (c) different inchoative alternation, (d) different stative alternation, (e) too specific, (f) too generic, (g) different entailment, (h) different coreness status, (i) missing FE and (j) other.
- Finally, in case we were unable to locate an appropriate frame, we left the LU under consideration aside making a note for future reference. This is the case of the LU *βασίζομαι.v*

(to be based on), for which the frames of the morphologically related lemmas could not be adopted and no synonymous word could be found.

It should be pointed out, however, that during the annotation process we found out that certain LUs could be assigned to more than one frames, as for example the LU *δημιουργικότητα.n* (creativity); using option (A) we located the LU *creation.n* that evokes the frame `Intentionally_create`. At the same time, an extensive search in the frames showed that the frame `Mental_property` is also applicable.

Finally, following common lexicographic practices, for each LU, we provided sense description, in the form of a short lexicographic gloss in English.

4.2. Corpus Annotation

After the LUs had been created, annotation proper was performed. At this stage, each sentence in the corpus was annotated at the following layers: (a) Frame and Frame Element (FE) layer, (b) Grammatical Function (GF) layer, and (c) Phrase Type (PT) annotation[1].

The major challenge was the identification of the correct LU already created (see section 4.1). Again, we also had to tackle polysemous lemmas by selecting the most appropriate LU to annotate. As a matter of fact, sense discrimination was often a challenge and fine distinctions between closely related frames made it difficult to spot the difference between them. In these cases, context was always helpful, especially in cases where the distinctions might be extremely fine. For example, the polysemous lemma *πηγαίνω.v* (to go) evokes more than one frames. However, as shown in example (1), given the context, the `Participation` frame has been selected based on the context – instead of the `Motion` one:

(1) "*Δεν πάτε συχνά σε πάρτι*"
Den pate   sichna se parti
Not go2.pr often   to parties
"You don't go to parties often"

LUs were then populated with information regarding the FEs found in the corpus and their realizations. At the next level, each FE was assigned the grammatical function it assumes in the sentence. The following grammatical relations are foreseen: Noun Subject (Nsubj), Object (Obj), Indirect Object (Iobj), Clause Subject (Csubj), Clause Complement (Ccomp), Xcomp, Head, Dep, Nmod, Appositive, Ext. These relations were adopted from Universal Dependencies (UD)[2]. Subsequently, Phrase

Types (PTs) chosen from UD tags were used to tag the realizations of FEs in the corpus. In the next section we will elaborate further on the results obtained, focusing on the creation of LUs and their annotation in the corpus.

In Figure 1, two examples of annotated sentences from the corpus are presented.

Είχαμε ΓΕΜΙΣΕΙ [GOAL το μέρος] [THEME με ατζέντηδες που φορούσαν μπλουζάκια] (Filling) (Implied AGENT: We)

Είχαμε γεμίσει το μέρος με ατζέντηδες [WEARER που] ΦΟΡΟΥΣΑΝ [CLOTHING μπλουζάκια] (Wearing)

Ihame   gemisi   to   meros   me agentides pou forousan   blouzakia

Had1.pl filled   the.acc   place.acc with agents.acc who wore3.pl   T-shirts.acc

"We had filled the place with agents wearing T-shirts"

[ADDRESSEE Σας] ΟΔΗΓΗΣΑΝ, πιθανότατα, [CONTENT μακριά από κάποια πράγματα στο σχολείο] όταν ήσασταν παιδιά, πράγματα που σας άρεσαν, [MEANS με τη δικαιολογία ότι δεν θα βρίσκατε ποτέ δουλειά κάνοντας αυτά], σωστά; (Talking_into) (Implied SPEAKER: They)

Σας οδήγησαν, πιθανότατα, μακριά από κάποια πράγματα στο σχολείο όταν ήσασταν ΠΑΙΔΙΑ, πράγματα που σας άρεσαν, με τη δικαιολογία ότι δεν θα βρίσκατε ποτέ δουλειά κάνοντας αυτά, σωστά; (People_by_age)

Σας οδήγησαν, πιθανότατα, μακριά από κάποια πράγματα στο σχολείο όταν ήσασταν παιδιά, [CONTENT πράγματα που] [EXPERIENCER σας] ΑΡΕΣΑΝ, με τη δικαιολογία ότι δεν θα βρίσκατε ποτέ δουλειά κάνοντας αυτά, σωστά; (Experiencer_focused_emotion)

Σας οδήγησαν, πιθανότατα, μακριά από κάποια πράγματα στο σχολείο όταν ήσασταν παιδιά, πράγματα που σας άρεσαν, με τη ΔΙΚΑΙΟΛΟΓΙΑ [EXPLANATION ότι δεν θα βρίσκατε ποτέ δουλειά κάνοντας αυτά], σωστά; (Justification)

Σας οδήγησαν, πιθανότατα, μακριά από κάποια πράγματα στο σχολείο όταν ήσασταν παιδιά, πράγματα που σας άρεσαν, με τη δικαιολογία ότι δεν θα ΒΡΙΣΚΑΤΕ [TIME ποτέ] [THEME δουλειά] κάνοντας αυτά, σωστά; (Getting) (Implied RECIPIENT: You)

Σας οδήγησαν, πιθανότατα, μακριά από κάποια πράγματα στο σχολείο όταν ήσασταν παιδιά, πράγματα που σας άρεσαν, με τη δικαιολογία ότι δεν θα βρίσκατε ποτέ δουλειά ΚΑΝΟΝΤΑΣ [ACT αυτά], σωστά; (Intentionally_act)

Sas   odigisan,   pithanotata,   makria apo   kapia pragmata   sto   scholio   otan isastan   pedia, pragmata   pou   sas   aresan,   me   ti

---

[1] Two more layers are also foreseen by the Shared Task organizers, namely, Other and Sentence. The layer Other involves annotation of relative pronouns and their antecedents, whereas, the Sentence layer features tags applicable to the whole sentence, and may include notes such as the existence of a metaphor, or how prototypical the sentence is. For the time being, we did not perform any annotations at these layers.

[2] https://universaldependencies.org/u/dep/index.html

dikaiologia oti den   tha   vriskate   pote
doulia   kanontas   afta,   sosta?

You.pl   were led   most likely   away   from
some.acc   things.acc   at the.acc   school.acc   when
were2.pl   children, things.nom   that   you.gen   were
liked,   with   the.acc   excuse.acc   that not would
find2.pl   never   job.acc   doing   them,   correct?

"They most likely led you away from certain things at
school when you were children, things you liked, with the
excuse that you would never find a job doing those things,
correct?

Figure 1: Examples of annotations from within the corpus

5. Preliminary Results

This being a work in progress, presented below are our
initial findings. After completing a certain part of the
annotation, the team got together and discussed their
findings. As will be shown below, there were several
issues, some of which pertain to the nature and structure
of the MG language as well as the translation of the text,
which, more often than not, was not optimal, while others
regard proposed additions or revisions of the FN frames
and FE structure. We did encounter several cases of
mistranslation or bad wording, some of which made it
impossible to assign frames and FEs, while in other cases
we had to make some uncommon decisions. Issues such
as annotation of multiword expressions and grammatical
differences between EN and EL will be discussed more
thoroughly below.

5.1. LU Creation: Results and Issues

In total, c. 603 LUs were created that evoke c. 250 frames;
regarding the verbs of the EL corpus, which are the main
focus, more than about 220 frames have been assigned to
the 167 unique verbs. In most cases, frame assignment via
the EN LUs was a laborious – yet straightforward – task
and the BFN 1.7 frames were proved a perfect fit,
whereas, in a number of cases, no frame seemed to be a
perfect fit. It should be noted that the already existing
BFN 1.7 frames worked very well in almost all cases of
commonly used phrases and words with a distinct and
specific meaning, even in cases of polysemy where the
word meanings were quite discrete.

Table 1 provides quantitative data on the frame
assignment of the LUs we have taken into account so far.
As one can see, the percentage of perfect fits is quite high
(87.8%), as opposed to the 8.6% of non-perfect fits and
the 3.7% percentage of the cases where no available frame
could be found. However, it should be noted that, in order
to achieve that satisfactory percentage, we often had to
diverge from the frames the BFN assigns to certain LUs
or make our own choices in cases of LUs that are not
indexed. The main causes for cases of non-perfect fits
were different perspective and different entailment,
followed by too specific or too general frame, missing FE
and different causative alternation.

No of existing LUs	626
No of LUs created	603
Perfect fits	549
Non-perfect fits	54
No frame assigned	23

Table 1: Quantitative results of frame assignment

A recurring issue that led us to sometimes taking unusual
initiatives or resulted in the assignment of non-optimal
frames are the cases of systematic polysemy, which is a
phenomenon encountered across languages and should be
considered by the FN team. Quite often, the FN catalogue
seems to take into account only a certain shade of the
occasional word's meaning, and does not assign it to other
frames that cover its different uses. This also led us to
speculate that there might be some important frames
missing from the FN catalogue. FN in general sometimes
does not seem to distinguish between subtle
differentiations in meaning, and there are words that in
certain contexts could easily be assigned to a frame, but
there are occasions where a perfect fit is impossible to
find. For example, LUs such as *πανεπιστήμιο.n*
(university) and *σχολείο.n* (school) fall in this category.
According to the FN index, these LUs evoke the frame
Locale_by_use, but this is merely one of their
meanings. This is a classic case of systematic polysemy,
as the words do not only denote the building itself, but
also the institution and the activities that take place there.

There were also other cases where the FN frame was more
or less a good fit, but we did notice some missing FEs that
would be useful in MG and perhaps other languages
(sometimes in English, as well) or cases where the
description of the frame contained FEs we consider
redundant or too specific. For example, the LU *παίζω.v*
(to play) evokes the frame Competition; however, a
game is not always competitive, and this is not captured in
the frame – or any other frame in BFN 1.7.

Another example is *χορεύω.v* (to dance). FN lists *dance*
under Self_motion, but the definition of the frame is:
"The SELF_MOVER, a living being, moves under its own
direction along a PATH. Alternatively, or in addition to
PATH, an AREA, DIRECTION, SOURCE, or GOAL for the
movement may be mentioned." There is clearly no
necessity for a PATH or DIRECTION when someone is
dancing. Another possible choice, not mentioned in the
English FN, would be Moving_in_place, which is
sometimes true for this specific activity and sometimes
not. Perhaps a more suitable frame would be one referring
to pastime activities.

A similar case is "Σε λίγο τα πτυχία δεν θα αξίζουν
τίποτα." A not very elegant, but closer to the EL text back
translation would be "In a while, the degrees will be worth
nothing." The LU *αξίζω.v* (to be worth) could be assigned
to the Deserving frame. The frame's definition
according to FN is "The existence of a
STATE_OF_AFFAIRS is sufficient reason for taking an
ACTION. The agent who is justified in taking the

suggested ACTION is not part of the immediate scene, however." Based on the phrase above, we believe that the ACTION is an optional element in the frame, since there is no reference to what ACTION would be taken if the STATE_OF_AFFAIRS (the degrees) were sufficient.

(2) "Σε λίγο τα πτυχία δεν θα αξίζουν τίποτα"
Se ligo ta ptihia den
tha axizoun tipota
In a little the.pl.nom degrees.nom not
will be worth nothing
"In a while the degrees will be worthless"

Another issue that caught our attention is that sometimes FN does not seem to distinguish between the procedure that leads to a certain result and the case where an LU denotes being in that certain state from the beginning. At least in EL, there are some LUs, mainly verbs, that could assume both meanings, depending on context. This distinction might appear too fine at first sight, it is however frame-defining, and we did notice the lack of available frames in such cases. This is the case of the LUs *ενώνω.v* (to connect, to join) and *χωρίζομαι.v* (to be separated, to be divided). Here are two similar cases: the LU *ενώνω.v* is not in this example a perfect fit for the Attaching frame, as shown in (3), since the frame refers to the process of joining, not the state of being joined.

(3) "Ενώνει τα δύο μισά του εγκεφάλου"
Enoni ta dyo misa tou
egefalou
Connects the.sg.acc two halves.acc the.sg.gen
brain.gen
"Connects the two halves of the brain"

On the other hand, the LU *χωρίζομαι.v* is not a perfect fit for Becoming_separated as shown in example (4), as the phrase refers to the state of being separated.

(4) "Δεν χωρίζεται σε διαμερίσματα"
Den horizete se diamerismata
Not divided3.sg.pass into compartments.acc
"It is not divided into compartments"

However, not all difficulties we encountered should be attributed to shortages in the FN index. Some issues arise from peculiarities and idiosyncrasies of the MG language, such as the middle voice, which are to be expected, since the BFN we take as a starting point was originally designed for the English language. Generally, passive (or non-active) morphology of some EL verbs is found in reflexive, anti-causative and passive structures. However, in some cases, the passive morphology of some verbs signifies usages/senses besides those entailed by the active morphology (Clairis & Babiniotis, 2005). These differences in meaning cannot be accounted for at early stages of processing; as a result, when attempting to assign an EL verb to a frame, the annotation tool treats the active and the middle voice of verbs as a single lemma. As expected, this presents a problem in several cases, as the active and middle forms of a verb might belong to a different frame. For example, the LU *εμφανίζω.v* (to reveal, to present) in active voice needs to be assigned to

different frame as opposed to its middle voice counterpart *εμφανίζομαι.v* (to appear or arrive). The middle voice of the verb can be assigned to frames such as Arriving or Becoming_visible, while the active voice *εμφανίζω.v* most certainly does not belong there. Similarly, the LU *ωφελούμαι.v* (to benefit from), which is middle voice in MG, and its active voice *ωφελώ.v* (which means *benefit* as in "These new courses will benefit the students") need to be indexed under different frames. The frame Cause_benefit_or_detriment certainly is not the best fit for the middle voice, while other frames only tangentially relate to the verb's meaning. This could imply that there's a missing frame in the FN catalogue, as we could not find one suitable to the middle voice form.

Similarly, non-perfect fits showcase differences in perspective between MG concepts and English ones, as shown with the verb *συνταξιοδοτώ.v*. In MG, the verb has both active and passive morphology, whereas the respective verb in English "to retire" corresponds to the passive voice; moreover, in MG, the verb has more specific connotations, as it means to leave one's job and get a pension, the pension being the core component of the verb's meaning.

The verbs *επιτρέπεται* (to be allowed) and *πρόκειται* (a rough translation would be "will" or "be about to") are analogous to *αρέσω.v* (discussed in 5.2). Regarding the first case, we encounter the phrase "Τα παιδιά χορεύουν όλη την ώρα, αν αυτό τους επιτρέπεται," which can be back translated as "Children dance all the time, if they are allowed to." This is the middle voice of *επιτρέπω.v* (to allow), and apart from the problems with frame assignment, there are some peculiarities in its use. A more literal translation of the phrase "αν αυτό τους επιτρέπεται" would be "if this is allowed to them" (consequently, it is not a perfect fit for Preventing_or_letting or Deny_or_grant_permission). A peculiarity of this verb, however, is that the middle voice of the verb appears only in the third person singular or plural, meaning that a certain act is allowed to some entity. Moreover, it should be noted that we couldn't find a suitable FE in the Preventing_or_letting frame denoting who is allowed or prevented from doing something. Furthermore, in MG the entity that is allowed to do something is realized as the object of the verb in the genitive case or as a complement of the preposition *σε* (e.g. *σε εμένα*, meaning "to me"), not as the subject, as is the case with the English verb *to be allowed*. The verb's antonym *απαγορεύεται.v* has the exact same properties as the ones just discussed.

(5) "Αν αυτό τους επιτρέπεται"
An afto tous epitrepete
If this.sg.nom they.gen is allowed
"If they are allowed to."

Regarding *πρόκειται.v*, here we have an even more noteworthy case. It is a middle voice verb that is used solely in the third person singular, and more often than not preceded by the negative particle *δεν* (not). An instance from our corpus is "δεν πρόκειται να γίνεις μουσικός" ("you will never become a musician"). We assigned the verb to the Destiny frame, even though we are not very satisfied with that choice, since the sense of fate is not always implied by this verb. What is interesting is that the core FEs (PROTAGONIST, ROLE, STATE_OF_AFFAIRS) are not realized as complements to the verb but as a subjunctive subordinate clause:

> (6) "Δεν πρόκειται να γίνεις μουσικός"
> Den prokite na ginis mousikos
> Not will3.sg to become2.sg.sbjv musician
> "You will never become a musician"

Furthermore, a number of ambiguous cases were identified. For example, the LU *κάνω.v* (to do or to make) was assigned to the frame Intentionally_act; however, this is not always the case. In some cases, there might be a different entailment, since doing something does not always imply intention to do it. In this respect, the frame is too specific.

Despite the variety of frames and LUs the BFN 1.7 offers, we encountered several instances where the FN-assigned frames do not cover all cases of the EL lemmas. One example is the EL noun *ιδέα.n* (idea: "να έχεις πρωτότυπες ιδέες" – "having original ideas"). The FN-assigned frame is Awareness. However, the particular meaning of the word is not covered by this frame. A possible candidate could be Coming_up_with, even though this frame is perhaps a bit too specific. This is a case were not all meanings of a word are covered. Similarly, the LU *ανταποδίδω.v* (to reciprocate or to return) in (7) was listed under the Request frame, although in this specific instance it does not mean inviting someone but returning a favour instead. *Reciprocate* is not indexed in FN and *return* is indexed only under different meanings.

> (7) "Δεν ανταποδίδουν την πρόσκληση"
> Den antapodidoun tin prosklisi
> Not return3.pl the.sg.acc invitation sg.acc
> "They don't invite you back"

Another instance was *χάνω.v* (in our case, to miss, but also to lose in other contexts): "Έχασα κάτι;" ("Did I miss something?"). We found it impossible to assign a frame to this meaning of the word. A possible candidate could be Perception, but *miss* does not imply modalities like hear or taste.

The LU *βρίσκω.v* (to find, to get) of the phrase "Δεν θα βρίσκατε ποτέ δουλειά" ("You would never find a job") posed a difficulty as well. The Getting frame implies the acquisition of an object or some property and the change of ownership. This is not the case here. On the other hand, the frame Being_employed, which would refer to the whole phrase and not just the verb (see cases of multiword expressions below), is not suitable either, because it does not refer to the process of acquiring a job.

> (8) "Δεν θα βρίσκατε ποτέ δουλειά"
> Den tha vriskate pote doulia
> Not will find3.pl.pret never job.acc
> "You would never find a job"

Last but not least, the LU *εισαγωγή.n* (in this case, university admission, but entrance or insertion in general – "είναι μια παρατεταμένη διαδικασία εισαγωγής στο πανεπιστήμιο"/"it is a prolonged university admission procedure") was also problematic. The word in this context cannot be assigned to Arriving, since the frame refers to a literal arrival at a place, but neither to Success_or_failure, as it is too specific. This is a case of a subtle differentiation in meaning which makes it difficult to find a suitable frame

5.2. Corpus Annotation: Results and Issues

In total, 222 out of the 251 sentences of the text were annotated, whereas, the annotation effort amounts to 620 annotation sets for verbs, nouns, adjectives, adverbs and numbers. The distribution of the annotated LUs per Part-of-Speech (POS) is depicted in Table 2.

POS	No
adjective	32
adverb	3
noun	157
num	7
verb	421
total	620

Table 2: Distributions of LUs per POS

It should be noted that MG is a pro-drop language, and consequently several core elements, such as the AGENT or the COGNIZER, appear to be missing from the sentences, while in reality they can be inferred from the verb form. This is a special case of constructional null instantiation that one can come across very frequently in languages that feature this syntactic characteristic, such as Greek, Spanish or the Slavic languages. For this reason, it is not possible to annotate all core FEs in the corpus, unless the annotation platform is modified as appropriate so as to take the peculiarities of pro-drop languages into account, since the labelling Null does not allow the annotator to define the FE that appears to be missing.

Moreover, the annotation process posed challenges due to the genre of the text; as a result, some sentences were not annotated at all since they present phenomena like ellipsis or pragmatic function. This is especially true for questions like the one presented in (9):

> (9) "Τι έγινε;"
> Ti egine?
> What became?
> "What happened?"

This meaning of the LU *γίνομαι.v* occurs only in the third person singular, which is a distinctive quality that should be noted.

From another perspective, the annotation at the GF and PT levels revealed further discrepancies and non-perfect fits. More precisely, we did notice some differences in the realization of the FEs in EN and EL that are worth pointing out; these could either pertain to the frame assignment itself or to differences between the structure and syntax of FEs within a given frame. An example of a

LU as compared to its translation in EN is depicted in Table 3. Following its EN counterpart, the EL LU *αρέσω.v* (to like) was created under the frame `Experiencer_focus`. However, this was proven to be a non-perfect fit, and was chosen only because no other frame seemed appropriate. The main difference between the verb *to like* and the EL verb *αρέσω.v* is that in English the EXPERIENCER is always realized as the Subject of the verb; in EL, however, the EXPERIENCER is realized either as the complement of the preposition or as the object complement in genitive case. Moreover, in a more general use/meaning, the verb can be used without a complement at all. Consequently, the CONTENT rather than the EXPERIENCER seem to be the focus of the verb; the EXPERIENCER might not even be present in the sentence, as will be shown in the examples below. The following table depicts the different realizations of the EN and EL verbs *αρέσω.v/to like.v*:

Experiencer focus		
	Realization	
	like.v	αρέσω.v
EXPERIENCER	Ext.NP	Obj.NP
CONTENT	Obj.NP	Nsubj

Table 3: Realization of the LUs *to like.v* and *αρέσω.v*

Usages of the verb *αρέσω* are depicted in examples (10) and (11) below:

(10) "Πράγματα που σας άρεσαν"
Pragmata   pou   sas   aresan
Things.nom that   you.pl.gen liked
"Things you liked"

(11) "Ο Γιάννης αρέσει"
O   Gianis   aresi
The.sg.nom Gianis.nom   is liked
"Giannis is liked" (meaning, by people in general – note the absence of the EXPERIENCER)

Finally, we should note again that there were a great many instances of mistranslation or bad wording in the EL text, which made the frame assignment very difficult or even impossible in certain cases. One such case, maybe the most characteristic one, is the phrase, "Αυτοί οι άνθρωποι που βγαίνουν από την κορυφή" ("These people who come out of the top"), which makes no sense and it was impossible to infer what the translator meant by it.

5.2.1. Multiword Expressions

Multiword expressions (MWEs) have long been regarded as a "pain in the neck" for NLP and translation alike, due to their idiosyncratic behaviour (Sag et al., 2002). In fact, they are lexical items characterized by lexical, syntactic, semantic, pragmatic or statistical idiosyncrasies. We did encounter such cases in the corpus which form solid semantic unities and cannot be treated on a word-by-word basis. Some cases are debatable; for example, collocations such as the noun phrases *καθηγητής πανεπιστημίου* (university professor) and *εκπαιδευτικό σύστημα* (educational system) could be either regarded as two distinct words or as a homogenous whole, as, for example, a university professor is a distinct vocation compared to, e.g., *καθηγητής αγγλικών.n* (English teacher), which both use the equivalent of the word professor in a totally different context. However, even if it would perhaps be preferable to assign these phrases to a single frame as a whole, it is quite straightforward to frame them word by word.

But not all cases are that simple. As a matter of fact, a number of idiomatic expressions found in the corpus can only be treated as single predicates. For example, the verbal MWE *δεν μας παίρνει* (we can't afford to) must be assigned as a whole to the `Capability` frame. However, as it is an idiomatic phrase, a word-by-word translation would be "it doesn't take us." Clearly there is no point in assigning the LU *take.v* to the `Taking` frame in this instance. This is also the case with a number or Light Verb constructions.

A fact that should be taken into account should the FN annotation platform make it possible to assign frames to MWEs is that MWEs are often discontinuous, as is often the case in MG. For example, the expression in (12), belonging to the `Attempt_suasion` frame, consists of fixed discontinuous elements and non-fixed ones:

(12) "Κάνε μου τη χάρη."
Kane mou   ti   hari
Do   I.gen the.sg.acc   favour.acc
"Do me this favour", also meaning "indulge me"

The expression is "κάνω τη χάρη" (do the favour), and the pronoun can be interposed in between, disrupting the continuity of the phrase.

6. Conclusion

We have presented work in progress towards developing the Greek section of the Global FrameNet Shared Task. In an attempt to prove the universal nature of frames, effort has been made to construct a frame-based lexical resource for MG and to annotate an EL corpus based on frames that already exist for the English language. This task has not always been an easy and straightforward one. In the paper we have reported on the progress made so far, and on the issues encountered. Future work is already planned towards enriching the EL data with new corpora and annotations and towards using the resource for aiding the translation process. In particular, a future prospect is to add comparable corpora to the data, in order to extend the lexical resource and avoid any inconsistencies that emerge from mistranslation or wrong wording of the translated corpus. As a matter of fact, the need of adding more frames or more FEs to FN, with which it would be possible to include the differentiated meanings of LUs of the MG language, has emerged, so that, in the future, the database can be used for the MG language. From another perspective, further work is planned towards making meaningful cross-lingual comparisons.

7. Acknowledgments

The authors would like to thank the anonymous reviewers and the editors for their valuable comments to the manuscript that contributed to improving the final version of the paper. The research leading to the results presented here was partially supported by the Translation and Interpreting MA programme of the Faculty of Turkish and Modern Asian Studies of the National and Kapodistrian University of Athens.

8. Bibliographical References

Ahlberg, M, Borin, L., Dannélls, D., Forsberg, M, Toporowska Gronostaj, M., Friberg Heppin, K., Johansson, R., Kokkinakis, D., Olsson, L.J., and Uppström, J. (2014): Swedish FrameNet++ The Beginning of the End and the End of the Beginning, in Proceedings of the Fifth Swedish Language Technology Conference, Uppsala, 13-14 November 2014.

Baker C. F., Fillmore C. J., and Lowe J. B. (1998). The Berkeley FrameNet Project. Proceedings of the 17th International Conference on Computational Linguistics – Volume 1 (COLING '98), Vol. 1. Association for Computational Linguistics, Stroudsburg, PA, USA: 86-90. https://dl.acm.org/citation.cfm?doid=980451.980860

Clairis, Chr., and Babiniotis, G. (2005). Grammar of the Modern Greek Language (In Greek). Athens: Ellinika Grammata.

Dalpanagioti, T. (2012). A Frame-driven Approach to Bilingual Lexicography: Lexical Meaning and Usage Patterns in Greek and English Motion Verbs. PhD Thesis. Εθνικό αρχείο διδακτορικών διατριβών. https://www.didaktorika.gr/eadd/handle/10442/27162

Fillmore, C. J. (1977). Scenes-and-frames Semantics. Book chapter in: Linguistic Structures Processing. Fundamental Studies in Computer Science, vol. 59. North Holland Publishing: 55-81.

Fillmore, C. J. (1982). Frame Semantics. Linguistics in the Morning Calm, ed. The Linguistic Society of Korea. Selected papers from SICOL-1981: 111-137.

Fillmore, C. J. (1885). Frames and the Semantics of Understanding. Quaderni di semantica. Vol. 6, no 2: 222-254.

Gotsoulia, V, Desipri, E., Koutsombogera, M., Prokopidis, P., Papageorgiou, H., and Markopoulos, G. 2007. Towards a Frame Semantics Lexical Resource for Greek. In Proceedings of the Sixth International Workshop on Treebanks and Linguistic Theories.

Matos, E. and Torrent, T. (2016). A Flexible Tool for an Enriched FrameNet. In Proceedings of the 9th International Conference on Construction Grammar (ICCG9), Juiz de Fora, Brazil, october. Federal University of Juiz de Fora (UFJF).

Ohara, K. H. (2009). Frame-based Contrastive Lexical Semantics in Japanese FrameNet: The Case of Risk and Kakeru: 163–182. Berlin/New York: Mouton de Gruyter.

Petruck, M. R. L. (1996). Handbook of Pragmatics. Jef Verschueren, Jan-Ola Östman, Jan Blommaert, and Chris Bulcaen (eds.). Philadelphia: John Benjamins.

Pilitsidou, V. (2018). Terminology: Application of Frame Semantics to the Thematic Field of Finance for the Creation of a Term Base, from a Translation Perspective. (Master's thesis, National and Kapodistrian University of Athens, Athens, Greece). Retrieved from https://pergamos.lib.uoa.gr/uoa/dl/object/2775104

Robinson, K. (2006). Do Schools Kill Creativity? TED Talk. Available at https://www.ted.com/talks/ken_robinson_says_schools_kill_creativity.

Sag, I., Baldwin, T., Bond, F., Copestake, A., and Flickinger, D. (2002). Multiword Expressions: A Pain in the Neck for NLP. In A. F. Gelbukh, ed. 2002. Proceedings of the Third International Conference on Computational Linguistics and Intelligent Text Processing (CICLing '02). Springer-Verlag, London, UK, UK, 1-15.

Salomão, M. M. M. (2009). Framenet brasil: um trabalho em progresso. Caleidoscópio 7(3): 171–182.

Straka, M. and Starková, J. (2017). Tokenizing, POS Tagging, Lemmatizing and Parsing UD 2.0 with UDPipe. Proceedings of the CoNLL 2017 Shared Task: Multilingual Parsing from Raw Text to Universal Dependencies. Association for Computational Linguistics: 8899. Vancouver, Canada. http://www.aclweb.org/anthology/K/K17/K17-3009.pdf

Subirats, C. (2009). Spanish FrameNet: A Frame-semantic Analysis of the Spanish Lexicon: 135–162. Berlin/New York: Mouton de Gruyter.

Tantos, A., Markantonatou, S., Anastasiadi-Symeonidi, A., and Kyriakopoulou, T. (2015). Computational Linguistics (in Greek). [E-book] Athens: Hellenic Academic Libraries Link. https://repository.kallipos.gr/bitstream/11419/2205/13/nlp2ndEdition.pdf

Torrent, T., Elsworth, M., Baker, C., da Silva Matos, E. E. (2018). The Multilingual FrameNet Shared Annotation Task: a Preliminary Report. In The International FrameNet Workshop 2018: Multilingual FrameNets and Constructions.

9. Language Resource References

FrameNet: https://framenet.icsi.berkeley.edu/fndrupal/
Glosbe: https://el.glosbe.com/
Merriam-Webster: https://www.merriam-webster.com/
Oxford Dictionaries: https://www.oxforddictionaries.com/
Portal for the Greek Language: http://www.greek-language.gr/greekLang/index.html
WordReference: http://www.wordreference.com/

Proceedings of the International FrameNet Workshop 2020: Towards a Global, Multilingual FrameNet, pages 56–62
Language Resources and Evaluation Conference (LREC 2020), Marseille, 11–16 May 2020

Using Verb Frames for Text Difficulty Assessment

John Lee, Meichun Liu, Tianyuan Cai

Department of Linguistics and Translation
City University of Hong Kong
{jsylee, meichliu, tianycai}@cityu.edu.hk

Abstract

This paper presents the first investigation on using semantic frames to assess text difficulty. Based on Mandarin VerbNet, a verbal semantic database that adopts a frame-based approach, we examine usage patterns of ten verbs in a corpus of graded Chinese texts. We identify a number of characteristics in texts at advanced grades: more frequent use of non-core frame elements; more frequent omission of some core frame elements; increased preference for noun phrases rather than clauses as verb arguments; and more frequent metaphoric usage. These characteristics can potentially be useful for automatic prediction of text readability.

Keywords: Mandarin VerbNet, verb frames, frame elements, readability

1. Introduction

FrameNet (https://framenet.icsi.berkeley.edu) and other similar resources have supported a large range of natural language processing (NLP) tasks including semantic role labeling (Gildea and Jurafsky, 2002), information extraction (Fader et al., 2011), sentiment analysis (Ruppenhofer and Rehbein, 2012) and language learning (Carrión, 2006; Xu and Li, 2011). However, they have yet to be exploited for analyzing text difficulty, which is also known as *readability assessment*. Given any text, the system is to predict its reading difficulty, by estimating the age or school grade (e.g., Grades 1 to 13) required for readers to understand the text; by assigning it a difficulty score, such as Lexile (Stenner, 1996); or by locating it on a proficiency scale, such as the six-level scale in the *Common European Framework of Reference for Language* (2001).

Previous research on automatic readability assessment has mostly relied on lexical and syntactic features. A common lexical feature is the level of vocabulary difficulty, for example according to the number of "difficult words" (Kincaid et al., 1975). Syntactic features may include parse tree patterns or, as a proxy, average sentence length. While lexical complexity and syntactic complexity have been shown to be effective predictors of text readability, they do not capture all aspects of reading difficulty. Consider the pairs of example sentences in Table 1. The sentences in each pair have comparable vocabulary difficulty and sentence length. Sentences (1a) and (1b) both have the verb 'worry'. The verb in (1a) takes as object a short clause 'you would get sick', but in (1b) it takes an abstract noun, 'your health', which may be more difficult to process. Likewise, sentences (2a) and (2b) are semantically similar, but the reason construction 'because [he] missed the exam' in the latter may make it harder to read than the former. Finally, sentence (3b) is likely more challenging to understand than (3a) due to a metaphorical usage.

Semantic analysis can be expected to improve the readability assessment for such sentences. While some existing assessment models already incorporate semantic features, they are mostly limited to anaphora patterns, word senses and semantic categories of individual words (Pilán et al., 2014; Sung et al., 2015; Schumacher et al., 2016). Salient features may potentially be derived from semantic frames,

such as those in FrameNet, Chinese Framenet (You and Liu, 2005), or Mandarin VerbNet (Liu, 2016; Liu and Chang, 2016; Liu, 2018; Liu, 2019). Based on Mandarin VerbNet, a verbal semantic database that adopts a frame-based approach, this paper investigates the correlation between verb frames and text difficulty.

2. Research Questions

We hypothesize that the verb usage patterns encoded in verb frames can be associated with different levels of reading difficulty. The distribution of frame-related attributes in a text may therefore be correlated with readability. More precisely, this paper tests the following hypotheses:

- H1: Non-core frame elements are more frequently used in more difficult texts (Section 5);

- H2: Core frame elements are more frequently omitted in more difficult texts (Section 6);

- H3: For verbs that can take either a noun phrase (NP) or a clause as argument, NPs are more frequently chosen in more difficult texts (Section 7).

- H4: Metaphor is more frequently used in more difficult texts (Section 8).

The rest of this paper is organized as follows. After a summary of previous research on readability assessment (Section 3), we describe our dataset (Section 4). We then present results on the four hypotheses above (Sections 5 to 8).

3. Previous Work

This section reviews the variety of lexical, syntactic and semantic features that have been explored for readability assessment.

3.1. Lexical Features

Most readability formulas rely on shallow features such as word length, sentence length, and vocabulary lists (Kincaid et al., 1975). The Lexile framework incorporates features derived from word frequencies, for instance lexical richness based on the type-token ratio (Stenner, 1996).

Sentence	Readability	Remarks
(1a) 我担心你会生病 'I worried you would get sick'	Less difficult	Clause argument for 'worry'
(1b) 我担心你的健康 'I worried about your health'	More difficult	Noun argument for 'worry'
(2a) 他很后悔错过了考试 'He regretted missing the exam.'	Less difficult	Clause argument for 'regret'
(2b) 他因为错过了考试十分后悔 'Because [he] missed the exam, he felt regretful.'	More difficult	Use of reason construction to express cause for regret
(3a) 他没有把书本放在桌上 'He did not put the book on the desk'	Less difficult	No metaphorical usage
(3b) 他没有把问题放在心上 'He did not care about (*lit.*, 'put on heart') this question'	More difficult	Metaphorical usage with 'put'

Table 1: Sentences with varying reading difficulty due to semantic complexity, despite similar lexical and syntactic complexity.

More recent work in NLP has made use of n-gram language models (Collins-Thompson and Callan, 2004; Petersen and Ostendorf, 2009), inflectional and derivational morphology (Hancke et al., 2012), verbal morphology, verb tense and mood-based features (Dell'Orletta et al., 2011; François and Fairon, 2012). Psycholinguistic properties, such as the concreteness, imageability and meaningfulness of words (Wilson, 1988), and the age of acquisition (Kuperman et al., 2012), have also been shown to be helpful.

3.2. Syntactic Features

Even if a sentence is composed of simple words, it can still be difficult to understand because of complicated syntactic structure. Early models often use sentence length and clause length as proxies for syntactic complexity. More recent ones incorporate part-of-speech (POS) features, including the frequency of coordination and subordination; the nominal ratio and the pronoun/noun ratio (Pilán et al., 2014); the number of different kinds of pronouns and conjunctions (Sung et al., 2015); and more generally, the percentage and diversity of POS tags (Vajjala and Meurers, 2014). Parse tree depth, parse scores, subtree patterns (Heilman et al., 2008; Schumacher et al., 2016) and dependency distance (Liu, 2008) have also been found to be useful.

3.3. Semantic Features

Lexical complexity and syntactic complexity do not cover all factors that influence readability. As discussed in Section 1, the (b) sentences in Table 1 can be expected to be more difficult to read than their (a) counterparts, despite their similar lexical and syntactic complexity.

Many readability models have therefore incorporated measures on semantic complexity. Common features include the average number of senses per word (Pilán et al., 2014); the ratio of active/passive voice (Graesser et al., 2011); the number of content words and the number of semantic categories in a sentence (Sung et al., 2015); the number of unique entities per document and the average number of words per entity; and the semantic probability of a sentence, according to a semantic network (vor der Brück et al., 2008).

4. Data

This section first presents Mandarin VerbNet and the verbs to be analyzed (Section 4.1), and then describes the corpus of graded texts on which our analysis is based (Section 4.2).

4.1. Mandarin VerbNet

Mandarin VerbNet is a verbal semantic database with annotation of frame-based constructional features (Liu and Chiang, 2008). In addition to frame elements, its frames make use of a schema-based meaning representation and constructional patterns. Adopting a hybrid approach to the semantic analysis of the lexical-constructional behavior of Chinese verbs, it incorporates tenets of Frame Semantics (Fillmore and Atkins, 1992) and Construction Grammar (Goldberg, 1995).

We selected ten verbs from three different frame categories for this study (Table 2). For more reliable statistics on frame distribution with respect to grade, we have deliberately chosen common verbs that are used in a wide range of grades.

4.2. Corpus of Graded Text

We performed our analysis on a corpus of Chinese language textbooks constructed at Ludong University, China.[1] The 5-million-character corpus consists of more than 6000 articles, taken from 368 textbooks spanning the twelve grades in the curriculum for Chinese language in mainland China. For analysis purposes, the grades are divided into three categories:

- **1-3**: Grades 1 through 3;
- **4-6**: Grades 4 through 6;
- **7+**: Grades 7 through 12.

Table 2 shows the number of sentences in which the ten verbs appear. We manually and exhaustively annotated the verb frame usage in these sentences.

5. Use of Non-core Frame Elements

Similar to FrameNet, Mandarin VerbNet distinguishes between "core" or "non-core" frame elements. Core frame

---

[1]We thank Prof. Xu Dekuan for providing access to this corpus.

Frame Category	Verb		# sentences			
			Grades 1-3	Grades 4-6	Grades 7+	Total
CAUSED-MOTION	放	*fàng* 'put'	24	26	49	99
	丢	*diū* 'cast away'	13	17	24	54
COGNITION	发现	*fāxiàn* 'discover'	125	323	404	852
	注意到	*zhùyìdào* 'notice'	5	18	56	79
	思考	*sīkǎo* 'reflect'	7	30	37	74
EMOTION	担心	*dānxīn* 'worry'	16	48	56	120
	吸引	*xīyǐn* 'attract'	19	50	49	118
	感动	*gǎndòng* 'be moved'	4	20	30	54
	着急	*zháojí* 'be anxious'	26	28	24	78
	后悔	*hòuhuǐ* 'regret'	9	18	18	45

Table 2: Verbs used in our analysis, and the number of sentences in which they appear in our corpus among texts of the lower and upper grades (see Section 4.2).

Verb	Frame Element	Lowest	Type	Selected examples
dānxīn 'worry'	Exp	1	Core	我[Exp] 担心 我会生病[Target-possible-situation]
	Target-Possible-Situation	1	Core	I[Exp] worried I would get sick[Target-possible-situation]
	Beneficiary	2	Non-core	我[Exp] 担心 你的健康[Target-entity]
	Target Entity	4	Core	I[Exp] worried about your health[Target-entity]
	Stim	7	Non-core	
gǎndòng 'be moved'	Affector	2	Core	观众[Affectee] 也都被感动了，大家拍着手[Result] …
	Affectee	2	Core	The audience[Affectee] were moved, clapping[Result] …
	Result	4	Non-core	他们[Affector] … 便 以死[Means] 来感动 …
	Means	6	Non-core	Through their death[Means], they[Affector] moved …
xīyǐn 'attract'	Affectee	1	Core	作者[Affector] 总是 用思想感情[Means] 吸引 你[Affectee]
	Act	1	Non-core	The author[Affector] attracts you[Affectee] with her emotions[Means] …
	Affector	2	Core	
	Means	4	Non-core	他[Affector] 吸引着 孩子的心[Affectee]，让人总在想着他呢[Result]
	Affectee Theme	6	Core	He[Affector] so attracted the kids[Affectee], making them think
	Result	7	Non-core	of him[Result] …
	Reason	7	Non-core	
fāxiàn 'discover'	Cognizer	1	Core	我[Cognizer] 在桌上[Medium] 发现 一本书[Topic]
	Phenomenon	1	Core	I[Cognizer] found a book[Topic] on the table[Medium]
	Means	1	Non-core	
	Topic	2	Core	从 瞄准镜[Instrument] 里, 发现 一个火球穿过[Phenomenon] …
	Medium	2	Non-core	From the telescope[Instrument], [we] discovered a fireball
	Instrument	7	Non-core	shooting[Phenomenon] …
hòuhuǐ 'regret'	Exp	2	Core	如果 不复习[Stim] 他[Exp] 会后悔的
	Expressor	2	Non-Core	He[Exp] would regret if [he] didn't review[Stim]
	Given-fact	3	Core	
	Reason	6	Non-Core	他[Affector] 因为错过了考试[Reason] 十分后悔
	Stim	7	Core	Because of missing the exam[Reason], he[Exp] felt regretful.
	Given-fact-description	10	Core	

Table 3: Verbs and their frame elements, showing the lowest grade in which the frame element appears.

elements are fundamental; they commonly appear as a necessary argument in a sentence and plays an essential role in the event frame. Non-core frame elements are optional; they are "potentially relevant", and can be added to a sentence as an adjunct (Liu and Chiang, 2008).

According to the first hypothesis (H1), non-core frame elements are used more frequently in more difficult text. As a preliminary investigation, we identified the lowest grade at

which a frame element occurs. As shown in Table 3, many non-core frame elements are found only at higher grades. For *xīyǐn* 'attract', for example, Result and Reason do not appear until Grade 7.

To test H1, we calculated the percentage of sentences with non-core frame elements at each grade. The verb *zhùyìdào* 'notice' does not employ non-core frame elements at any grade level in our dataset. As shown in Table 4, the overall

Verb	Grades		
	1-3	4-6	7+
zhùyìdào 'notice'	0%	0%	0%
diū 'cast away'	0%	5.9%	**8.3%**
sīkǎo 'reflect'	0%	7.0%	**22.0%**
gǎndòng 'be moved'	0%	**55.0%**	40.0%
fàng 'put'	4.2%	**7.7%**	2.0%
dānxīn 'worry'	6.3%	**12.5%**	10.7%
hòuhuǐ 'regret'	**11.1%**	0%	5.6%
zhāojí 'be anxious'	15.4%	**35.7%**	20.8%
xīyǐn 'attract'	26.3%	18.0%	**42.9%**
fāxiàn 'discover'	40.8%	32.2%	**46.0%**

Table 4: (H1) Percentage of sentences with non-core frame elements.

Verb	Grades		
	1-3	4-6	7+
gǎndòng 'be moved'	100%	100%	100%
xīyǐn 'attract'	100%	100%	100%
zhùyìdào 'notice'	**100%**	**100%**	85.7%
hòuhuǐ 'regret'	**100%**	**100%**	97.2%
dānxīn 'worry'	**100%**	95.8%	71.4%
zhāojí 'be anxious'	**96.2%**	78.6%	79.2%
fàng 'put'	**91.7%**	69.2%	42.9%
fāxiàn 'discover'	**91.2%**	87.3%	76.0%
sīkǎo 'reflect'	**85.7%**	80.0%	67.6%
diū 'cast away'	**84.6%**	82.4%	66.7%

Table 5: (H2) on subjects: Percentage of sentences with frame elements serving as the subject of the verb.

Verb	Grades		
	1-3	4-6	7+
fàng 'put'	100%	100%	100%
diū 'cast away'	100%	100%	100%
fāxiàn 'discover'	**100%**	**100%**	99.4%
zhùyìdào 'notice'	**100%**	94.4%	98.2%
gǎndòng 'be moved'	**100%**	70.0%	86.7%
xīyǐn 'attract'	94.7%	90.0%	**98.0%**
dānxīn 'worry'	**75%**	66.7%	67.6%
hòuhuǐ 'regret'	44.0%	**66.7%**	**66.7%**
sīkǎo 'reflect'	14.3%	23.3%	**32.5%**
zhāojí 'be anxious'	0%	10.7%	**16.7%**

Table 6: (H2) on objects: Percentage of sentences with frame elements serving as the direct object of the verb.

statistics of the remaining verbs lend support to the hypothesis. Eight of the verbs[2] exhibit a lower percentage of sentences with non-core frame elements at grades 1-3 than at higher grades. Consider *gǎndòng* 'be moved' as an example: non-core frame elements for this verb[3] do not appear in grades 1-3, but account for 55.0% of the sentences in grades 4-6 and 40.0% in higher grades. The difference between grades 4-6 and 7+, however, is less clear-cut. Five of the verbs exhibit higher rates of non-core frame elements in grades 7+, while four exhibit lower rates. More fine-grained analysis is necessary to account for the underlying differences.

6. Omission of Core Frame Elements

To reduce repetition, a writer may omit a verb argument from a sentence, expecting the reader to infer the information from the context. This phenomenon is frequent in Chinese even for some core arguments; for example, pro-dropped subjects account for more than 36% of the subjects in Chinese sentences (Kim, 2000). The number of zero pronouns is likely correlated with the effort needed for resolution. According to the second hypothesis (H2), omission of core frame elements is more frequent in more difficult texts.

6.1. Subjects

We first examine frame elements that normally occupy the subject position before the verb. Table 5 shows the proportion of sentences containing these frame elements.[4] For the verbs *gǎndòng* 'be moved' and *xīyǐn* 'attract', this proportion is constant since all of their sentences at all grades contain subjects. The hypothesis is however supported by the remaining eight verbs. Generally, more sentences lack subjects in the higher grades than in the lower ones. The gap between grades 4-6 and 7+ is usually larger than the

gap between 1-3 and 4-6.[5]

6.2. Objects

We next investigate frame elements that normally occupy the object position after the verb. Table 6 shows the proportion of sentences containing these frame elements.[6] Two of the verbs, *fàng* 'put' and *diū* 'cast away', always have explicit objects in sentences at all grades, as the frame element Figure is indispensable for their semantic expression. Among the remaining eight verbs, the trend is more nuanced compared to the omission of subjects. We will focus on comparing grades 1-3 with the higher grades. Consistent with H2, four of these verbs — *fāxiàn* 'discover', *zhùyìdào* 'notice', *gǎndòng* 'be moved' and *dānxīn* 'worry' — have more sentences in grades 1-3 containing objects. In contrast, for the other four verbs, the sentences in grades 1-3 are more likely to omit the object. These results sug-

---

[2]With the exception of *hòuhuǐ* 'regret'.

[3]See Table 3 for example sentences for the non-core frame elements Result and Means.

[4]Among the ten verbs analyzed, depending on their frame category, these frame elements can be Agent, Cognizer, Exp, Placer, Affector or Affectee.

[5]For the verb *dānxīn* 'worry', for example, all sentences in grades 1-3 have subjects, as do 95.8% of the sentences in grades 4-6. However, the figure drops to 71.4% at grades 7+. The only exception to this trend is observed for *zhāojí* 'be anxious'.

[6]Among the ten verbs analyzed, depending on their frame category, these frame elements can be Affectee, Figure, Given_Fact, Given_Fact_Description, Phenomenon, Topic, Target, Target_Empathy, Target-Entity, Target-Situation or Target-Possible-Situation.

Verb	Argument	Grades		
	type	1-3	4-6	7+
zhùyìdào	clause	**80%**	55.6%	41.1%
'notice'	NP	20%	38.9%	**53.6%**
fāxiàn	clause	**78.4%**	57.6%	55.2%
'discover'	NP	21.6%	**51.7%**	44.1%
dānxīn	clause	**75.0%**	58.3%	53.6%
'worry'	NP	0%	8.3%	**14.3%**
hòuhuǐ	clause	44.4%	**66.7%**	50.0%
'regret'	NP	0%	0%	**16.7%**

Table 7: (H3) Percentage of sentences with clause or noun phrase as argument to the verb.

gest that the impact of the object on text difficulty differs according to usage patterns of individual verbs. The presence of objects in the verbs *zhāojí* 'be anxious' and *hòuhuǐ* 'regret', for instance, can make a sentence harder to read. Since these verbs do not take objects in most instances, the absence of the object should perhaps not be considered an omission.

7.　Clause vs. Noun Phrase

As illustrated by the verb *dānxīn* 'worry' in sentences (1a) and (1b) in Table 1, some verb arguments can be either a noun phrase (NP) or a clause. The distinction is reflected by the frame element. Sentence (1a), which contains the clause 'you would get sick' as object, has the frame element `Target-possible-situation`. In contrast, sentence (1b), with the NP 'your health' as object, has the `Target-entity` element. Similar distinctions are made in other frame categories, for example with `Phenomenon` (clause) vs. `Topic` (NP), and `Given-fact` (clause) vs. `Given-fact-description` (NP).

According to the third hypothesis (H3), given a choice between NP and clause for an eventive complement, NP or event nominal is more often used in difficult texts than in easier ones. We analyzed the four verbs in our dataset that offer this choice, and the overall statistics support the hypothesis (Table 7). For all four verbs, sentences in grades 1-3 substantially prefer clause over NP, and the gap narrows in grades 7+; in the case of *zhùyìdào* 'notice', clauses are even outnumbered by NPs in grades 7+. This observation suggests that for these verbs, a clause may be easier for less proficient readers to understand than a noun, especially when it expresses an abstract meaning.

When taking grades 4-6 into account, the statistics are not always consistent with H3. Consider the case of *fāxiàn* 'discover'. While the preference for clause over NP decreases from grades 1-3 (a difference of 56.8%) to grades 4-6 (a difference of 5.9%), it unexpectedly increases again from grades 4-6 to grades 7+ (a difference of 11.1%).

8.　Metaphor

Metaphorical usage which involves cognitive transfer from one domain to another tends to make a sentence harder to read, even when the vocabulary and syntactic structures are simple. Consider the example sentences (3a) and (3b) in

Verb	Grades		
	1-3	4-6	7+
fàng 'put'	0.0%	19.2%	**30.60%**
diū 'cast away'	0.0%	11.8%	**33.30%**

Table 8: (H4) Percentage of sentences with metaphoric usage.

Table 1. In (3a), the verb 放 *fàng* 'put' is used in its regular sense, 'put a book on the table'. In (3b), however, it is used in the metaphorical sense in the verb phrase 放在心上 ('remember'; literally, "put on the heart"), which is more difficult to interpret.

Our analysis centered on the two verbs in our dataset — *fàng* 'put' and *diū* 'cast away' — that are more productive in metaphorical usage. In non-metaphorical usage, the frame elements `Ground-Location` (for *fàng* 'put') and `Figure` (for *diū* 'cast away') typically expect physical locations and objects. That is not necessarily the case in metaphorical usage, which allows abstract entities such as 'worry' (e.g., "cast away one's worry") or 'heart' ("put on the heart").

The fourth hypothesis (H4) predicts metaphorical usage to be more frequent in more difficult texts. Table 8 presents evidence for this hypothesis. For both verbs, no metaphor is employed in the texts for grades 1-3. The percentage of metaphorical usage increases to 19.2% and 11.8%, respectively, at grades 4-6. The higher grades see even more substantial amount of metaphorical usage, at 30.60% and 33.30%.

9.　Conclusions

We have presented the first investigation on the correlation between verb frames and text difficulty. Based on Mandarin VerbNet (Liu, 2016; Liu and Chang, 2016; Liu, 2018; Liu, 2019), our analysis of ten common Chinese verbs showed that at higher grades, there is generally more frequent use of non-core frame elements; more frequent omission of core frame elements that normally occupy the subject position before the verb; increased preference for a noun phrase over a clause as verb argument; and more frequent metaphorical usage. These patterns can potentially help improve a readability assessment model.

We plan to pursue two directions in future work. First, we plan to expand our analysis to a larger set of verbs from diverse frame categories. Second, we intend to incorporate frame patterns as features in a system for readability prediction.

10.　Acknowledgements

We thank Prof. Dekuan Xu for providing access to the corpus of Chinese-language textbooks, and Tianqi He and Yingying Ye for their assistance. We gratefully acknowledge support from a grant (Project #9360163) from the Hong Kong Institute for Data Science at City University of Hong Kong.

11. Bibliographical References

Carrión, O. B. (2006). Framenet as a Corpus Tool for the Learning of Second Languages and for the Lexical Awareness of one's First Language. *Porta Linguarum*, 6:67–76.

CEFR. (2001). *Common European Framework of Reference for Languages: Learning, Teaching, Assessment.* Cambridge University Press, Cambridge.

Collins-Thompson, K. and Callan, J. (2004). A language-modelling approach to predicting reading difficulty. In *Proc NAACL-HLT*, Boston, MA.

Dell'Orletta, F., Montemagni, S., and Venturi, G. (2011). Read-it: Assessing Readability of Italian Texts with a View to Text Simplification. In *Proc. 2nd Workshop on Speech and Language Processing for Assistive Technologies.*

Fader, A., Soderland, S., and Etzioni, O. (2011). Identifying Relations for Open Information Extraction. In *Proc. EMNLP.*

Fillmore, C. J. and Atkins, B. T. (1992). Towards a Frame-based organization of the lexicon: the semantics of RISK and its neighbors. In Adrienne Lehrer et al., editors, *Frames, Fields, and Contrasts: New Essays in Semantics*, pages 75–102, Hillsdale. Lawrence Erlbuan.

François, T. and Fairon, C. (2012). An "AI Readability" Formula for French as a Foreign Language. In *Proc. EMNLP-CONLL.*

Gildea, D. and Jurafsky, D. (2002). Automatic Labeling of Semantic Roles. *Computational Linguistics*, 28(3):245–288.

Goldberg, A. E. (1995). *Constructions: A Construction Grammar Approach to Argument Structure.* University of Chicago Press, Chicago.

Graesser, A. C., McNamara, D. S., and Kulikowich, J. M. (2011). Coh-metrix providing multilevel analyses of text characteristics. *Educational Researcher*, 40(5):223–234.

Hancke, J., Vajjala, S., and Meurers, D. (2012). Readability Classification for German using Lexical, Syntactic and Morphological Features. In *Proc. 24th International Conference on Computational Linguistics (COLING).*

Heilman, M., Collins Thompson, K., and Eskenazi, M. (2008). An Analysis of Statistical Models and Features for Reading Difficulty Prediction. In *Proc. Third Workshop on Innovative Use of NLP for Building Educational Applications.*

Kim, Y.-J. (2000). Subject/object drop in the acquisition of Korean: A cross-linguistic comparison. *Journal of East Asian Linguistics*, 9:325–351.

Kincaid, J. P., Fishburne, R. P., Rogers, R. L., and Chissom, B. S. (1975). Derivation of new readability formulas (automated readability index, fog count, and flesch reading ease formula) for Navy enlisted personnel. In *Research Branch Report 8–75*. Chief of Naval Technical Training: Naval Air Station Memphis.

Kuperman, V., Stadthagen-Gonzalez, H., and Brysbaert, M. (2012). Age-of-Acquisition ratings for 30,000 English words. *Behavior Research Methods*, 44(4):978–990.

Liu, M. and Chang, J.-C. (2016). Semantic annotation for Mandarin verbal lexicon: A frame-based constructional approach. In Minghui Dong, et al., editors, *Proc. International Conference on Asian Language Processing (IALP)*, pages 30–36. New York: Institute of Electrical and Electronics Engineers (IEEE).

Liu, M. and Chiang, T. Y. (2008). The construction of mandarin verbnet: A frame-based study of statement verbs. *Language and Linguistics*, 9(2):239–270.

Liu, H. (2008). Dependency Distance as a Metric of Language Comprehension Difficulty. *Journal of Cognitive Science*, 9(2):159–191.

Liu, M. (2016). Emotion in lexicon and grammar: lexical-constructional interface of Mandarin emotional predicates. *Lingua Sinica*, 2.4.

Liu, M. (2018). A frame-based morpho-constructional approach to verbal semantics. In Chunyu Kit et al., editors, *Frontiers of Empirical and Corpus Linguistics*. China Social Sciences Press, Beijing, China.

Liu, M. (2019). The construction and annotation of a semantically enriched database: The mandarin verbnet and its nlp application. In *From Minimal Contrast to Meaning Construct: Corpus-based, Near Synonym Driven Approaches to Chinese Lexical Semantics (Vol. 9, Frontiers in Chinese Linguistics Book Series)*, pages 257–272. Springer-Nature and Peking University Press.

Petersen, S. E. and Ostendorf, M. (2009). A machine learning approach to reading level assessment. *Computer Speech and Language*, 23(1):89–106.

Pilán, I., Volodina, E., and Johansson, R. (2014). Rule-based and Machine Learning Approaches for Second Language Sentence-level Readability. In *Proc. 9th Workshop on Innovative Use of NLP for Building Educational Applications.*

Ruppenhofer, J. and Rehbein, I. (2012). Semantic Frames as an Anchor Representation for Sentiment Analysis. In *Proc. 3rd Workshop in Computational Approaches to Subjectivity and Sentiment Analysis (WASSA)*, pages 104–109.

Schumacher, E., Eskenazi, M., Frishkoff, G., and Collins-Thompson, K. (2016). Predicting the relative difficulty of single sentences with and without surrounding context. In *Proc. Conference on Empirical Methods in Natural Language Processing (EMNLP)*, pages 1871–1881.

Stenner, A. J. (1996). Measuring reading comprehension with the Lexile framework. In *Proc. Fourth North American Conference on Adolescent/Adult Literacy.*

Sung, Y.-T., Lin, W.-C., Dyson, S. B., Chang, K.-E., and Chen, Y.-C. (2015). Leveling L2 Texts Through Readability: Combining Multilevel Linguistic Features with the CEFR. *The Modern Language Journal*, 99(2):371–391.

Vajjala, S. and Meurers, D. (2014). On Assessing the Reading Level of Individual Sentences for Text Simplification. In *Proc. 14th Conference of the European Chapter of the Association for Computational Linguistics (EACL).*

vor der Brück, T., Hartrumpf, S., and Helbig, H. (2008). A Readability Checker with Supervised LEarning using Deep Syntactic and Semantic Indicators. In *Proc. 11th International Multiconference: Information Society.*

Wilson, M. D. (1988). The MRC Psycholinguistic Database: Machine Readable Dictionary, Version 2. *Behavioral Research Methods, Instruments and Computers*, 20:6–11.

Xu, F. and Li, T. (2011). Semantic Frame and EVT for Chinese EFL Learners. *Journal of Language Teaching and Research*, 2(3):649–654.

You, L. and Liu, K. (2005). Building Chinese FrameNet Database. In *Proc. IEEE NLP-KE*.

Proceedings of the International FrameNet Workshop 2020: Towards a Global, Multilingual FrameNet, pages 63–69
Language Resources and Evaluation Conference (LREC 2020), Marseille, 11–16 May 2020

Deriving a PropBank Corpus from Parallel FrameNet and UD Corpora

Normunds Gruzitis, Roberts Dargis, Laura Rituma, Gunta Nespore-Berzkalne, Baiba Saulite
Institute of Mathematics and Computer Science, University of Latvia
Raina bulv. 29, LV-1459, Riga, Latvia
{normunds.gruzitis, roberts.dargis, laura.rituma, gunta.nespore, baiba.valkovska}@lumii.lv

Abstract

We propose an approach for generating an accurate and consistent PropBank-annotated corpus, given a FrameNet-annotated corpus which has an underlying dependency annotation layer, namely, a parallel Universal Dependencies (UD) treebank. The PropBank annotation layer of such a multi-layer corpus can be semi-automatically derived from the existing FrameNet and UD annotation layers, by providing a mapping configuration from lexical units in [a non-English language] FrameNet to [English language] PropBank predicates, and a mapping configuration from FrameNet frame elements to PropBank semantic arguments for the given pair of a FrameNet frame and a PropBank predicate. The latter mapping generally depends on the underlying UD syntactic relations. To demonstrate our approach, we use Latvian FrameNet, annotated on top of Latvian UD Treebank, for generating Latvian PropBank in compliance with the Universal Propositions approach.

Keywords: PropBank, FrameNet, Universal Dependencies, Universal Propositions, Latvian

1. Introduction and Related Work

Proposition Bank or PropBank (Palmer et al., 2005) is (i) a shallow semantic representation for the annotation of predicate-argument structures, (ii) a lexicon of English verbs and their semantic predicates (frames) and semantic arguments (roles), and (iii) a large annotated text corpus of English, where the semantic roles of each predicate instance are added to the syntactic structures of the underlying treebank.

Since PropBank uses a small set of semantic roles which are defined on a verb-by-verb basis, and the annotated corpus provides broad-coverage training data, it is an attractive approach for robust automatic semantic role labelling, SRL (Cai and Lapata, 2019). This has also encouraged extensive use of PropBank framesets (coarse-grained verb senses each having a specific set of semantic arguments or roles) in the whole-sentence Abstract Meaning Representation (AMR) approach (Banarescu et al., 2013).

Following the work on English, PropBank-style corpora have been created for a number of languages. Apart from other aspects, creation of a propbank depends on a fundamental decision: whether to define language-specific framesets or to re-use the English PropBank framesets.

In most projects, language-specific framesets have been defined and used in the manual or semi-automatic corpus annotation workflow, e.g. for Chinese (Xue, 2008), Hindi/Urdu (Bhatt et al., 2009) and Finnish (Haverinen et al., 2015). Few attempts have been made to create a non-English propbank by reusing the English PropBank framesets. An example to the latter approach is Brazilian Portuguese PropBank (Duran and Aluisio, 2012), although the use of English framesets was intended only as an intermediate step on the way to define language-specific framesets. Another consideration is the underlying syntactic representation – syntactic structures to which the semantic roles are added. In the case of phrase structure trees (e.g. the English and Chinese treebanks), semantic roles are added to constituents (phrases). In the case of dependency trees (e.g. the Finnish treebank), semantic roles are added to dependencies (syntactic roles of the root tokens of the respective subtrees). For some languages (e.g. Hindi/Urdu and Brazilian Portuguese) both kinds of syntactic representations and both kinds of PropBank-treebank mappings are available.

While dependency trees are often considered a more convenient and straightforward intermediate representation for robust automatic SRL, as it has been proved by state-of-the-art SRL parsers (Cai and Lapata, 2019), the use of a common inventory of PropBank framesets would facilitate cross-lingual SRL and the downstream applications like cross-lingual information extraction.

The Universal Propositions (UP) project[1] proposes to use the English PropBank framesets for universal SRL, on top of the Universal Dependencies (UD) syntax trees. The underlying UD representation (Nivre et al., 2016) facilitates cross-lingual semantic parsing even more.

Akbik et al. (2015) present a method for automatic projection of English framesets to a target language, and they have applied this method to generate UP propbanks for multiple languages. In this paper, we present our work which contributes to the UP initiative. We propose an alternative approach for generating accurate and consistent UP propbanks for languages that have a FrameNet-annotated corpus where FrameNet annotations are specified on top of a UD treebank, or a dependency treebank in general.

To some extent, our approach is similar to the one applied to convert the SALSA Corpus for German into a PropBank-like corpus for the CoNLL 2009 shared task (Hajič et al., 2009). The SALSA corpus (Burchardt et al., 2006) uses semantic roles in the FrameNet paradigm (Fillmore et al., 2003), annotated on top of a treebank, which were semi-automatically converted to the respective PropBank arguments. The semantic predicates, however, remain German-specific in the converted SALSA corpus. In contrast, we reuse semantic predicates from the English PropBank (following the UP approach), which was the most challenging part in the Latvian FrameNet-to-PropBank conversion. The

---

[1]`https://github.com/System-T/`
`UniversalPropositions`

LEMMA	UPOS	PRED$_{FN}$	PRED$_{PB}$
mācīt	VERB	Education_teaching	teach.01
mācīties	VERB	Education_teaching	study.01
mācīties	VERB	Memorization	learn.01
dzīvot	VERB	Residence	reside.01
dzīvot	VERB	Dead_or_alive	live.01
dzīvot	VERB	Living_conditions	live.02

Table 1: Sample mapping from lexical units (verb-frame pairs) in Latvian FrameNet (FN) to English PropBank (PB) predicates (verb sense-specific translation equivalents).

PRED$_{FN}$	APRED$_{FN}$	DEP	PRED$_{PB}$	APRED$_{PB}$
Education_teaching	Student	nsubj	study.01	A0
Education_teaching	Student	obj	teach.01	A2
Education_teaching	Student	iobj	teach.01	A2
Education_teaching	Subject	obj	study.01	A1
Education_teaching	Subject	obj	teach.01	A1
Education_teaching	Teacher	obl	study.01	A2
Education_teaching	Teacher	nsubj	teach.01	A0
Education_teaching	Institution	obl	study.01	AM-LOC
Education_teaching	Institution	obl	teach.01	AM-LOC
Education_teaching	Level	obl	study.01	AM-LOC
Education_teaching	Time	obl	study.01	AM-TMP
Education_teaching	Time	obl	teach.01	AM-TMP

Table 2: Mapping from FrameNet (FN) frame elements to PropBank (PB) semantic roles, taking UD dependency relations (syntactic roles) into account.

consecutive conversion of FrameNet roles into PropBank roles is rather straightforward, although it depends on the underlying UD roles.

On the one hand, FrameNet defines a set of more abstract semantic frames (compared to PropBank predicates) that can be evoked by different target words. On the other hand, FrameNet uses more fine-grained semantic roles (frame elements), some of which are often not expressed in a sentence as direct syntactic arguments of the predicate. Therefore our proposed FrameNet-to-PropBank conversion approach is unidirectional, i.e., a rather complete PropBank corpus can be derived from an existing FrameNet corpus (with parallel dependency annotations), however, it would not be possible to derive a complete FrameNet corpus from an existing PropBank corpus without additional annotation work.

To demonstrate our approach, we use Latvian UD Treebank (Gruzitis et al., 2018b) and Latvian FrameNet (Gruzitis et al., 2018a) for generating Latvian PropBank, compliant to the Universal Propositions approach.

2. Mapping Configuration

Semantic roles in PropBank are much more robust compared to FrameNet frame elements, and the overall PropBank annotation systematically follows the syntactic verb-argument structure. Therefore the PropBank layer of such a multi-layer text corpus can be semi-automatically derived from the existing FrameNet and UD layers of the corpus, by providing (i) a mapping configuration from lexical units (LU) in [a non-English language] FrameNet to [English language] PropBank predicates (see Table 1), and (ii) a mapping configuration from FrameNet frame elements to PropBank semantic arguments for the given pair of a FrameNet frame and a PropBank predicate, i.e., independently from LUs (see Table 2).

We are building on the previous work on SemLink (Palmer, 2009) and Predicate Matrix (Lopez de Lacalle et al., 2016), although none of the two data sets provide complete mapping suggestions, especially for less frequently used lexical units, since the suggestions are corpus-driven. We use the suggested mapping alternatives between English FrameNet and English PropBank as a draft configuration. The manual task for a linguist is to map the LUs from Latvian FrameNet to the semantic predicates of English PropBank, and to verify the mapping between FrameNet frame elements (FE) and PropBank semantic roles, which generally depends on the underlying syntactic relations. The successive generation of a PropBank annotation layer is a straightforward automation.

Since the FrameNet annotation is semantically richer, and it can be non-projective w.r.t. the underlying dependency tree, some FrameNet frame elements are not transferred to the PropBank layer, if they are not syntactic arguments of the target verb.

To ensure productive work on defining the language-specific mapping configuration (Latvian FrameNet to English PropBank via Latvian UD Treebank), we have developed a convenient and predictive user interface that exploits a simple but efficient method for sorting candidate suggestions for LU-to-predicate mapping (Section 2.1) and for FE-to-argument mapping (Section 2.2). Note that both kinds of mapping are done on the type level, i.e., no individual occurrences are mapped. Affected corpus examples, however, are dynamically selected and displayed, which helps the annotator to verify the choices made.

2.1. LU-to-predicate mapping

Figure 1 partially illustrates the interface for mapping FrameNet lexical units (verb-frame pairs) to the corresponding PropBank predicates.

In total, there are nearly 11,000 English PropBank framesets, therefore an efficient method to narrow down the LU-to-predicate mapping candidates is necessary.

Mapping suggestions are extracted from two existing data sets. First, the SemLink data set was parsed to extract suggested FrameNet frame candidates (if any) for each PropBank predicate. Second, additional mapping alternatives between FrameNet frames and PropBank predicates were similarly extracted from the Predicate Matrix data set. Overall, the two data sets provide suggestions for about 90% of Berkeley FrameNet frames reused in Latvian FrameNet. Although the ultimate mapping must be provided between the language-specific LUs (verb-frame pairs) and the PropBank predicates, not just between FrameNet frames and PropBank predicates, the candidate predicates are proposed based on the FrameNet frame.

In addition to SemLink and Predicate Matrix, we also used

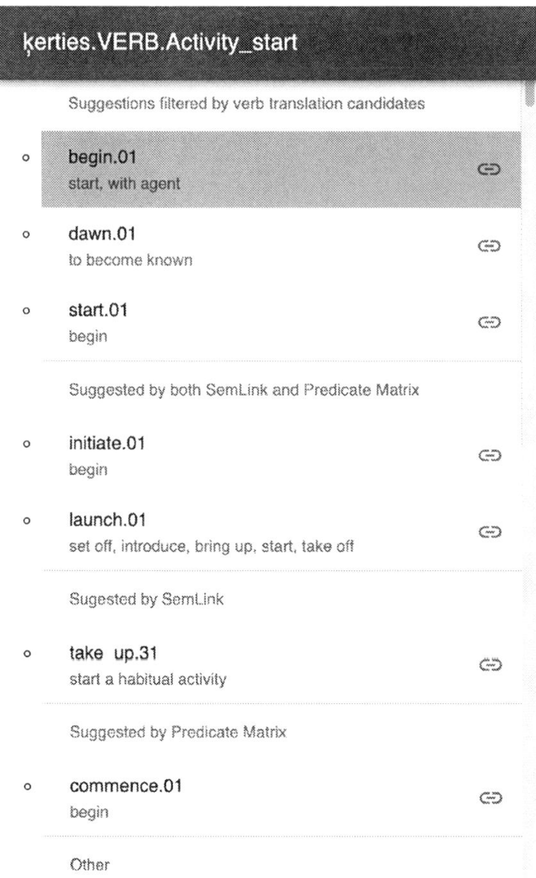

Figure 1: User interface for mapping a LU in Latvian FrameNet (the verb 'ķerties' in the *Activity_start* sense) to a PropBank predicate (*begin.01*). Candidate predicates are sorted depending on the sources that have suggested this candidate: translation candidates are the most probable, followed by suggestions by SemLink and Predicate Matrix (if not already proposed as translation candidates).

a state-of-the-art Latvian-English machine translation (MT) system[2] to acquire translation candidates for Latvian verbs (lexical units in Latvian FrameNet). Translation candidates that correspond to PropBank predicates or their aliases (alternative lexical units, or target verbs, suggested by Predicate Matrix) are used to reorder the final suggestions. As it has turned out, the MT-supported suggestions are the most useful and accurate ones.

To make the choice for a linguist easier, the PropBank predicate suggestions are split in the user interface into four priority groups (see Figure 1). Each lower priority group contains suggestions that are not contained by any of the higher priority groups.

The first group contains LU-to-predicate suggestions that are supported by Latvian-English verb translation candidates. This group is provided for 61% of all LUs in Latvian FrameNet, suggesting 2.6 PropBank predicates per LU on

---

[2]https://hugo.lv

average. When this group of predicate candidates is available, a mapping suggestion proposed by this group is accurate in 79% of the cases.

The second group contains suggestions which are an intersection of suggestions proposed by both SemLink and Predicate Matrix. Although this group is provided for 71% of all LUs in Latvian FrameNet, it is the first group of suggestions only in 23% of the cases (when no MT-supported suggestions are available). On average, there are 5 suggestions per LU contained in this group. When this group is the first available one, a suggestion proposed by this group is accurate in 27% of the cases.

The remaining groups contain suggestions that are supported only by SemLink or by Predicate Matrix. One of these two groups is the first priority group only for 7% of all LUs.

Note that for 10% of all LUs, the ultimately selected PropBank predicate was not present in any of the suggestion groups, and the linguist had to find an appropriate predicate on its own.

Also note that each FrameNet frame has 15 PropBank predicate suggestions on average due to the highly abstract FrameNet frames that each can be evoked by different target verbs. Consequently, for all LUs of the same frame, the same 15 candidates (on average) are suggested for PropBank predicate mapping, except that these candidates are grouped differently, based on translation candidates of the target verb. For example, the FrameNet frame *Body_movement* can be evoked by many target verbs, and therefore it has 70 PropBank predicate suggestions, such as *clap.01*, *close.01*, *kneel.01*, *nod.01*, and *wave.01*. However, if we consider, for instance, the LU *aizvērt.VERB.Body_movement*, the predicate *close.01* is the top suggestion, while for *pamāt.VERB.Body_movement* the top suggestion is *wave.01*.

2.2. FE-to-argument mapping

When a lexical unit (LU) is mapped between FrameNet and PropBank at the frame-predicate level, the next step is to map FrameNet frame elements (FE) to PropBank semantic arguments.

Figures 2 and 3 partially illustrate the interface for mapping FrameNet frame elements to the corresponding PropBank arguments, depending on the underlying syntactic relations. In case of FE-to-argument mapping, we consult only the Predicate Matrix data set (in addition to the PropBank data set itself) to extract and group FE-to-argument mapping suggestions, since Predicate Matrix is a more recent data set, and it provides mapping suggestions directly between FrameNet and PropBank, instead of the indirect SemLink mappings via VerbNet (Schuler et al., 2000).

For each PropBank frameset, core and non-core arguments are extracted and grouped separately. The group of core arguments is prioritised over the group of non-core arguments.

Suggestions supported by Predicate Matrix are separated in the highest priority group. Such priority suggestions are available for 51% of the required FE-to-argument mappings, typically containing only one suggestion. If this group is present, it always contains the accurate mapping

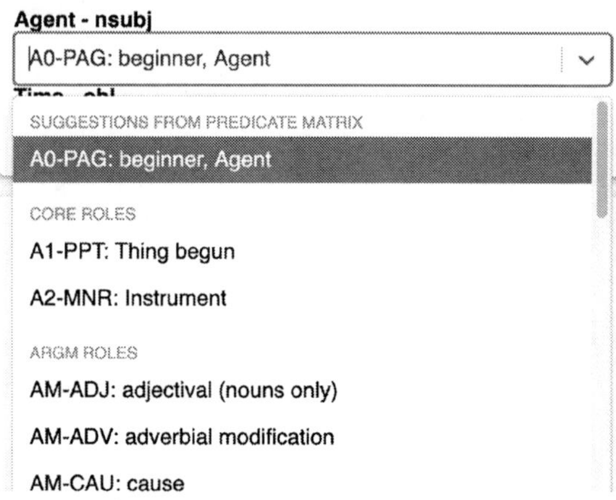

Figure 3: Candidate PropBank argument mappings for the selected pair of a FrameNet frame element (*Agent*) and a UD dependency relation (*nsubj*).

As Figure 2 illustrates, the linguist who verifies the mapping configuration also sees all corpus examples for the given LU. This not only helps to make decisions in both LU-to-predicate mapping and FE-to-argument mapping, but also helps to notice inconsistencies and errors in the underlying annotation layers. Such sentences can be marked with a *FixMe* tag, indicating the annotation layer and the type of the issue.

We have identified three types of typical issues so far:

- An incorrect UD relation associated with a FrameNet frame element, which means that most likely there is an error in the UD annotation layer. The FrameNet-to-PropBank mapping user interface allows to filter all corpus examples (along with their sentence identifiers) containing this error. The mapping configuration of LUs containing such issues is left unfinished until the issues are fixed and the mapping can be finalised.

- An incorrect root node of a subtree of the underlying UD tree is selected for a FrameNet frame element. It can also be the case that the whole FrameNet frame is chosen incorrectly for a particular sentence, and the PropBank perspective has helped to notice that. Again, the user interface allows to filter the problematic corpus examples, and the mapping configuration for the particular LUs is left unfinished until the issues are fixed.

- The mapping process also encourages to reconsider the whole LU – whether the selected FrameNet frame is best suited for the particular verb sense. For instance, we have observed that different verbs are annotated in Latvian FrameNet using the *Give_impression* frame, however, SemLink suggests the *Appearance* frame for the respective PropBank predicates. This helps to achieve a better consistency for both Latvian FrameNet and Latvian PropBank.

Figure 2: User interface for mapping FrameNet frame elements to PropBank semantic arguments for the given LU (*ķerties.VERB.Activity_start*) / predicate (*begin.01*). In general, the choice depends on the underlying UD relation.

candidate, and a linguist had to make a choice between two or three candidates only in 10% of the cases; the rest of the cases were unambiguous.

In 49% of all cases when no Predicate Matrix suggestions are available for a given FE, a linguist first considers the group of PropBank core arguments defined for the particular frameset. This group contains 3 candidates on average. Note that Latvian FrameNet mostly contains annotations of core FEs; non-core FEs are annotated rarely (for the time being). Therefore one of these suggestions is typically the correct one, and it is easy to make the choice.

The remaining group of non-core PropBank arguments (the *ArgM* roles) is always present, containing all the possible *ArgM* options regardless the particular frameset (except if already included in the priority group of Predicate Matrix suggestions). However, this group of suggestions is seldom consulted by a linguist because of the above mentioned nature of Latvian FrameNet.

2.3. Elimination of FrameNet and UD errors

A very important side result of the FrameNet to PropBank mapping process is that it has unveiled a number of annotation errors and inconsistencies both in Latvian FrameNet and in Latvian UD Treebank.

3.   Results

The Latvian FrameNet to PropBank mapping process is nearly finished: we have so far specified mappings for 92% of the LUs in the latest version of Latvian FrameNet. A corresponding Latvian PropBank corpus is automatically derived, and all the annotation layers of the multi-layer corpus are released as open data.[3]

3.1.   Data set

Current statistics of the parallel Latvian FrameNet and Latvian PropBank corpora is as follows:

- **Lexical units** For 2,377 (out of 2,577) LUs represented in Latvian FrameNet, a mapping configuration to PropBank has been specified (92.2%). These LUs represent word senses of 1,322 (out of 1,358) frequently used verbs represented in Latvian FrameNet (97.3%).

- **FrameNet frames** For 521 (out of 540) Berkeley FrameNet frames reused in Latvian FrameNet, at least one LU has been mapped to PropBank so far (96.5%). Latvian FrameNet, in turn, covers 44.2% of 1,222 frames defined in Berkeley FrameNet v1.7.

- **PropBank predicates** Current LU-to-predicate mappings cover 1,033 (out of 10,687) English PropBank v3.1 predicates (9.7%).

- **Corpus examples** The LU-to-predicate and FE-to-argument mappings specified so far cover 20,054 (out of 20,879) annotation sets in Latvian FrameNet (96.0%).

Latvian PropBank consists of two data sets: (i) a machine-readable mapping configuration for each LU in Latvian FrameNet, and (ii) a set of annotated corpus examples in an extended CoNLL-U format, compliant to Universal Propositions. Latvian FrameNet is a single data set of annotated corpus examples in an extended CoNLL-U format.

3.2.   Inter-annotator agreement

To conduct an inter-annotator agreement (IAA) experiment, we selected 30 random LUs from Latvian FrameNet to be mapped to PropBank by three linguists experienced in treebanking as well as in frame semantics. The 30 LUs cover 205 corpus examples (annotation sets). First, we measured IAA w.r.t. LU-to-predicate mapping, then – w.r.t. FE-to-argument mapping.

LU-to-predicate Statistically, only in 13 cases out of 30 (43.3%) all 3 annotators have agreed on the corresponding PropBank predicate for a given LU. In 13 more cases, at least 2 annotators agreed on the same predicate, thus, at least 2 of 3 annotators could agree on a predicate in 86.6% of the cases. In the remaining 4 cases, no two annotators could agree on the same predicate. The qualitative analysis, however, shows that the cause of disagreement was mostly due to different preferences when deciding between close translation equivalents (having an equivalent argument structure). For instance, the LU

dauzīties.VERB.Impact was mapped to three different predicates: *beat.02*, *bang.02* and *thud.01*. In general, all three predicates represent a situation when something hits something making a sound. However, each alternative has a slightly different meaning. Another example – the LU *noslaucīt.VERB.Emptying* – first annotator has selected a rather abstract predicate (*clear.01*), second annotator – a more specific predicate (*wipe.01*), while third – even a more specific one (*wipe-off.03*). These differences illustrate that the annotator's sense of the second language plays an important role.

FE-to-argument Given that annotators have agreed on a predicate, the mapping of FrameNet frame elements to PropBank semantic arguments is straightforward. Our IAA experiment shows that annotators can agree in 95.2% of the cases. The remaining 4.8% are cases where at least one annotator has tagged the given FrameNet frame element or UD dependency relation as an annotation error to be fixed in the FrameNet or UD layer respectively.

4.   Discussion

This section summarises discussion of linguistic issues regarding LU-to-predicate and FE-to-argument mapping.

4.1.   LU-to-predicate mapping

If there are several predicates with similar meaning in PropBank, it is not always clear which of them should be chosen. If we consider, for instance, the LU *parādīties.VERB.Circumscribed_existence*, its meaning roughly corresponds to PropBank predicates *appear.01*, *show_up.02* and *emerge.02*. In such cases, we choose the predicate with an argument structure that best matches the argument structure of the Latvian verb, i.e., the predicate that covers as many core FEs of the corresponding FrameNet frame as possible.

In some cases, more than one PropBank predicate corresponds to the meaning of a LU in Latvian FrameNet – the meaning of the FrameNet frame is more general than the meaning of the candidate PropBank predicates. For instance, the LU *izvirzīt.VERB.Choosing* covers corpus examples *izvirzīt merķi* ('to set a goal') and *izvirzīt kandidatu* ('to nominate a candidate'), but PropBank does not provide a predicate that covers both meanings. In such cases, we consider the possibility of making the sense split at the FrameNet layer, if possible, by applying different FrameNet frames to represent these differences. Another example: the LU *slēgt.VERB.Closure*. The FrameNet frame *Closure* covers LUs of both meanings: opening and closing something. In PropBank, there are different predicates for each of the two meanings. In Latvian, however, these both meanings can be expressed by the same verb, using different adverbial modifiers: *slēgt ciet* ('to close') and *slēgt vaļā* ('to open'). We do not have a good solution for this issue yet, although such cases are quite rare.

There are some cases when a LU does not have an appropriate PropBank predicate for mapping, and would require a constructicon kind of a sense inventory. For instance, the LU *klusēt.VERB.Volubility* is expressed in English as the predicate adjective construction 'to be/keep silent'.

A related issue are several Latvian verbs with modal meaning, which are not considered as modal verbs. In English PropBank, modal verbs like *must* and *can* are not annotated as predicates, therefore we cannot select a verbal predicate for a Latvian verb with such a meaning. However, we can choose an adjectival predicate, for instance, *able.01* or *unable.01*.

For around 25% of LUs in Latvian FrameNet, it was challenging to select the corresponding semantic predicate from English PropBank. In such cases, it took up to 1 hour for a linguist to decide the best fitting mapping, sometimes resulting in no mapping at all (see Section 3.1). In the remaining 75% of cases, it took up to 5 minutes for a linguist to decide the mapping. Overall, it took around 1 person month (PM) to map the easy cases (around 1,933) and 4 PMs to map the difficult cases (around 644).

4.2. FE-to-argument mapping

There are cases when it is impossible to assign a PropBank argument to a core FE of a FrameNet frame:

- In a syntax tree, the potential argument of a PropBank predicate is not a syntactic argument of this predicate. For example, consider the sentence *ļauj man paskatīties* 'let me look': the argument *ARG0* of the predicate *look.01* semantically is *man* ('me'), but syntactically this is an argument of the verb *ļaut* ('to let').

- Similarly, there are cases when a syntax subtree with a verb as its root node depends on another part of the sentence which represents a semantic argument of the verb but is not its syntactic argument. Consider, for instance, the sentence *kā pastāstīja organizācija, nebija iespējams lietot elektrības ģeneratoru* ('as it was told by the organization, it was impossible to use the power generator'). The verb *pastāstīt* ('to tell') corresponds to the PropBank predicate *tell.01* that has the argument *ARG1: utterance*, but the utterance itself is represented by the root node of the whole syntax tree on which the instance of *tell.01* depends.

- A core FE of a FrameNet frame is not defined as a core argument of the corresponding PropBank predicate. A typical example is the frame *Change_position_on_a_scale*: in FrameNet, there are two core FEs – *Item* (the entity that has a position on the scale) and *Attribute* (a scalar property that the *Item* possesses) – that both correspond to one argument of a corresponding PropBank predicate. Consequently, the FE *Item* is not mapped to an argument, if both *Item* and *Attribute* are present in the sentence.

The time spent to provide mapping at the semantic role level is included in the estimated time spent to provide mapping from lexical units in Latvian FrameNet to English PropBank predicates (see Section 4.1).

5. Conclusion

We have demonstrated in practice that a quality PropBank-compliant lexical database and annotated text corpus can be consistently and rapidly derived from an existing multi-layer corpus that contains both FrameNet and UD annotation layers (or equivalent annotation layers). While mapping lexical units from a non-English FrameNet to English PropBank predicates is often (around 25% cases) a linguistically challenging task, the mapping at the semantic role level is straightforward, although it depends on the syntactic roles in general. Note that neither SemLink nor Predicate Matrix mappings contain information about the corresponding syntactic roles. This kind of information is created in our approach, and it could be added to these resources.

Although it is often the case that a PropBank corpus is created before a FrameNet corpus, as a layer on top of a treebank, since PropBank closely follows the syntactic verb-argument structure, it has paid us off to start with the manual creation of the more abstract FrameNet annotation layer from which the PropBank layer can be derived semi-automatically. It would not be possible the other way around.

It is also often the case that language-specific framesets are defined in advance to create language-specific FrameNet or PropBank annotations. Our design decision to reuse the existing framesets of English FrameNet and English PropBank, although introduce some cross-lingual issues, allow for cross-lingual linguistic studies and for the development of cross lingual semantic parsers.

6. Acknowledgements

This work has received financial support from the European Regional Development Fund under the grant agreements 1.1.1.1/16/A/219 and 1.1.1.2/VIAA/1/16/188. Later development was supported by the Latvian Council of Science under the grant agreement lzp-2018/2-0216.

7. Bibliographical References

Akbik, A., Chiticariu, L., Danilevsky, M., Li, Y., Vaithyanathan, S., and Zhu, H. (2015). Generating high quality proposition banks for multilingual semantic role labeling. In *Proceedings of the 53rd Annual Meeting of the Association for Computational Linguistics and the 7th International Joint Conference on Natural Language Processing*, pages 397–407, Beijing, China.

Banarescu, L., Bonial, C., Cai, S., Georgescu, M., Griffitt, K., Hermjakob, U., Knight, K., Koehn, P., Palmer, M., and Schneider, N. (2013). Abstract Meaning Representation for Sembanking. In *Proceedings of the 7th Linguistic Annotation Workshop and Interoperability with Discourse*, pages 178–186, Sofia, Bulgaria.

Bhatt, R., Narasimhan, B., Palmer, M., Rambow, O., Sharma, D., and Xia, F. (2009). A Multi-Representational and Multi-Layered Treebank for Hindi/Urdu. In *Proceedings of the 3rd Linguistic Annotation Workshop*, pages 186–189, Suntec, Singapore.

Burchardt, A., Erk, K., Frank, A., Kowalski, A., Padó, S., and Pinkal, M. (2006). The SALSA Corpus: a German Corpus Resource for Lexical Semantics. In *Proceedings of the 5th International Conference on Language Resources and Evaluation (LREC)*, Genoa, Italy.

Cai, R. and Lapata, M. (2019). Semi-Supervised Semantic Role Labeling with Cross-View Training. In *Proceedings of the 2019 Conference on Empirical Methods in Natural Language Processing and the 9th International Joint Conference on Natural Language Processing (EMNLP-IJCNLP)*, pages 1018–1027.

Duran, M. S. and Aluisio, S. M. (2012). Propbank-Br: a Brazilian Treebank annotated with semantic role labels. In *Proceedings of the 8th International Conference on Language Resources and Evaluation*, pages 1862–1867, Istanbul, Turkey.

Fillmore, C. J., Johnson, C. R., and Petruck, M. R. (2003). Background to FrameNet. *International Journal of Lexicography*, 16(3):235–250.

Gruzitis, N., Nespore-Berzkalne, G., and Saulite, B. (2018a). Creation of Latvian FrameNet based on Universal Dependencies. In *Proceedings of the International FrameNet Workshop 2018: Multilingual FrameNets and Constructicons (IFNW)*, pages 23–27, Miyazaki, Japan.

Gruzitis, N., Pretkalnina, L., Saulite, B., Rituma, L., Nespore-Berzkalne, G., Znotins, A., and Paikens, P. (2018b). Creation of a Balanced State-of-the-Art Multilayer Corpus for NLU. In *Proceedings of the 11th International Conference on Language Resources and Evaluation (LREC)*, pages 4506–4513, Miyazaki, Japan.

Hajič, J., Ciaramita, M., Johansson, R., Kawahara, D., Martí, M. A., Màrquez, L., Meyers, A., Nivre, J., Padó, S., Štěpánek, J., Straňák, P., Surdeanu, M., Xue, N., and Zhang, Y. (2009). The CoNLL-2009 Shared Task: Syntactic and Semantic Dependencies in Multiple Languages. In *Proceedings of the 13th Conference on Computational Natural Language Learning (CoNLL): Shared Task*, pages 1–18.

Haverinen, K., Kanerva, J., Kohonen, S., Missilä, A., Ojala, S., Viljanen, T., Laippala, V., and Ginter, F. (2015). The Finnish Proposition Bank. *Language Resources and Evaluation*, 49(4):907–926.

Lopez de Lacalle, M., Laparra, E., Aldabe, I., and Rigau, G. (2016). A Multilingual Predicate Matrix. In *Proceedings of the 10th International Conference on Language Resources and Evaluation*, pages 2662–2668, Portoroz, Slovenia.

Nivre, J., de Marneffe, M.-C., Ginter, F., Goldberg, Y., Hajič, J., Manning, C. D., McDonald, R., Petrov, S., Pyysalo, S., Silveira, N., Tsarfaty, R., and Zeman, D. (2016). Universal Dependencies v1: A Multilingual Treebank Collection. In *Proceedings of the 10th International Conference on Language Resources and Evaluation*, pages 1659–1666.

Palmer, M., Gildea, D., and Kingsbury, P. (2005). The Proposition Bank: An Annotated Corpus of Semantic Roles. *Computational Linguistics*, 31(1):71–106.

Palmer, M. (2009). SemLink: Linking PropBank, VerbNet and FrameNet. In *Proceedings of the Generative Lexicon Conference*, pages 9–15, Pisa, Italy.

Schuler, K. K., Dang, H. T., and Palmer, M. (2000). Class-Based Construction of a Verb Lexicon. In *Proceedings of the 17th National Conference on Artificial Intelligence (AAAI)*.

Xue, N. (2008). Labeling Chinese Predicates with Semantic Roles. *Computational Linguistics*, 34(2):225–255.

Proceedings of the International FrameNet Workshop 2020: Towards a Global, Multilingual FrameNet, pages 70–76
Language Resources and Evaluation Conference (LREC 2020), Marseille, 11–16 May 2020

Building the Emirati Arabic FrameNet

A. Gargett(1), T. Leung(2)

(1) Hartree Centre (Science & Technology Facilities Council),
United Kingdom (andrew.gargett@stfc.ac.uk)
(2) United Arab Emirates University,
United Arab Emirates (leung@uaeu.ac.ae)

Abstract

The Emirati Arabic FrameNet (EAFN) project aims to initiate a FrameNet for Emirati Arabic, utilizing the Emirati Arabic Corpus. The goal is to create a resource comparable to the initial stages of the Berkeley FrameNet. The project is divided into manual and automatic tracks, based on the predominant techniques being used to collect frames in each track. Work on the EAFN is progressing, and we here report on initial results for annotations and evaluation. The EAFN project aims to provide a general semantic resource for the Arabic language, sure to be of interest to researchers from general linguistics to natural language processing. As we report here, the EAFN is well on target for the first release of data in the coming year.

Keywords: Emirati Arabic, FrameNet, corpus linguistics

1. Introduction

The Emirati Arabic FrameNet (EAFN) project aims to initiate a FrameNet for Emirati Arabic, utilizing the Emirati Arabic Corpus (EAC, Halefom et al. 2013). The goal is to create a resource comparable to the initial stages of the Berkeley FrameNet (Baker et al. 1998). A FrameNet (FN) is a corpus-based resource, documenting the semantics of a natural language by linking the "lexical units" (or form-meaning pairings) of the language, such as words, to "frames". Frames represent the background knowledge against which lexical units are understood. This background knowledge typically surfaces in how a lexical unit is used in some situation, together with syntactically related units, termed "frame elements". For example, lexical units such as accuse, blame and esteem all have in common a JUDGEMENT frame, since they typically involve "a Cognizer making a judgment about an Evaluee" (such frame elements are usually presented capitalized).

This notion of a "Frame Semantics" has been pursued by Charles Fillmore and colleagues for over 4 decades, with a vast body of research to support the approach (e.g. Fillmore 1982. Fillmore et al. 2003), much of which can be accessed from the Berkeley FrameNet website.[1] Fillmore's key insight is that an individual's use of specific items in their language is structured by the background knowledge referred to above. Thus, expressing notions of judging draws upon a "'domain' of vocabulary whose elements somehow presuppose a schematization of human judgment and behavior involving notions of worth, responsibility, judgment, etc." (Fillmore 1982). This enables generalizations to be made about natural language patterns in terms of frames, which the FN seeks to capture.

A FN for a natural language thereby provides a rich and highly nuanced model of the syntactic and semantic patterns of the language. A FN project has the potential to add a number of valuable component resources to any existing corpus:

a) Fine-grained information about grammatical roles and relations.
b) A searchable database of semantically oriented annotations.

c) Easily accessible and semantically organized example sentences, especially useful for language learning and teaching.
d) Detailed annotations in a gloss language, such as English in the case of the EAFN project, also a significant resource for language learning and teaching.

The EAFN will be an invaluable resource for primary theoretical research on Emirati Arabic, as well as for additional forms of research crossing a number of disciplines, including natural language processing, information retrieval, corpus linguistics, second language acquisition teaching and research, machine translation, psycholinguistics, and artificial intelligence. FNs are currently available for such major languages as English, German (Rehbein et al. 2012) and Japanese (Ohara 2012). FNs typically accompany a corpus resource of some description, in the target language, and the EAFN will employ data from the EAC for this purpose.

1.1 The Emirati Arabic Corpus

The Corpus of Emirati Arabic (EAC) was established and licensed by the Department of Linguistics at the United Arab Emirates University (Halefom et al. 2013). The EAC is a three-million-word corpus of Emirati Arabic. The data of the EAC was drawn from various naturalistic sources such as radio and TV interviews, and daily conversations. It also consists of some scripted conversations such as TV dramas and documentaries.

While the current size of the EAC is incomparable with other full-fledged corpora (e.g. British National Corpus), the EAC is the first annotated corpus of spoken Arabic (cf. other annotated corpora which are based on Modern Standard Arabic). It also serves as a useful tool for other potential research.

The EAC is fully annotated using the International Phonetic Alphabet (IPA). Narrow transcriptions are used in which detailed phonetic information instead of the citation form is described. In addition to the phonetic details, the EAC also provides further annotation including morphological boundaries (\mb), glossing (\ge), part of speech (\ps), and translation (\ft). For in-stance, Tables 1 and 2 contain two annotated examples from the EAC.

---

[1] https://framenet.icsi.berkeley.edu/fndrupal/

\ref	EAC002.3						
\tx	do:k	hawi:h	ʃu:	jalɛs	jso:lɛf	wja	lɛħma:r
\mb	do:k	hawi:h	ʃu:	jalɛs	jso:lɛf	wja	lɛ-ħma:r
\ge	look	Hawih	what	doing	talk	with	the-donkey
\ps	v	N	wh	v	v	prep	d-n
\ft	look, hawih is talking with the donkey						

Table 1: Example from the EAC

\ref	EAC002.59
\tx	wɛsʕalt
\mb	wɛsʕal-t
\ge	arrived-2sp
\ps	v-pro
\ft	Did you arrive?

Table 2: Example from the EAC

1.2 The Emirati Arabic FrameNet Project

The EAFN project aims to describe the range of semantic and syntactic combinations of each word in our collection in each of its senses. As mentioned earlier, this collection is a sub-corpus extracted from the EAC. To add FN information, annotators perform computer-assisted annotation of example sentences, these annotations then being collected in the EAFN database.

Currently, the Berkeley English FrameNet (BEFN), which began in 1997, consists of in excess of 13,000 entries for senses of lexical units, over 190,000 manually annotated sentences, rep-resenting more than 1200 frames. Started in 2015, the EAFN project originally planned for the initial 2-year phase to collect 1000 senses of lexical units, and up to 10,000 annotated sentences, and an expectation of over 100 frames for Emirati Arabic. However, while a substantial amount of these initial objectives was met, the project was delayed until earlier this year, due to a change in circumstances for the first author. We are currently planning to complete the project by the end of this current year. Delivery of this database will represent a huge advance in knowledge about the language, and lay the groundwork for development of a rich array of corpus-based and other resources, including descriptive, computational and teaching and learning resources, for Emirati Arabic.

Our project aims to make a significant contribution to the level of resources for Arabic, and especially Emirati Arabic. The only comparable work to date is from outside the region, for example, the Leeds University Corpus, where within the Computer Science Department, the Corpus of Quranic Arabic has been developed. However, our project differs from such previous work, in that it aims to deliver large-scale information about deep-level syntactic (grammatical roles) as well as semantic (argument roles) information for this dialect of Arabic. This will involve developing novel collection materials, much of which involves using the BEFN.

Regarding research outcomes, the project aims to deliver a store of primary linguistic information about syntactic and semantic patterns of Emirati Arabic, in a detailed and searchable database of such patterns in this language. The information stored in this database will include:

1) Raw sound files (from the current Emirati Arabic Corpus).
2) Arabic and English Transcriptions of the data (a variety of texts in Emirati Arabic).
3) Annotations in the International Phonetic Alphabet of the files listed in (1) above (from the current Emirati Arabic Corpus).
4) FrameNet annotations, including Frame Element (FE) components for each lexical unit:
   a) Frame Element (FE) name for lexical unit
   b) Grammatical function (e.g. subject, object, etc)
   c) Phrase type (e.g. noun phrase)

2. Method

The annotation in this project combines manual and automatic annotation techniques, and integrates these at several points, as explained below.

2.1 FrameNet Annotation

Formally, FN annotations are sets of triples that represent the FE realizations for each annotated sentence, each consisting of the frame element's name (for example, Food), a grammatical function (say, Object) and a phrase type (say, noun phrase). Working these out for a newly encountered language requires a range of decisions to be made. The first stage of our project involved developing a manual annotation protocol, as well as preparing the sub-corpus of EAC texts for annotation (e.g. extracting citation forms for lexical units).

Developing a FN typically proceeds as follows (Fillmore and Atkins 1998, Fillmore et al. 2003, Boas 2009):

1) Select the words to be analyzed.
2) Starting from the primary corpus (for the proposed project, this is the Emirati Arabic Corpus), define frame descriptions for these words by:
   a) first, providing in simplified terms a description of the kind of entity or situation represented by the frame,

b) next, choosing labels for the frame elements (entities or components of the frame),

c) finally, collecting words that apparently belong to the frame.

3) Next, focus on finding corpus sentences in the primary corpus that illustrate typical uses of the target words in specific frames.

4) Then, the sentences from (3) are annotated by tagging them for frame elements.

5) Finally, lexical entries are automatically prepared and stored in the database.

Building a FN for a language from scratch involves a range of decisions, both linguistic and non-linguistic, raising questions about having sufficient data, about the kind of information to include (dependent on the size and scale of the project aims), and also about the tools required to carry out the work. Relatedly, there are questions about the overall approach to building the FN, such as, whether to employ largely manual or automatic techniques, there being advantages and disadvantages on both sides. As can be seen from the above outlines of a procedure for annotating frames, the complexity of annotating se-mantic information means manual annotation would be expected to yield higher quality data, although relatively much more expensively, whereas automatic annotation would potentially yield much more, lower quality data albeit far more cheaply.

In our project, we have combined manual and automatic annotation procedures, to maximize quality and yield, over the longer term of the project itself. Having a foundation of manually annotated frames provides for the EAFN a solid core on which to build our database. On the other hand, we faced a lengthy lead-in time for developing suitable software tools for the automatic annotation, and so having the manual annotation track enabled an immediate start on frame collection. Further, and perhaps more importantly, the manually collected gold-standard can be used to evaluate the output of automatic annotation, and in turn, manual annotators are able to evaluate the results of automatic annotation.

It might at first seem counter-intuitive that such a resource can indeed be constructed automatically, given the semantic complexity of natural language. Ambiguity abounds in daily communication, making the proposal that a computer system could somehow automatically perform accurate and reliable annotation a somewhat dubious one. However, it turns out that a key factor in being able to achieve this is the generality of the notion of frame, in particular its definition in usage-based terms: this definition leads us to expect that there is a significant overlap between the set of frames in one language and a completely unrelated language, since a frame consists of knowledge about the situations in which a specific language is used, and a significant number of such situations are common across languages. For example, while currencies and even protocols for proper financial arrangements may differ from country to country, the Transaction frame, wherein goods are exchanged for tokens or other goods of equal worth, is ubiquitous across language settings, covering a range of activities, such as buying, selling, bartering, trading, and the like. The automatic side of the project aims to build resources able to leverage this generality of frames, and thereby interface the English FN with an Arabic language resource, in order to capture frames common across each language. Of course, this generality is known to be limited (e.g. Boas 2009), although, we have anticipated this with the manual annotation side of our project, which provides a capacity within our project for discovering frames unique to (Emirati) Arabic. Of course, we acknowledge the difficulty of the challenge involved in being able to build such a resource for generating frames across distinct languages (on this, see e.g. recent work by Czulo et al. 2019).[2] However, we are heartened by a range of results, particularly using more recent, scaled up data-driven approaches to Machine Translation, where Deep Neural Networks are making significant gains in automating the task of relating the semantics of one language to another,[3] and such work is already yielding impressive results (e.g. ElJundi et al. 2019).

2.1.1 Manual annotation

One standard approach to building a large-scale resource like a FN is to construct a representative sample of the language, to carry out any required corpus analysis. Manual annotation on the EAFN follows this route, and starts from a sub-corpus specially selected from the EAC for this task.

In spring 2014, a research collaboration was established between the UAE University and the University of Birmingham with the aim of enriching the EAC by providing frame annotations. In particular, the research purpose is to annotate the EAC by adopting the framework laid out by the Berkeley FN (Baker et al. 1998). Researchers at the UAEU manually annotated the EAC with frames. Manual annotation was initiated with native Arabic speaker annotators being trained by the main EAFN researchers in frame annotation, in line with the protocols established by the Berkeley English FN (see section 2.1 above). Annotators then carried out annotation of sentences sample from the EAC.

Below are two examples of the same lexical unit ʔəmʃii which stems from the tri-consonantal root mʃʔ. All conceptual frames are arrived at through corpus-driven techniques, rather than through native speaker introspection. Note that for these initial stages of the EAFN, labels for frames and FEs have been largely drawn from the Berkeley English FN, although we fully anticipate this will need to be revised as the project further develops.

---

[2] We would like to thank an anonymous reviewer for pointing this out (complete with reference).

[3] For a very recent example of this, see work by the Tsinghua University Natural Language Processing Group (https://github.com/THUNLP-MT/THUMT/)

\entryid	EAC001.2
\root	m ʃ ʔ
\lexeme	ʔəm ʃ ii
\gloss	Walk
\pos	verb
\frame	Self-Motion
\corefe1_label	Goal
\corefe1_item	Deliila
\corefe1_gloss	Deliila
\corefe2_label	Path
\corefe2_item	xəTTi
\corefe2_gloss	along with
\example	ʔəm ʃ ii ʕalaa xəTTi deliila
\free_trans	I walk on the path to Deliila

Table 3: Example from the EAFN

\entryid	EAC0016
\root	m ʃ ʔ
\lexeme	ʔam ʃ ii
\gloss	Walk
\pos	verb
\frame	Self_Motion
\corefe1_label	Path
\corefe1_item	fi ha Siihra
\corefe1_gloss	in the desert
\example	ʔam ʃ i fi ha Siihra
\free_trans	I will walk in this desert.

Table 4: Example from the EAFN

The initial annotation process was carried out iteratively in two phases. During the initial development phase, annotators built the database using backslash entries, as demonstrated in Tables 1 to 4. In the second phase this backslash database was converted into an XML database using custom built parsers; for this phase, the initial annotation protocol can be refined, involving reconsideration of the range of categories required for annotating frames in Emirati Arabic, as well as the procedures for this annotation. For this first round of annotations, these phases gave rise to the foundation of the EAFN database; subsequent rounds of annotations continue to employ both phases, enabling a relatively flexible arrangement. Furthermore, this approach to building a database requires a minimal setup of a laptop on which to run a text editor, making the task highly mobile and relatively technology independent, with annotators employing relatively lightweight tools. Note that the flexibility of such a set-up potentially facilitates collecting such data in a more typical fieldwork type setting. Finally, by extending the custom parsers for the backslash database, we can extract the required information as XML, thereby making our database (re)usable in a range of ways.

2.1.2 Automatic annotation

This side of the project brings together a variety of Natural Language Processing tools, aiming to construct a state-of-the-art system for automatically generating frames for Emirati Arabic. There have been a variety of attempts to use the Berkeley English FN to help build FNs in other languages (De Cao et al. 2008, Tonelli et al. 2009), often by linking existing electronic resources, such as a dictionary, in a target language to the English FN in some way, in order to label items from this language with frames from the English FN.

Along these lines, our approach makes use of the English FN (i.e. the Berkeley English FN), and the English and Arabic Wiktionaries. In order to link these resources, we have customized available NLP tools, and also built such tools from scratch, in order to use these resources to derive candidate frames for the EAFN, based on those from the English FN. A major part of this work has involved using the tools made available by the Ubiquitous Knowledge Processing (UKP) Lab at the University of Darmstadt in Germany.[4] In particular, we employed tools for parsing the English and Arabic Wiktionaries, the Java-based Wiktionary Library (JWKTL),[5] and the UBY database[6] (Gurevych et al. 2012).

Considering the UBY database first, we built tools for extracting information from the UBY database, in order to bridge the English Wiktionary and the English FN. This database stores a wealth of Wiktionary-related information across a range of languages, such as English and Arabic, as well as links to other resources, in particular the English FN. We extracted the following information from this:

1) For each English Wiktionary lexeme:
   a) Its written form
   b) Its sense
2) For each English FrameNet lexical unit matched to an English Wiktionary lexeme:
   a) Its index in the English FN
   b) Its UBY definition [essentially a gloss]

As well as supplying a ready-made parser for the English Wiktionary, the JWKTL library provides the means for customizing a parser for the Arabic Wiktionary; while wiktionaries largely overlap in their format, there can be significant differences from one language to another.

Actual entries in individual language wiktionaries contain information about a specific lexeme in that language, but also, importantly for our purposes, links to translations of this lexeme in wiktionaries of other languages; e.g. the English Wiktionary entry for book links to the Arabic Wiktionary entry for كتاب (this Arabic word being a direct translation of the English).

Using the newly customized parser for the Arabic Wiktionary, and the one already available for the English Wiktionary, we were able to collect information from both wiktionaries, as follows – for each lexeme in the English Wiktionary, we collected:

1) Word form
2) Part-of-speech
3) All possible definitions for this lexeme

---

[4] https://www.informatik.tu-darmstadt.de/ukp/
[5] https://dkpro.github.io/dkpro-jwktl/
[6] https://dkpro.github.io/dkpro-uby/

4) The lexeme in the Arabic Wiktionary which the English lexeme has been linked to. For each of these Arabic lexemes, we also collected:
   a) Word form
   b) Part-of-speech
   c) Definition [supplied in English]

Now, these links between the English to Arabic Wiktionaries are one-to-many, in that there are many possible Arabic word forms for each English lexeme. This means we need to carry out a disambiguation of some kind, if we are to properly align the FN and Wiktionary resources. Taking this need for disambiguation into account, we proceed with the alignment in two stages:

1) First, for each English Wiktionary lexeme from the UBY database, we split the list of English Wiktionary definitions, and calculate a measure of the similarity between this lexeme's UBY definition and its Wiktionary definition. For this work, we used the Gensim word2vec tools,[7] and trained models for this based on the so-called "1 Billion Word Language Model Benchmark".[8] We use this similarity measure as part of an automatically derived overall confidence score, which we later use when comparing competing frame entries in the database.

2) Second, we align the English Wiktionary definitions with the Arabic Wiktionary definitions, again calculating a similarity measure between these definitions (with the same set-up for Gensim word2vec referred to above), as another automatically derived component of the above-mentioned confidence score.

The automatically collected frame annotations of items from the Arabic Wiktionary, currently consist of lexical units (i.e. pairing of lemma and frame), including confidence measure derived from measuring the strength of the match between the English FN and Wiktionary definitions, on the one hand, and between English and Arabic gloss-es/definitions, on the other. Future work will involve extending this work to include annotations of Frame Elements.

2.2 Corpus progress

While the initial release of the EAFN is still un-der development, immediately below we provide a snapshot of the current data collection, for the initial stages of each collection track. In the next section, we present more detailed evaluations of both the automatic and manual collection efforts.

Currently the EAFN covers verbs only. For manually gathered entries, we have collected 29 frames, and 360 LUs. As we show later in this section, in initial evaluation studies, we have found reasonably high inter-annotator agreement for the manual annotation. We have also implemented a fully automatic procedure for collecting entries, for which we have gathered 630 frames and 2100 LUs. Of course, such results need to be treated with a great deal of caution, and indeed initial evaluation of this data suggests only a fraction of this data is expected to be of sufficient quality to justify its being retained for the initial release of the EAFN database.

While we are listing manually and automatically collected entries separately at this stage, these will be collected together for the initial release of the database.

Finally, we should also emphasize that the two sources of language are different in dialectal terms: the manual track works directly from the EAC, and so the yield is dialect-based, whereas the automatic track works from the Wiktionary, which is in fact closer to the Modern Stand Arabic dialect. This combination of dialects within the same resource raises many issues, and we intend to begin addressing these during the latter part of the current project, which constitutes the initial development stage of the EAFN. However, it is likely that more comprehensive solutions to the issues raised will be solved in later stages of the EAFN, once we have completed the initial release of the database.

3. Evaluation

Semantic annotation is fraught with issues regarding lack of reliability and accuracy, making quality control of data a key component of any project in this area. While our project is still at an early stage of development, we are working toward an initial release of our data, for which we are developing a comprehensive evaluation regime, incorporating both the manual and automatic annotation tracks. A description of this, as well as some early results, are included in the rest of this section.

3.1 Manual track

3.1.1 Procedure

We are currently piloting several evaluation tasks, targeting accuracy of judgements about frames and the core elements of those frame. For these tasks, we first extract a random sample from the EAC, and annotators then carry out annotation of this data according to the annotation protocols we have developed (see Section 2 above). We then proceed to apply various measures of agreement between the annotators

We have several measures of the quality of this data, centering on degrees of overlap in the annotations of two of the annotators currently involved in the collection efforts at the UAEU. The statistic we are using here is Cohen's kappa coefficient k:

$$k = \frac{\Pr(a) - \Pr(e)}{1 - \Pr(e)}$$

Where $\Pr(a)$ models the probability of observed agreement among raters, and $\Pr(e)$ captures chance agreement; the higher the value for k, the better the agreement between annotators. There are various interpretations of such scores, for example, 0.60 is often considered a threshold, with

---

[7] https://radimrehurek.com/gensim/

[8] http://www.statmt.org/lm-benchmark/

scores above this being taken to indicate "substantial agreement" (Landis & Koch 1977). k enables quantifying the inter-annotator agreement (IAA), particular for qualitative data, which is closer to our evaluation task, involving as it does detailed semantic knowledge.[9]

3.1.2 Results

For comparison of frame annotations on our sample, we achieve the following: $k = 0.790$ (p-value $\ll$ .001, $N = 31$). For annotation of core FEs, we achieve, $k = 0.899$ (p-value $\ll$ .001, $N = 31$). This shows that using the protocol we have devised, annotators are achieving very good levels of agreement for judgements about FEs, and acceptable agreement for judgements about frames.

3.2 Automatic track

3.2.1 Procedure

Evaluating the automatic annotation provides a key point of convergence between the two tracks. For this, the manual annotators evaluated the output of the automatic system, their responses to the automatically generated frames requiring them to draw on their intuitions, which have their foundations in their direct experience building the manual collection of frames. Feedback from the annotators is crucial to pinpoint where further development on the automatic system will be required. In this way, our aim is that the automatic track more closely approximates the results from the manual track.

The procedure we followed here involved manual annotators going through individual, automatically generated LUs, complete with brief information about the target LU, as well as the frame assigned to this LU. Each annotator was given a total of 198 randomly sampled lexical units to evaluate. Annotators rated this on the following 5-point scale: 1 = Completely correct, 2 = Mostly correct, 3 = Acceptable, 4 = Mostly incorrect, 5 = Completely incorrect. The sample was further split according to two conditions: either (1) the rendering of the lexical unit in Arabic script included vowel information, or (2) it did not. For Arabic script, information about vowels can help disambiguate LUs, and potentially influence the ratings assigned for any specific LU. We are interested in investigating such aspects of the automatic collection process more closely.

The key statistic we are using here is Cohen's kappa coefficient, the same statistic used for measuring agreement during evaluation of the manual annotation task. The difference for the task of evaluating the automatic annotation, is that this task results in ordered data (a likert scale), and so we need to use weighted kappa coefficients; specifically, we are using squared weights, whereby disagreements are weighted according to their squared distance from perfect agreement.

3.2.2 Results

Table 5 presents the results of this evaluation, with evaluation categories used by both annotators across the top and down the leftmost column, and inside the table showing how scores matched for each item. From this, we can see that by far the largest number of matches is where annotators agree that an item is "completely correct", and the next highest being where one an-notator thought that an item was "mostly correct" and the other annotator thought the same item was "completely correct".

When ignoring the vowel vs. no-vowel condition, we achieve the following: $k = 0.443$ (p-value value $\ll$ .001, $N = 198$). However, when taking into consideration the vowel vs. no-vowel condition, this score improved somewhat: $k = 0.602$ (p-value value $\ll$ .001, $N = 83$).

Overall, we can see that general agreement be-tween annotators is quite low, despite the overall largest match being "completely correct". This suggests possible problems and indeed errors for many of the automatically collected frames. On the other hand, when we partition the data set, and extract those items with vowel information, for this subset, the IAA improves considerably, suggesting that such information is an important component to incorporate in future automatically acquired collections for the EAFN.

	1	2	3	4	5
1	24	15	4	1	1
2	2	7	0	2	0
3	1	1	0	2	0
4	1	3	1	3	1
5	2	2	0	1	9

Table 5: Evaluation of automatic track (**1** = Completely correct, **2** = Mostly correct, **3** = Acceptable, **4** = Mostly incorrect, **5** = Completely incorrect)

4. Conclusion

We have presented early results for the first iteration of the Emirati Arabic FrameNet (EAFN). The EAFN is a general semantic resource for the Arabic language, which is sure to be of interest to a range of researchers, from those in linguistics, to others working within natural language processing. The project is divided into manual and automatic tracks, based on the predominant techniques being used to collect frames in each track. Despite a hiatus, work on the EAFN has recommenced; we have here reported on initial results for annotations and evaluation of these annotations which have been carried out in both tracks. The EAFN is well on target for the first release of data in the coming year.

5. Acknowledgements

We would like to thank S. Al Helou and W. Ghaban for help with the evaluation. We would also like to thank M.

---

[9] For all of this, we have used the **irr** package in R, which has been specifically designed for modelling "interrater reliability and agreement."

Elkaref for some early technical help with the JWKTL library, as well as valuable discussions about carrying out computational linguistic modelling of Arabic. Finally, we would also like to thank J. Ruppenhofer for discussions about the English FrameNet.

6. Bibliographical References

Baker, C. F., Fillmore, C. J., & Lowe, J. B. (1998). The Berkeley Framenet project. In Proceedings of the 17th international conference on Computational linguistics-Volume 1 (pp. 86-90). Association for Computational Linguistics

Boas, H. C. (Ed.). (2009). Multilingual FrameNets in computational lexicography: methods and ap-plications (Vol. 200). Walter de Gruyter.

Czulo, O., Torrent, T. T., da Silva Matos, E. E., da Costa, A. D., & Kar, D. (2019). Designing a Frame-Semantic Machine Translation Evaluation Metric. In 2nd Workshop on Human-Informed Translation and Interpreting Technology (HiT-IT 2019) (pp. 28-35).

De Cao, D., Croce, D., Pennacchiotti, M., & Basili, R. (2008). Combining word sense and usage for modeling frame semantics. In Proceedings of the 2008 Conference on Semantics in Text Processing (pp. 85-101). Association for Computational Linguistics.

ElJundi, O., Antoun, W., El Droubi, N., Hajj, H., El-Hajj, W., & Shaban, K. (2019). hULMonA: The Universal Language Model in Arabic. In Proceedings of the Fourth Arabic Natural Language Processing Workshop (pp. 68-77).

Fillmore, C. (1982). Frame semantics. Linguistics in the morning calm, (pp. 111-137). Seoul, South Korea: Hanshin Publishing Co.

Fillmore, C. J., & Atkins, B. S. (1998). FrameNet and lexicographic relevance. In Proceedings of the First International Conference on Language Resources and Evaluation, Granada, Spain (pp. 28-30).

Fillmore, C.J., C.R. Johnson, and M.R. L. Petruck. (2003). "Background to FrameNet." International Journal of Lexicography. 16.3: 235-250.

Gurevych, I., Eckle-Kohler, J., Hartmann, S., Matuschek, M., Meyer, C. M., & Wirth, C. (2012). Uby: A large-scale unified lexical-semantic resource based on LMF. In Proceedings of the 13th Conference of the European Chapter of the Association for Computational Linguistics (pp. 580-590). Association for Computational Linguistics.

Halefom, G, T. Leung and D. Ntelitheos. (2013). A Corpus of Emirati Arabic. NRF Grant 31 H001, United Arab Emirates University.

Landis, J.R. and G.G. Koch (1977). The measurement of observer agreement for categorical data. Biometrics. Vol. 33, pp. 159—174.

Ohara, K. (2012). Semantic Annotations in Japanese FrameNet: Comparing Frames in Japanese and English. In LREC (pp. 1559-1562).

Rehbein, I., Ruppenhofer, J., Sporleder, C., & Pinkal, M. (2012). Adding nominal spice to SALSA-frame-semantic annotation of German nouns and verbs. In Proceedings of the 11th Conference on Natural Language Processing (KONVENS'12) (pp. 89-97).

Tonelli, S., & Giuliano, C. (2009). Wikipedia as frame information repository. In Proceedings of the 2009 Conference on Empirical Methods in Natural Language Processing: Volume 1-Volume 1 (pp. 276-285). Association for Computational Linguistics

Proceedings of the International FrameNet Workshop 2020: Towards a Global, Multilingual FrameNet, pages 77–84
Language Resources and Evaluation Conference (LREC 2020), Marseille, 11–16 May 2020
© European Language Resources Association (ELRA), licensed under CC-BY-NC

Exploring Crosslinguisitic FrameNet Alignment

Collin F. Baker, Arthur Lorenzi

International Computer Science Institute
1947 Center St. Suite 600
Berkeley, CA, 94704, U.S.A.
`{collinb,lorenzi}@icsi.berkeley.edu`

Abstract

The FrameNet (FN) project at the International Computer Science Institute in Berkeley (ICSI), which documents the core vocabulary of contemporary English, was the first lexical resource based on Fillmore's theory of Frame Semantics. Berkeley FrameNet has inspired related projects in roughly a dozen other languages, which have evolved somewhat independently; the current Multilingual FrameNet project (MLFN) is an attempt to find alignments between all of them. The alignment problem is complicated by the fact that these projects have adhered to the Berkeley FrameNet model to varying degrees, and they were also founded at different times, when different versions of the Berkeley FrameNet data were available. We describe several new methods for finding relations of similarity between semantic frames across languages. We will demonstrate ViToXF, a new tool which provides interactive visualizations of these cross-lingual relations, between frames, lexical units, and frame elements, based on resources such as multilingual dictionaries and on shared distributional vector spaces, making clear the strengths and weaknesses of different alignment methods .

Keywords: frame semantics, lexical semantics, semantic frames, multilingual lexical resources

1. Introduction

1.1. Frame Semantics and FrameNet

NLP researchers have long sought to develop tools and resources to build meaning representations beyond the word or syntax level, and many have looked to Charles J. Fillmore's theory of Frame Semantics (Fillmore, 1977b; Fillmore, 1977a) as part of the solution. Fillmore and his colleagues founded the FrameNet (FN) Project (Fillmore and Baker, 2010; Fontenelle, 2003) at the International Computer Science Institute (ICSI) in 1997 with the goal of establishing a general-purpose resource for frame semantic descriptions of English language text. FrameNet's lexicon is organized not around words, but **semantic frames** (Fillmore, 1976), which are characterizations of events, static relations, states, and entities. Each frame provides the conceptual basis for understanding a set of word senses, called **lexical units (LUs)**, that **evoke** the frame in the mind of the hearer; LUs can be any part of speech, although most are nouns, verbs, or adjectives. FrameNet now contains roughly 1,200 frames and 13,600 LUs.

FrameNet provides very detailed information about the syntactic-semantic patterns that are possible for each LU, derived from expert annotations on naturally occurring sentences. These annotations label the phrases that instantiate the set of roles involved in the frame, known as **frame elements (FEs)**. An example of a simple frame is **Placing**, which represents the notion of someone (or something) placing something in a location; this frame is **evoked** by LUs like *place.v, put.v, lay.v, implant.v,* and *billet.v* and also *bag.v, bottle.v,* and *box.v,* The core frame elements of **Placing** are the AGENT who does the placing (or the CAUSE of the placing), the THEME that is placed, and the GOAL. An example of a more complex frame is **Revenge**, which has FEs AVENGER, INJURED PARTY, INJURY, OFFENDER, and PUNISHMENT.

The FrameNet lexical database, in XML format, has been downloaded more than 3,000 times by researchers and developers around the world; the well-known NLP library NLTK (Loper and Bird, 2002) also provides API access to FrameNet (Schneider and Wooters, 2017). FrameNet's main publications have been cited over 2,500 times according to Google Scholar, and it has been an important basis for at least 14 PhD dissertations.

The wide use of FrameNet in NLP depends on the success of systems for automatic semantic role labeling (ASRL) of unseen text, trained on the FrameNet annotation data. ASRL then enables (or improves) downstream NLP applications, such as

- Question Answering (Shen and Lapata, 2007; Sinha, 2008)
- Information Extraction (Surdeanu et al., 2003)
- Text-to-scene generation (Coyne et al., 2012)
- Dialog systems (Chen et al., 2013)
- Social network extraction (Agarwal et al., 2014)
- Knowledge Extraction from Twitter (Søgaard et al., 2015)

In fact, automatic semantic role labeling has become one of the standard tasks in NLP, and several freely available FrameNet-based ASRL systems have been developed, including SEMAFOR (Das et al., 2010; Das et al., 2014) and open-sesame (Swayamdipta et al., 2018). The latter jointly exploits PropBank-based (Palmer et al., 2005) semantic role labeling and FrameNet to train a neural net (NN) to do frame and FE discrimination without run-time parsing. Other recent FrameNet-based ASRL systems have tried a variety of new approaches:

- FitzGerald et al. (2015) train a NN representing joint embeddings of PropBank and FrameNet roles,
- Kshirsagar et al. (2015) use structured features and the frame hierarchy,
- Roth and Lapata (2015) predict roles based both on the

entire document and on recent role assignments, and

- Peng et al. (2018) jointly model FrameNet roles and dependency parses.

1.2. Multilingual FrameNet

Since the beginning of Frame Semantics, the question has arisen as to whether semantic frames represent "universals" of human language or are language specific. Despite many language-specific patterns of expression, the conclusion from the FrameNet experience has been that many frames are applicable across different languages, especially those for basic human experiences, like eating, drinking, and sleeping. Even some cultural practices are similar across languages: e.g. in every culture, commercial transactions involve the roles BUYER, SELLER, MONEY, and GOODS (or services).

Since the Berkeley FrameNet (hereafter BFN) project began releasing its data, researchers in many countries have expressed interest in creating comparable resources for other languages; in fact, the BFN team is in contact with about a dozen FrameNets in languages other than English [1]. The methods used in building these FrameNets have differed, and each has created frames based on their own linguistic data, but all at least have an eye to how their frames compare with those created for English at ICSI (Boas, 2009).

Given that so much research has been conducted in building separate lexical databases for many languages, it is natural to ask whether these lexical databases can be aligned to form a multilingual FrameNet lexical database connecting all of the languages (as well as new FrameNets that may arise in the future), while also accounting for language-specific differences and domain-specific extensions to FrameNet. The results produced so far suggest that this is possible. It is also urgent to carry out this harmonization process as soon as possible, to take better advantage of the experience of each language project, to avoid duplication of effort, and to unify the representational format as much as possible. A number of FrameNet groups, led by FrameNet Brasil have also established the Global FrameNet[2] project to improve communication between FrameNets.

Despite differences among the FrameNet projects, all agree on the concept of semantic frames as their organizing principle and all have found the set of frames defined in BFN to be generally applicable to their language. For example, all languages have ways to express directed self-motion, which involves the frame elements MOVER, SOURCE, PATH and GOAL (although it is rare for all of these to be expressed in the same clause). Likewise, whenever a communicative act occurs, we can identify the FEs SPEAKER, ADDRESSEE, and TOPIC or MESSAGE, which are common to all the communication frames. Semantic frames thus should provide useful generalizations both over lexical units within a language and across languages.

However, the projects have adhered to the Berkeley FrameNet (BFN) model to different degrees: The Spanish, Japanese, and Brazilian Portuguese FNs have followed BFN rather closely, using BFN frames as templates, whereas the SALSA Project (for German), French FN, Swedish FrameNet++ and Chinese FN have diverged further from BFN, either adding many new frames and/or modifying the BFN-derived ones.[3]

More fundamentally, there is no reason to assume that cross-linguistic frame relations will be limited to equivalence. Frames in other languages can be broader or narrower than the nearest English frame, or similar situations may require a different point of view in different languages. For example, English *I like X*, where *like*.v is in the **Experiencer_focused_emotion** frame (along with *adore, dread* and *regret*), is regularly translated as Spanish *Me gusta X*, 'X pleases me' where *gustar*.v is in the **Experiencer_object** frame (along with *asombrar* 'astound', *chocar* 'shock', and *molestar* 'bother', cf. Subirats-Rüggeberg and Petruck (2003)). Other well-attested differences in information structure between languages are similarly reflected in differences in choice of frames, such as that between satellite-framed languages like English and German and verb-framed languages like Spanish and Japanese (Slobin, 1996). There will also be cultural differences, which may mean that equivalent frames do not exist, such as frames for religions or legal processes, which differ widely from country to country.[4] The Multilingual FrameNet project (Gilardi and Baker, 2018) is studying the relations between frames in different languages and will distribute a database of alignments between FrameNets. We have developed several approaches to calculating frame similarity to produce the cross-lingual alignments; these are described in Sections 2.1. through 2.4.. In order to compare these approaches and to evaluate their strengths and weaknesses under various settings of parameters, we have also built an interactive tool for visualization of frame alignments, called ViToXF (for "visualization tool across FrameNet"). We describe this tool in Sec. 3., and will demonstrate it at the workshop. Finally, Sec. 4. offers some qualitative evaluations of the alignment methods and discusses directions for future research.

2. Cross-lingual alignment and Visualization Techniques

Table 1 gives counts for frames and LUs for the six languages included in the preliminary version of the visualization tool; in some cases, these numbers may understate the total in each project, due to certain difficulties in importing the data.

2.1. Alignment by frame name/ID

At first glance, the alignment problem seems trivial: if the other FrameNets have largely used BFN frames, one might

---

[1] https://framenet.icsi.berkeley.edu/fndrupal/framenets_in_other_languages

[2] https://www.globalframenet.org

[3] At this time, the MLFN effort is not trying to align the Italian, Arabic, or Hebrew data, for various reasons, including availability and coverage, among others.

[4] Of course, languages frequently develop, borrow, or calc terms and frames for concepts that are not "native" to the language, in order to discuss other cultures.

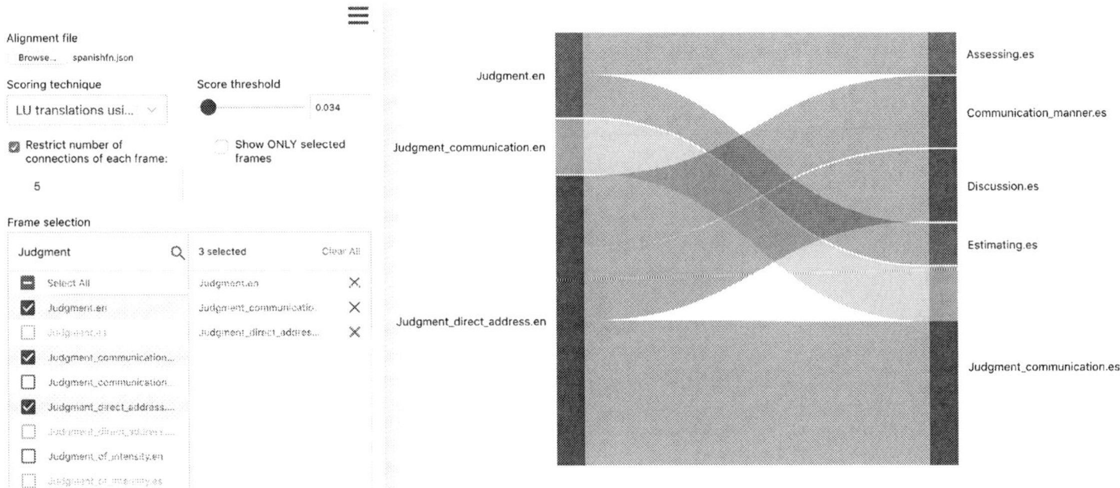

Figure 1: Visualization tool, showing user controls and resulting Sankey diagram of English Judgment frames aligned with Spanish Frames using LU translation by linking synsets at a high score threshold (see Sec. 2.2. for details)

Project	Frames	Lexical Units
FrameNet (ICSI) = BFN	1,224	13,675
Chinese FN	1,259	20,551
FN Brasil (PT)	1,092	2,896
French FN (Asfalda)	148	2,590
German FN	1,023	1,826
Japanese FN	984	3392
Spanish FN	1,196	11,352
Swedish FN	1,186	38,749

Table 1: Frame and LU counts of FrameNets now in ViToXF

just assume that a frame in another language with the same name as a BFN frame represents the same concept, and ignore any that don't have matching names. However, as might be expected, some of the other languages have used frame names in the target language, rather than English; this would mean aligning the frame names themselves across languages. In some cases, their frame data also includes a field for the BFN name or BFN ID, which can be used for alignment, even when the frame names are not in English. Furthermore, even when the names (or IDs) match, the non-English frame may be defined differently or have more or fewer core frame elements than the BFN frame, which, strictly speaking, makes it a different frame.

2.2. Alignment by LU translation

A second way of approaching alignment is to take all the lexical units from a source language frame and find translation equivalents in the target language. To the extent that frames are equivalent across languages, we would expect all the translations of LUs in one source language frame to fall into one target language frame. Of course, this depends on the accuracy of the translations. By definition, a lexical unit in a frame represents one sense of a lemma, so in theory that should greatly narrow the range of possible translations; however, exactly how to use information from frames and frame relations in the translation process is still to be determined.

The Open Multilingual WordNet (OMWN) (Bond and Foster, 2013) contains multilingual synsets, combining lemmas from WordNets for dozens of languages, data from Wiktionary, and the Common Locale Data Repository.[5] We are currently using it to find a set of translation equivalents between languages. The first step is to create a mapping $S(\ell)$ from each LU in each language to a set of OMWN synsets that represent its senses. That mapping is created by searching OMWN for synsets that contain the lemma (with the correct part of speech) of the LU. More formally, let e be a frame in the source language and f a frame in the target language; let L_e and L_f be the lists of the LUs in frames e and f respectively. Then any two LUs a and b in L_e and L_f (respectively) match if they occur together in at least one synset; this matching function can be expressed by Equation 1.

$$\mathrm{m}(L_e, L_f) = \{a \in L_e \mid b \in L_f : S(a) \cap S(b) \neq \emptyset\} \quad (1)$$

When evaluating the alignment between two frames, this function was used to calculate three different scores. The first is a metric that takes into consideration LUs from both frames (Equation 2); however, this gives frames containing more LUs more influence over the result. To avoid this problem, we decided to break the alignment into two other scores taking into account the direction of alignment, i.e., the score of the alignment from English to the target language can be different from the reverse. The basic formula for those scores is presented in Equation 3. (Note that the two scores can be obtained by simply swapping the arguments

---

[5] http://cldr.unicode.org/

in the equation.)[6]

$$s_1(L_e, L_f) = \frac{|m(L_e, L_f)| + |m(L_f, L_e)|}{|L_e| + |L_f|} \quad (2)$$

$$s_2(L_e, L_f) = \frac{|m(L_e, L_f)|}{|L_e|} \quad (3)$$

We also explored another alternative scoring method that is available in the visualization tool by selecting the "Synset count" scoring method. This score is calculated using Equation 3.

$$s_3(L_e, L_f) = \frac{\left| \bigcup_{a \in L_e} S(a) \cap \bigcup_{b \in L_f} S(b) \right|}{\left| \bigcup_{a \in L_e} S(a) \right|} \quad (4)$$

2.3. Alignment by frame element similarity

By definition, for two frames to be the same across languages, they must have the same number and type of frame elements (FEs). Some FrameNets (such as Spanish FN and Japanese FN) have simply copied the FEs from Berkeley FrameNet, so that their names and definitions are still identical to BFN. Others, such as Chinese FN, have translated or created both the names and the definitions in the target language; in those cases, we need to align the FEs by using the proximity of the names and definitions from the two languages in a shared vector space. French FN created FE names and definitions in English, even though many of their frames do not correspond to BFN. Swedish has FE names in English, but no definitions; since they state that the frames and FEs with English names are intended to be identical to the BFN frames and FEs of the same name, the English definitions should also apply to them. Finally, both Brazilian Portuguese and German (SALSA) have FEs in a mixture of English and the target language. In those two cases, we group the FEs according to whether they are in English or the target language,[7] calculate the similarity separately for the two groups, and then combine the scores.

2.4. Alignment by distributional similarity of LUs

Another approach to alignment is to use cross-lingual word embeddings to obtain translations equivalents. The current iteration of the visualization tool uses the FastText word embeddings from FaceBook Research, which were trained on Wikipedia data from various languages and aligned to a single embedding space (Bojanowski et al., 2017). The spaces were aligned by an unsupervised method that uses an adversarial approach, where the discriminator tries to predict the embedding origin and the generator aims to create transformations that the former is not able to accurately classify (Conneau et al., 2017). The transformed FastText vectors of many languages mapped to English space were made publicly available in the MUSE library.[8] We are currently using these pre-trained cross-lingual word embeddings for

two different scoring techniques. The first, "LU translations using MUSE", like those discussed above based on OMWN, uses the word embeddings as a way to obtain translation equivalents: we define the neighborhood around the vector embedding of a target language word as $n(\vec{v}, k, t)$, that is, the k-neighborhood of $\vec{v}$ in the target language with a cosine similarity greater than t. Then we define the alignment score between a pair of frames given their LU lists L_e and L_f by Equation 5.

$$s_4(L_e, L_f) =$$
$$\frac{|\{a \in L_e \mid b \in L_f : \vec{v}(b) \in n(\vec{v}(a), k, t)\}|}{|L_e|} \quad (5)$$

The second scoring technique, "LU centroid similarity using MUSE", calculates the alignment between two frames by finding the average of the vectors of their LUs (i.e. the centroid vector of each frame) and computing the cosine similarity of those two centroids, similar to the approach of Sikos and Padó (2018).

3. Alignment Visualization Tool

3.1. Frame Alignment example

We will demonstrate the alignment of three related English frames with Spanish, **Judgment, Judgment_communication**, and **Judgment_direct_address**. The **Judgment** frame applies whenever a person (the COGNIZER) forms an opinion (good or bad) about someone or something (the EVALUEE). In the **Judgment_communication** frame, the COGNIZER, now called the COMMUNICATOR expresses that opinion, possibly to an ADDRESSEE. In the frame **Judgment_direct_address**, the ADDRESSEE is also the one being evaluated, so this frame contains LUs like *congratulate,harangue, scold, take to task* and *tell off*. The relations between these frames and their frame elements are spelled out in detail in FrameNet; the **Judgment_communication** frame **uses** two frames, **Judgment** frame and **Statement**, and **Judgment_direct_address** **inherits** from **Judgment_communication**.

3.2. Visualization modes

In its current iteration, the system has two visualization modes, one that uses a Sankey diagram to show alignments between frames and another that displays the translations between the LUs of a frame pair in a different type of graph.

Frame Alignment Visualization: Fig. 1 shows the main visualization mode of the tool. It is an interactive bipartite Sankey diagram where English frames are displayed on the left side and target language frames on the right. The width of each band in the diagram is proportional to the alignment score between the frame pair.

Due to the number of lexical units in the FrameNet projects, the resulting diagram can be very dense, making analysis difficult. To alleviate this problem, ViToXF allows both frame selection and band filtering. Frames to be shown can be selected from a list of all the English and target language frames, (marked with a two-letter suffix, *en* for English, *es* for Spanish and so forth). By default, the system will display any match that includes one of the selected frames.

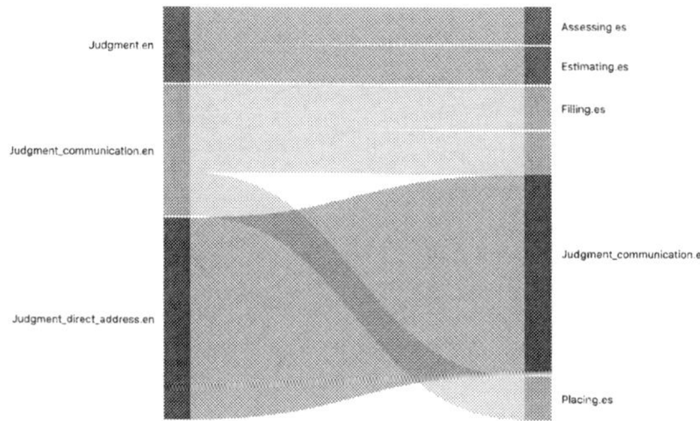

Figure 2: Frame Alignment: English ⇒ Spanish for Judgment-related Frames, matched using synsets at a lower score threshold

This can be further restricted by checking "Show ONLY selected frames"; in that case, it displays only connections where **both** frames are selected.

To filter which bands are displayed in the diagram, the user can also set an alignment score threshold (so that weaker alignments will not be shown) and/or set a limit on the number of connections from each frame. When the number of connections is restricted, those with the highest scores will always be displayed first.

When the "LU-based using MUSE vectors" is selected as the scoring technique for LU matching between frames, the parameters k (neighborhood size) and t (distance threshold) of the function $n(\vec{v}, k, t)$ described in Subsection 2.4., Eq. 5 can be modified, potentially changing alignment scores and hence, the graph displayed. Fig. 1 shows the sidebar, where all of these parameters can be controlled by the user.

Fig. 2 shows the same English-Spanish alignment of frames related to judgment, with a slightly lower similarity threshold than in Fig. 1. Note that alignments to two additional frames **Placing** and **Filling** have now appeared; this will be explained in the following section.

Lexical Unit Translation Visualization: This visualization mode is intended to demonstrate exactly how translations were found for the LUs of a frame pair, and can be accessed by clicking on any band in the Sankey diagram. ViToXF provides two methods for aligning frames and LUs across languages, one based on synsets, the other on vector embeddings; depending on which method is used for the Sankey diagram, the LU translation visualization will be somewhat different.

In both cases, the translation visualization is a tripartite graph with vertices organized in three columns: the left column is composed of the LUs of the BFN frame, the right column of the LUs of the target language frames. In the case of the synset-based LU translation method, the middle column lists the names of synsets, and edges are drawn between the synsets and the LUs in each language whose lemma+POS occurs in that synset. If an English LU and a target language LU both match a lemma+POS in a synset, the name of that synset (or LU depending on the scoring method) is shown in green, and the overall matching score is raised. If an LU from one language matches the synset but not from the other language, the synset name or LU is yellow; this adds to the denominator of Equations 2, 3, 4 and 5 reducing the overall matching score. Synsets which match no LU in the source language are colored black; they do not influence the score.

When the vector embedding method is being used, the left and right columns are as described above, but the center column now represents wordforms; edges are connected to LUs in either language whose lemma lies within the neighborhood of the wordform in the embedding space. If the FastText vectors are used, this means that subparts of words play a role, and that may help connect the various wordforms of a lemma, but may also lead to false positives. Part of speech is not used. The meanings of the colors in the central column are as described above.

Continuing with our example of aligning from English to Spanish in the Judgment-related frames using LU translation via synsets, Fig. 3 shows how the LUs in each language link to the lemmas in the synsets of OMWN. Fig. 3 also shows what can go wrong: the lemma *charge*.v appears in the BFN **Judgment_communication** frame, but in OMWN it also appears in a synset with English *load*.v and Spanish *cargar*.v, defined as 'provide (a device) with something necessary'. Thus it links erroneously to the **Filling** frame in both languages; this problem is discussed further in the next section.

4. Discussion

Each new FrameNet constitutes an experiment in cross-linguistic Frame Semantics. Motivated by the fundamental research question "To what extent are semantic frames similar across languages?", ViToXF provides an intuitive, graphical, interactive tool to study a variety of methods for finding the relations between frames and lexical units across different languages. It also highlights some of the problems that need to be solved to create meaningful alignments that are useful for a wide range of NLP tasks. We do not yet have not results from testing these alignments against standard NLP tasks, but this section offers some qualitative evaluations of the methods and results so far.

4.1. Evaluating Synset-based methods

The alignment methods that depend on WordNet synsets have the merit that they take advantage of large-scale curated groupings of lemmas (by part of speech). However, they also make clear one problem with WordNets: for many common words, the number of senses given is simply too high. We noted in the preceding section some problems with the polysemy of *charge*.v; in fact, Princeton WordNet lists 31 senses for the verb alone! Some of the major divisions are clear:

- charge#1, bear down#3 (to make a rush at or sudden attack upon, as in battle) *He saw Jess charging at him with a pitchfork*

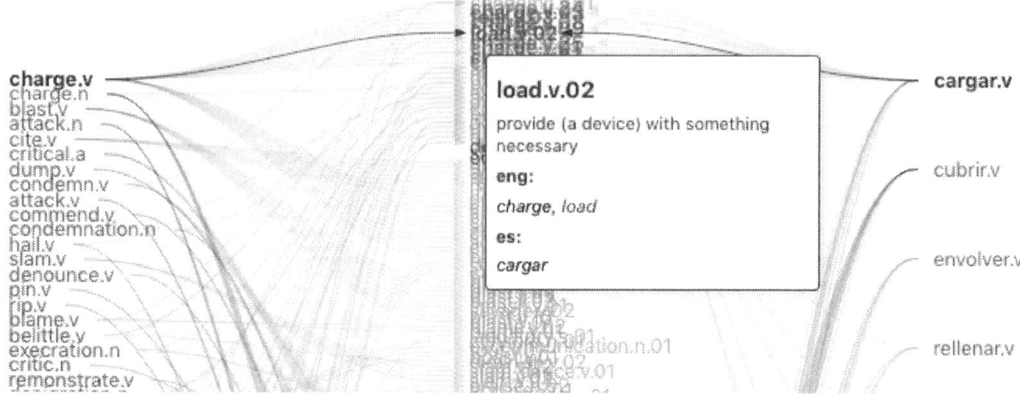

Figure 3: Lexical unit translation: English ⇒ Spanish for Judgment-related Frames, matched using synsets at a lower score threshold. In addition to the expected alignment to **Judgment_communication**, *charge*.v is also mapped to a synset in the **Filling** frame.

- charge#3, bill#1 (demand payment)*Will I get charged for this service?*
- appoint#2, charge#5 (assign a duty, responsibility or obligation to) *She was charged with supervising the creation of a concordance*
- charge#6, lodge#3, file#4 (file a formal charge against) *The suspect was charged with murdering his wife*
- charge#24 (energize a battery by passing a current through it in the direction opposite to discharge) *I need to charge my car battery*

But some senses are hard for humans to distinguish, let alone algorithms; compare for example:

- charge#2, accuse#2 (blame for, make a claim of wrongdoing or misbehavior against) *He charged the director with indifference* and
- charge#7 (make an accusatory claim) *The defense attorney charged that the jurors were biased.*

Are these separate from each other? How are they related to #6?

- charge#8 (fill or load to capacity) *charge the wagon with hay* and
- load#2, charge#16 (provide (a device) with something necessary) *He loaded his gun carefully.*

Are these the same as #24? Is #24 just a special case of charge#16?

The Ontonotes lexical resource (Pradhan et al., 2013), which is based on combining WordNet senses so that annotators can reliably distinguish the classes, may provide a coarser but more reliable list of senses for English and Chinese, but it does not include the other FrameNet language pairs.

4.2. Evaluating Vector-based methods

The alignment methods based on vector embeddings have the advantage of making it possible to measure distances between uses, distances which are arguably semantic; however these distances are not easily converted to "senses" that humans can understand. Also, the MUSE embeddings, like most distributional embeddings, are based on word forms, and do not generalize to the level of lexemes (e.g. most lexicographers would expect the verb *go* to be represented by a single vector that covers *go, went, gone, goes*, and *going*, rather than separate vectors for the five word forms). These embeddings also do not include Chinese and Japanese.

The major shortcoming of the current distributional embeddings, however, is that they provide only one vector per word form, with no distinction of senses. However, there have been encouraging results on finding embeddings for word **senses**, such as Upadhyay et al. (2016) who use multilingual corpora to learn sense-specific embeddings. They point out that often patterns of polysemy are similar across languages; continuing with the preceding example, English *charge* and Spanish *cargar* can both mean either 'file charges in court' or 'fill a battery with electricity'. However, adding an unrelated language such as Chinese often gives completely different translations:

4.3. Applications and Future Work

A major limitation of ViTOXF is simply that most FrameNets are rather small in comparison with other lexical resources, primarily because of the amount of human curation needed to produce them. However, interest in Frame Semantics continues to grow and new FrameNet projects are appearing frequently, so there may be a continuing interest in finding alignments for them. There are also numerous approaches to automatically or semi-automatically adding lexical units to FrameNets (e.g. Pavlick et al. (2015), Fossati et al. (2013),Hartmann and Gurevych (2013),Green (2004)), offering the prospect of much larger, if less precise, lexical inventories.

We expect that alignments produced by the methods outlined here and refined by the use of ViTOXF will prove useful to

- translators and second language learners seeking to understand cross-linguistic differences in framing;
- developers of MT systems, parsers, and grammars (especially for languages for which FrameNets already

exist) (e.g. Czulo et al. (2019)); and, of course,

- cognitive linguists and researchers creating new FrameNets.

Since FastText does not provide cross-linguistic embeddings for English-Japanese and English-Chinese, we will attempt to train some ourselves, to make that type of alignment available for them. We may be able to find ways to use the annotated sentences themselves to align frames, possibly using methods related to BERT vector embeddings, such as those of Zhang et al. (2020).

As just mentioned, instances of similar polysemy can usually be split apart by looking simultaneously at more languages, especially if the languages are unrelated. We therefore plan to look for frames which align well across three or more languages, making for highly robust alignments. Our immediate goal is to incorporate as many of the current FrameNet projects as possible.

We also plan to explore methods for creating sense-specific vectors in all the languages, and better techniques for finding translation equivalents; for example, a smaller number of translations from an MT system may prove more accurate than those from OMWN synsets. Finally, it should be clear that there are many ways to combine the similarity scores from the different methods to get an overall score between two frames. We plan to test the advantages and disadvantages of various weighted linear combinations of scores for different applications. The current code for the visualizer is essentially an alpha version; we welcome suggestions for improving the user interface. We will make the code for ViToXF available on Github; a demo version of the visualizer is available now at https://icsi-berkeley.github.io/framenet-multilingual-alignment/.

Acknowledgments

This material is based in part upon work supported by the U.S. National Science Foundation under Grant No. 1629989. Any opinions, findings, and conclusions or recommendations expressed in this material are those of the authors and do not necessarily reflect the views of the National Science Foundation. We also received support in the form of access to virtual machines from the NSF-funded XSEDE program and machine time and systems support from Ely Matos and Tiago Torrent of FrameNet Brasil, which supported a separate experiment in cross-lingual annotation, reported in Gilardi and Baker (2018) Finally, of course, we are especially grateful to all the FrameNets mentioned above for providing their data for this study.

Bibliographical References

Agarwal, A., Balasubramanian, S., Kotalwar, A., Zheng, J., and Rambow, O. (2014). Frame semantic tree kernels for social network extraction from text. In *EACL*, pages 211–219.

Hans C. Boas, editor. (2009). *Multilingual FrameNets in Computational Lexicography: Methods and Applications*. Mouton de Gruyter.

Bojanowski, P., Grave, E., Joulin, A., and Mikolov, T. (2017). Enriching word vectors with subword information. *Transactions of the Association for Computational Linguistics*, 5:135–146.

Bond, F. and Foster, R. (2013). Linking and extending an Open Multilingual Wordnet. In *Proceedings of the 51st Annual Meeting of the Association for Computational Linguistics (Volume 1: Long Papers)*, pages 1352–1362, Sofia, Bulgaria, August. Association for Computational Linguistics.

Chen, Y.-N., Wang, W. Y., and Rudnicky, A. I. (2013). Unsupervised induction and filling of semantic slots for spoken dialogue systems using frame-semantic parsing. In *Automatic Speech Recognition and Understanding Workshop*, pages 120–125. IEEE.

Conneau, A., Lample, G., Ranzato, M., Denoyer, L., and Jégou, H. (2017). Word translation without parallel data. *arXiv preprint arXiv:1710.04087*.

Coyne, B., Klapheke, A., Rouhizadeh, M., Sproat, R., and Bauer, D. (2012). Annotation Tools and Knowledge Representation for a Text-To-Scene System. In *COLING 2012, 24th International Conference on Computational Linguistics, Proceedings of the Conference: Technical Papers*, pages 679–694.

Czulo, O., Torrent, T., Matos, E., Costa, A. D. d., and Kar, D. (2019). Designing a frame-semantic machine translation evaluation metric. In *Proceedings of the Human-Informed Translation and Interpreting Technology Workshop (HiT-IT 2019)*, pages 28–35, Varna, Bulgaria, September. Incoma Ltd., Shoumen, Bulgaria.

Das, D., Schneider, N., Chen, D., and Smith, N. A. (2010). Probabilistic Frame-Semantic Parsing. In *Proceedings of the North American Chapter of the Association for Computational Linguistics Human Language Technologies Conference*, Los Angeles, June.

Das, D., Chen, D., Martins, A. F. T., Schneider, N., and Smith, N. A. (2014). Frame-Semantic Parsing. *Computational Linguistics*, 40(1).

Fillmore, C. J. and Baker, C. F. (2010). A Frames Approach to Semantic Analysis. In Bernd Heine et al., editors, *Oxford Handbook of Linguistic Analysis*, pages 313–341. OUP. This is Chapter 13 in 1st edition, 33 in 2nd edition.

Fillmore, C. J. (1976). Frame semantics and the nature of language. *Annals of the New York Academy of Sciences: Conference on the Origin and Development of Language and Speech*, 280(1):20–32.

Fillmore, C. J. (1977a). Scenes-and-frames semantics. In Antonio Zampolli, editor, *Linguistic Structures Processing*, number 59 in Fundamental Studies in Computer Science. North Holland Publishing.

Fillmore, C. J. (1977b). The need for a frame semantics in linguistics. In Hans Karlgren, editor, *Statistical Methods in Linguistics*. Scriptor.

FitzGerald, N., Täckström, O., Ganchev, K., and Das, D. (2015). Semantic role labeling with neural network factors. In *EMNLP*, pages 960–970.

Thierry Fontenelle, editor. (2003). *International Journal of Lexicography–Special Issue on FrameNet*, volume 16. Oxford University Press.

Fossati, M., Giuliano, C., and Tonelli, S. (2013). Outsourcing FrameNet to the Crowd. In *Proceedings of the 51st Annual Meeting of the Association for Computational Linguistics (Volume 2: Short Papers)*, pages 742–747, Sofia, Bulgaria, August. Association for Computational Linguistics.

Gilardi, L. and Baker, C. F. (2018). Learning to align across languages: Toward Multilingual FrameNet. In Tiago Timponi Torrent, et al., editors, *Proceedings of the International FrameNet Workshop 2018: Multilingual FrameNets and Constructicons*, pages 13–22. LREC.

Green, R. (2004). *Inducing Semantic Frames from Lexical Resources*. Ph.D. thesis, University of Maryland, College Park.

Hartmann, S. and Gurevych, I. (2013). FrameNet on the Way to Babel: Creating a Bilingual FrameNet Using Wiktionary as Interlingual Connection. In *Proceedings of the 51st Annual Meeting of the Association for Computational Linguistics (Volume 1: Long Papers)*, pages 1363–1373, Sofia, Bulgaria, August. Association for Computational Linguistics.

Kshirsagar, M., Thomson, S., Schneider, N., Carbonell, J., Smith, N. A., and Dyer, C. (2015). Frame-Semantic Role Labeling with Heterogeneous Annotations. In *Proceedings of the 53rd Annual Meeting of the Association for Computational Linguistics and the 7th International Joint Conference on Natural Language Processing (Volume 2: Short Papers)*, pages 218–224, Beijing, China, July. Association for Computational Linguistics.

Loper, E. and Bird, S. (2002). NLTK: The natural language toolkit. In *In Proceedings of the ACL Workshop on Effective Tools and Methodologies for Teaching Natural Language Processing and Computational Linguistics. Philadelphia: Association for Computational Linguistics*.

Palmer, M., Gildea, D., and Kingsbury, P. (2005). The proposition bank: An annotated corpus of semantic roles. *Computational Linguistics*, 31(1):71–106.

Pavlick, E., Wolfe, T., Rastogi, P., Callison-Burch, C., Dredze, M., and Van Durme, B. (2015). FrameNet+: Fast Paraphrastic Tripling of FrameNet. In *Proceedings of the 53rd Annual Meeting of the Association for Computational Linguistics and the 7th International Joint Conference on Natural Language Processing (Volume 2: Short Papers)*, pages 408–413, Beijing, China, July. Association for Computational Linguistics.

Peng, H., Thomson, S., Swayamdipta, S., and Smith, N. A. (2018). Learning joint semantic parsers from disjoint data. In *Proceedings of the 2018 Conference of the North American Chapter of the Association for Computational Linguistics: Human Language Technologies, Volume 1 (Long Papers)*, pages 1492–1502. Association for Computational Linguistics.

Pradhan, S., Moschitti, A., Xue, N., Ng, H. T., Björkelund, A., Uryupina, O., Zhang, Y., and Zhong, Z. (2013). Towards robust linguistic analysis using OntoNotes. In *Proceedings of the Seventeenth Conference on Computational Natural Language Learning*, pages 143–152, Sofia, Bulgaria, August. Association for Computational Linguistics.

Roth, M. and Lapata, M. (2015). Context-aware Frame-Semantic Role Labeling. *Transactions of the Association for Computational Linguistics*, 3:449–460.

Schneider, N. and Wooters, C. (2017). The NLTK FrameNet API: Designing for discoverability with a rich linguistic resource. In *Proceedings of the 2017 Conference on Empirical Methods in Natural Language Processing: System Demonstrations*, pages 1–6, Copenhagen, Denmark, September. Association for Computational Linguistics.

Shen, D. and Lapata, M. (2007). Using Semantic Roles to Improve Question Answering. In *Proceedings of the 2007 Joint Conference on Empirical Methods in Natural Language Processing and Computational Natural Language Learning (EMNLP-CoNLL)*, pages 12–21.

Sikos, J. and Padó, S. (2018). Using embeddings to compare framenet frames across languages. In *Proceedings of the First Workshop on Linguistic Resources for Natural Language Processing*, pages 91–101. Association for Computational Linguistics. Collocated with COLING 2018.

Sinha, S. (2008). *Answering Questions about Complex Events*. Ph.D. thesis, EECS Department, University of California, Berkeley, Dec.

Slobin, D. I. (1996). Two ways to travel: Verbs of motion in English and Spanish. In M. S. Shibatani et al., editors, *Grammatical constructions: Their form and meaning*, pages 195–220. Clarendon Press, Oxford.

Subirats-Rüggeberg, C. and Petruck, M. R. L. (2003). Surprise: Spanish FrameNet! In Eva Hajičová, et al., editors, *Proceedings of the Workshop on Frame Semantics, XVII International Congress of Linguists (CIL)*, Prague. Matfyzpress.

Surdeanu, M., Harabagiu, S., Williams, J., and Aarseth, P. (2003). Using Predicate-Argument Structures for Information Extraction. In Erhard Hinrichs et al., editors, *Proceedings of the 41st Annual Meeting of the Association for Computational Linguistics*, pages 8–15.

Swayamdipta, S., Thomson, S., Lee, K., Zettlemoyer, L., Dyer, C., and Smith, N. A. (2018). Syntactic scaffolds for semantic structures. In *Proceedings of the 2018 Conference on Empirical Methods in Natural Language Processing*, pages 3772–3782, Brussels, Belgium, October-November. Association for Computational Linguistics.

Søgaard, A., Plank, B., and Alonso, H. M. (2015). Using Frame Semantics for knowledge extraction from Twitter. In *Proceedings of the Twenty-Ninth AAAI Conference on Artificial Intelligence*.

Upadhyay, S., Faruqui, M., Dyer, C., and Roth, D. (2016). Cross-lingual models of word embeddings: An empirical comparison. *CoRR*, abs/1604.00425.

Zhang, Z., Wu, Y., Zhao, H., Li, Z., Zhang, S., Zhou, X., and Zhou, X. (2020). Semantics-aware BERT for language understanding. In *Proceedings of the Thirty-Fourth AAAI Conference on Artificial Intelligence (AAAI-2020)*.

Proceedings of the International FrameNet Workshop 2020: Towards a Global, Multilingual FrameNet, pages 85–92
Language Resources and Evaluation Conference (LREC 2020), Marseille, 11–16 May 2020
© European Language Resources Association (ELRA), licensed under CC-BY-NC

Building Multilingual Specialized Resources Based on FrameNet:
Application to the Field of the Environment

Marie-Claude L'Homme*, Benoit Robichaud*, Carlos Subirats**

*Observatoire de linguistique Sens-Texte (OLST), Université de Montréal, C.P. 6128, succ. Centre-ville, Montréal
Québec, H3C 3J7, CANADA
**Departamento de Filología Española. Facultad de Filosofía y Letras. Campus Universidad Autonoma de Barcelona,
Edifici B, Carrer de la Fortuna, 08193 Bellaterra, SPAIN
{mc.lhomme, benoit.robichaud}@umontreal.ca
carlos.subirats@uab.cat

Abstract

The methodology developed within the FrameNet project is being used to compile resources in an increasing number of specialized fields of knowledge. The methodology along with the theoretical principles on which it is based, i.e. Frame Semantics, are especially appealing as they allow domain-specific resources to account for the conceptual background of specialized knowledge and to explain the linguistic properties of terms against this background. This paper presents a methodology for building a multilingual resource that accounts for terms of the environment. After listing some lexical and conceptual differences that need to be managed in such a resource, we explain how the FrameNet methodology is adapted for describing terms in different languages. We first applied our methodology to French and then extended it to English. Extensions to Spanish, Portuguese and Chinese were made more recently. Up to now, we have defined 190 frames: 112 frames are new; 38 are used as such; and 40 are slightly different (a different number of obligatory participants; a significant alternation, etc.) when compared to Berkeley FrameNet.

Keywords: terminology, FrameNet, Frame Semantics, multilingual resource, environment

1. Introduction

Frame Semantics (Fillmore 1982), and more specifically the methodology developed within the FrameNet project (Fillmore and Atkins 1992; Ruppenhofer et al. 2016) is being used for the development of resources in an increasing number of specialized fields of knowledge. Projects can lead to stand-alone resources based on FrameNet or to proposals to increase the lexical coverage of Berkeley FrameNet with the addition of specialized terminology. These projects deal with various fields of knowledge, such as biology (Dolbey et al. 2006), football (Schmidt 2009; Dicionário da copa de mundo 2020), law (Pimentel 2013), computing (Ghazzawi 2016), linguistics (Malm et al. 2018), and the environment (the resource presented in this article). Other terminology projects, such as EcoLexicon (Faber et al. 2016) in the field of the environment, apply Frame Semantics without referring explicitly to the FrameNet methodology.

For designers of specialized resources, the FrameNet methodology is especially appealing as it first allows them to capture the conceptual background of domain-specific knowledge. As pointed out by Fillmore and Baker (2010), acquiring new specialized concepts requires a background of other, more familiar concepts:

> […] as with the mathematical concept mantissa, which requires previous familiarity with such concepts as base, power, logarithm, decimal point, and, of course, the conceptual prerequisites of each of these in turn. (Fillmore and Baker 2010:317)

Authors also point out that the process of acquiring specialized concepts require "a lengthy chain of prior learning as a prerequisite to attaining the new concept." (Fillmore and Baker 2010:317)

Additionally, the FrameNet methodology allows designers of specialized resources to account for the linguistic properties of terms and to connect these properties to a conceptual background. Traditionally, specialized resources have focused on providing explanations (in some cases, very detailed ones) about the knowledge conveyed by terms, giving very few details about the linguistic behavior of these terms. It is often assumed that this information can be found in other, perhaps more general resources. Things are changing though as work on corpora emphasizes the need for a deeper understanding of linguistic behavior.

This paper presents a methodology for the development of a multilingual resource that accounts for environment terms. The resource, called *Framed DiCoEnviro* (2020), covers various topics, such as climate change, renewable energy, transport electrification, endangered species, and sustainable agriculture. It includes Chinese, English, French, Portuguese (Lamberti 2019) and Spanish terms.[1] (The coverage varies considerably from one language to another as some projects started only recently). Additionally, besides French and English, topics covered in different languages vary.

After listing some lexical and conceptual differences that must be managed in domain-specific resources (Section 2), we describe the steps of our methodology and explain to what extent the FrameNet methodology needed to be

---

[1] The terminological resource also contains Italian terms, but these have not been linked to the Framed DiCoEnviro yet.

adapted (Section 3). We conclude by providing some figures regarding the work we have done up to now and mention some directions we wish to take in the future.

2. Why Developing "FrameNets" in Specialized Fields of Knowledge is not a Trivial Task

Specialized knowledge and terms used to express it can be unknown to the layperson, as is the case with *mantissa* mentioned in the previous section. However, such clear-cut cases do not exhaust all possible ways to convey specialized knowledge. Indeed, specialized and common knowledge interact in various situations and influence each other in different ways. In addition, terms are often based on the lexical stock of languages and share with lexical units a complex set of relationships (L'Homme and Polguère 2008).

A common mechanism to create terms consists in adding new meanings to existing lexical items (e.g. *green* meaning "that is less damageable to the environment"). Other, much subtler changes can also affect the way lexical items are used in specialized situations. Fillmore pointed out that, although the concepts of INNOCENT and GUILTY can be known to laypeople, they are conceptualized differently when considered from the perspective of law.

> In both everyday language and legal language there is a contradictory opposition between INNOCENT and GUILTY. In everyday language, the difference depends on whether the individual in question did or did not commit the crime in question. In legal language, by contrast, the difference depends on whether the individual in question has or has not been declared guilty by the court as a result of a legal action within the criminal system. (Fillmore 1982:127)

Such differences can be observed in many other fields of knowledge. In the environment, which is the field that we are concerned with in this article, situations that may seem familiar at first sight are considered in a way that contrasts with what we will call *everyday situations*. We examine a simple example, i.e. a situation that involves species that live in a specific location, and consider it from the perspective of endangered species. We will compare this situation to a similar one captured in FrameNet (which is considered here, although this is not entirely the case, as a reference for "everyday situations").[2]

In contrast with the *mantissa* example, everybody has at least basic knowledge about this situation.[3] We could assume that it is closely related to the situation captured in the RESIDENCE Frame, which is defined as follows:

> This frame has to do with people (the Residents) residing in Locations, sometimes with a Co-resident (FrameNet 2020).

In both cases, living entities make use of locations for shelter and to carry out daily activities. However, a closer

look soon reveals that many differences can be spotted between the situation as it is described in FrameNet and a situation in which species are involved. The first one is that the perspective taken in FrameNet concerns human beings. Other differences are listed below.

Lexical content of frames. It appears that some lexical units that can evoke the RESIDENCE frame cannot apply to species. Indeed, some lexical units only apply to human beings (*e.g. resident, squatter*) and others only to species (*e.g. nest*) (Table 1).

RESIDENCE in FrameNet	RESIDENCE in the environment
bivouac.n, bivouac.v, camp.n, camp.v, camped.a, camper.n, dwell.v, dweller.n, inhabit.v, inhabitant.n, live.v, lodge.v, occupant.n, occupy.v, reside.v, resident.n, room-mate.n, room.v, shack up.v, squat.v, squatter.n, stay.v, tenant.n	*inhabit, live, nest, nesting, occupy*

Table 1. Different lexical contents for the RESIDENCE frame

Core and non-core frame elements (FEs). Core and non-core frame elements can vary when considering the RESIDENCE situation from the perspective of endangered species. The Co-resident core FE has no correspondence in the field of endangered species. On the other hand, the range in which a given species can be found is often specified.

Relations between frames. When considering a residence situation from the point of view of endangered species, the fact of living in a given area is closely linked to other situations that concern the state of this species. Species can spread in small or large areas; they can also settle in locations in larger and larger numbers. Species are also vulnerable to certain threats that will cause them to be less abundant in an area or even disappear. Finally, measures can be taken to place species in an area so they can start occupying it again. In other words, the relations shared by situations from the point of view of endangered species differ sharply from those described in FrameNet (Figure 1).

This simple example is by no means an exceptional case. Many more examples could be mentioned in which situations are similar or do not differ drastically from other more common situations. However, differences emerge at many descriptive levels (lexicon, frame as was discussed above) given that entities and events can be conceptualized differently in specialized fields of knowledge.

On a lexical level, differences in conceptualization result in subtle "meaning modulations"[4] that we differentiate from polysemy *per se* and are much more difficult to pinpoint using standard lexico-semantic criteria. For instance, the

---

[2] More differences between Berkeley FrameNet and the Framed DiCoEnviro are listed in L'Homme et al. (2016).

[3] This being said, some technical aspects of the situation might be only known by the expert.

[4] These phenomena are linked to what Cruse (2011) called *microsenses*.

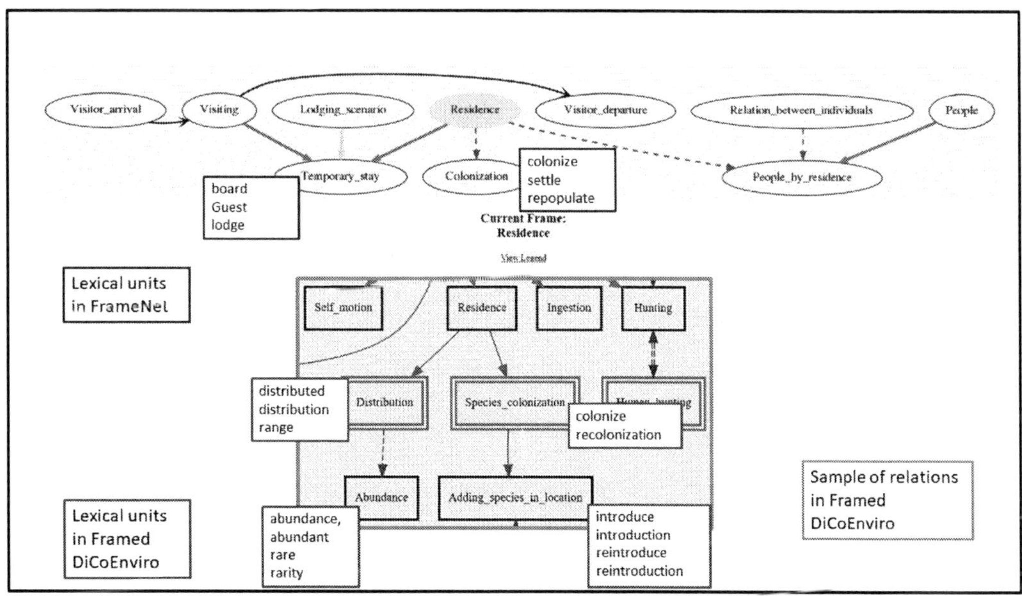

Figure 1 Relations shared by the RESIDENCE frame in FrameNet and the Framed DiCoenviro

verb *introduce* denotes an activity whereby someone places a species in an area where it can live and reproduce (*Toad populations, predatory fish should not BE INTRODUCED into breeding ponds*). It is related to *reintroduce* and *introduction* and is opposed to *eliminate* and *extirpate*. In everyday language, *introduce* includes many more activities in which someone places something in a given location. Given the use of *introduce* in everyday language, it is linked to a much larger set of different lexical units (LUs) (such as *imbed, implant, insert, place,* etc.). It would be difficult to contend that we are dealing with a completely new meaning in the field of endangered species (as was the case with *green* mentioned earlier).

Furthermore, some distinctions can be relevant when considering lexical units from the perspective of a specialized domain but would not be made in other contexts. For instance, the verb *hunt* lends itself to two different uses in corpora that deal with the environment. One corresponds to the activity whereby a meat eater chases, captures and kills other animals for food; the second corresponds to the activity carried out by modern human beings that consists in chasing animals for other kinds of reasons, this activity having a negative impact on the conservation of species. *Hunt₁* is linked to other terms, such as *predation*, and *to prey*; while *hunt₂* is linked to *poach, capture,* and *fish* (Figure 2).

In order to account for these phenomena, designers of specialized resources can build stand-alone resources for specific fields of knowledge. This strategy certainly has the advantage of allowing designers and users of these resources to focus exclusively on the way situations are conceptualized in a given area of knowledge. However, the relationship with common knowledge and the general lexical stock of languages is lost. This strategy also implies that stand-alone resources need to be compiled each time a new domain or topic is targeted.

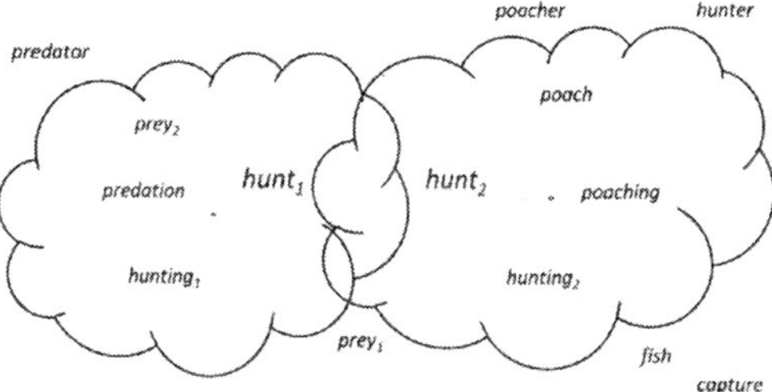

Figure 2 Distinguishing *hunt* in the environment

Another approach – which is the one taken in this work – consists in situating terminology within the broader spectrum of the lexicon. This will allow us to connect specialized meanings and usage to a more "general" lexicon. By doing so, we must also attempt to better define what is specific to a given field of knowledge and what this field of knowledge shares with language in general.

3. A Methodology Adapted to Specialized Fields of Knowledge

Our methodology is bottom-up (Schmidt 2009) as in many other terminology projects. Terminologists are not experts of the fields they are asked to account for, especially when they recently embarked on a project. They must rely on knowledge sources to identify relevant terms and describe them. The first five steps of the methodology consist in compiling terminological entries. This part of the work is heavily based on Explanatory Combinatorial Lexicology (Mel'čuk et al. 1995) and is implemented in a terminological resource called the *DiCoEnviro* (2020). Once these entries contain enough linguistic data, we proceed to define frames based on the knowledge acquired during these first steps. Frames are modelled in a resource called the *Framed DiCoEnviro* (2020). Both resources are interlinked.

Compiling terminological entries:

1. Compilation of specialized corpora
2. Identification of terms (semi-automated)
3. Selection and extraction of contexts
4. Definition of the argument structure
5. Annotation of contexts

Finding frames among lexical entries:

6. Definition of semantic frames
7. Encoding of frames
8. Definition of relations between frames

As was mentioned above, our resources account for terms in different languages and more could be added in the future. The first five steps of the methodology are applied to languages separately. Native speakers or near native speakers of each language are responsible for building lexical entries. The definition of semantic frames can take into account terms in different languages.

3.1 Compilation of Corpora

Since terminologists are seldom experts of the field they describe, they rely heavily on the contents of corpora to locate relevant terms and information about their uses. Hence, all terminological projects start with the compilation of a corpus. Since the field of the environment encompasses a wide range of subjects and that the terminology and the number of occurrences of given terms can vary quite drastically from one subject to another, we work on separate topics and compile a corpus accordingly.

When we embark on a new project, we start with corpora of about 500,000 words (this corresponds roughly to 30-40 different texts of varying sizes ranging between 1,000 to 50,000 occurrences). Corpora are often enriched at a later stage (for instance, our English corpus on endangered species now amounts to around 1,060,000 tokens and comprises 88 different texts).

3.2 Identification of Terms

Once a corpus on a specific topic is compiled, we proceed to identify relevant terms. We first approach this task with an automated method that produces a list of candidate-terms.

We submit our corpus to a term extractor, called *TermoStat* and developed by Drouin (2003), and have it search for nouns, verbs, adjectives and adverbs. The term extractor compares the content of a specialized corpus to a reference corpus. For English, the latter is a combination of the British National Corpus (BNC) and the American National Corpus (ANC). More specifically, the extractor compares lemmatized and part of speech tagged units in both corpora and produces a list of candidate terms ranked according to their specificity in the specialized corpus. This specificity is a reflection of the unusual frequency of the unit in the specialized corpus. The hypothesis underlying this method is that unusually frequent units correspond to terms. Table 2 shows the first results of this method applied to our corpus of endangered species.

Canonical form	Frequency	Specificity score	Variants
specie[5]	3710	202.96	*specie, species*
species	3046	185.74	*species*
habitat	2614	173.96	*habitat, habitats*
conservation	1388	112.76	*conservation*
recovery	1142	108.22	*recovery, recoveries*
endangered	928	103.71	*endangered*
population	1621	98.61	*population, populations*
threaten	943	84.46	*threaten, threatens, threatened, threatening*
extinction	603	81.63	*extinction, extinctions*
endanger	504	72.48	*endanger, endangered, endangering*
status	866	71.86	*status*
nest	422	69.94	*nest, nests, nested, nesting*
threat	789	67.43	*threat, threats*

Table 2. First term candidates extracted from a corpus on endangered species

Terminologists must then analyze this list, keep those candidates that correspond to relevant terms, and ignore other lexical items. Although some cases do not raise problems (e.g. *species, habitat*), others might be more problematic (e.g. *recovery*). Terminologists look up problematic cases in the corpus to examine the context in which they appear.

3.3 Extraction of Contexts

The third step of the methodology consists in going back to the corpus and retrieving contexts that will be placed in lexical entries. These contexts are extremely useful to analyze terms and complete other parts of their description. Contexts are also annotated, as will be seen further on.

For each term, terminologists extract 15 to 20 different contexts. These are selected according to the richness of the information they contain (presence and number of participants, argumental or circumstantial status of each participant, explanations of the meaning, etc.). Experience has shown that 15 to 20 contexts per meaning are sufficient to give a clear picture of how terms behave in a specialized corpus. Beyond that point, the information becomes redundant.

At this stage, terminologists might make meaning distinctions they missed during the previous step. Since different meanings are described in separate entries,

---

⁵ Since lemmatization and POS tagging are automated, there might be some erroneous entries

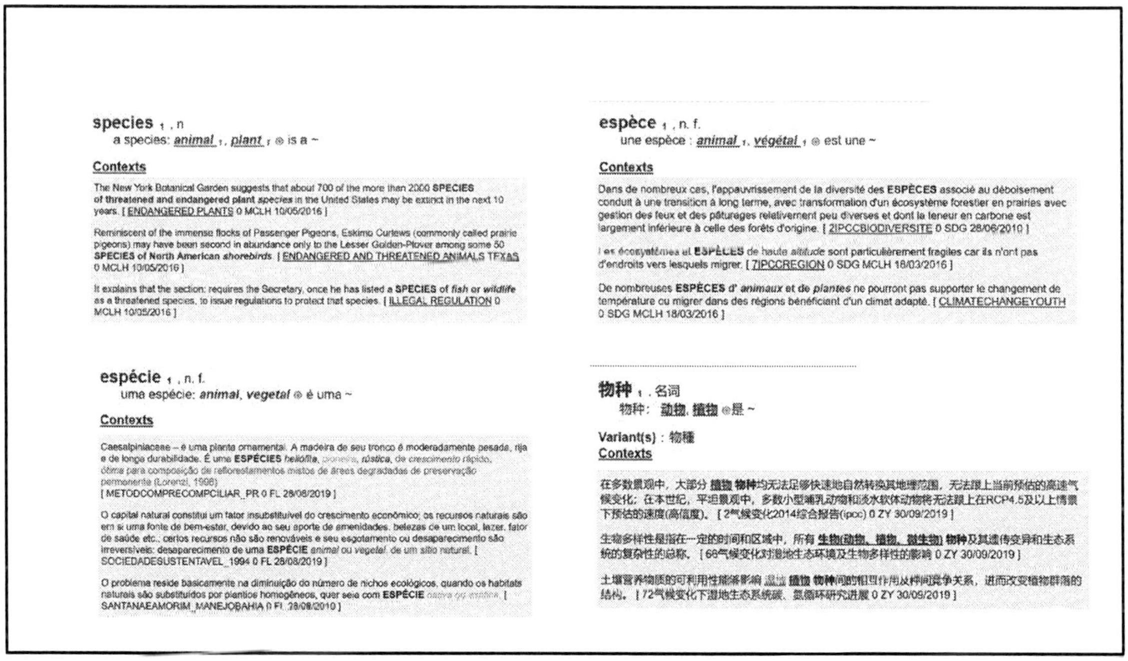

Figure 3: Entries in English, French, Portuguese and Chinese in the DiCoEnviro (2020)

contexts must reflect these distinctions and be placed in the right entry.

3.4 Definition of Argument Structure

The fourth step consists in defining the argument structure of terms. This step – albeit central in our methodology – does not apply to terms that are non-predicative (e.g., *animal, organism, plant, wolf*). At this stage, terminologists determine how many arguments a term has and state these arguments in the entry (*habitat* of X; X *inhabits* Y).

Arguments are represented with two different systems. We first label them with semantic roles that express the relationship between the term and its arguments. The labels used for the arguments of *inhabit* are: Patient *inhabits* Location.[6] An additional label states what we call the *typical term* (Species *inhabits* Area). This typical term is designed to give the user an idea of the kinds of terms that can instantiate the arguments.

3.5 Annotation of Contexts

Once the argument structure is defined, terminologists proceed to annotate the set of contexts based on the methodology devised for the FrameNet project (Ruppenhofer et al. 2016).

The examples selected below represent a sample of the annotated contexts for the term *inhabit*.

> This is primarily a species of the lowlands of central and southwest Arizona and adjacent areas, where it is a permanent resident along desert rivers and streams (Tweit and Finch 1994). It is found in New Mexico only in Grant and Hidalgo counties primarily in the Gila Valley and at San Simon Cienega, where it[Patient] INHABITS riparian thickets and similar native habitats[Location].

> Young or small fish[Patient] are noted to INHABIT gravel riffles[Location], and all individuals may move to deeper waters to overwinter

> Current populations, especially young[Patient], are much reduced and INHABIT more restricted areas of the lake[Location].

> Other species of pupfish in the Pecos River system[Patient] INHABIT more saline waters[Location].

> The highly endangered Alabama beach mouse[Patient] once[Time] INHABIT most of Alabama's Gulf Coast[Location].

Once these first five steps are completed, we obtain terminological entries that contain a statement of the argument structure and up to 20 annotated contexts (Figure 3). Terminologists then proceed to identify terms that are likely to evoke the same frame.

3.6 Definition of Semantic Frames

Given that our methodology is bottom-up, the identification of frames is first guided by different lexico-semantic properties of terms that are described in their entries:

- The same number of arguments: e.g., *inhabit, live* and *occupy* have two arguments.
- Arguments of a similar nature: e.g. the arguments of *inhabit, live* and *occupy* are labelled as Patient

---

[6] It should be said at this point that the labels used in our terminological resources differ from those used in FrameNet (L'Homme (2015). Frame elements in FrameNet are relevant within a specific frame. In our resources, labels should be applied to large sets of terms.

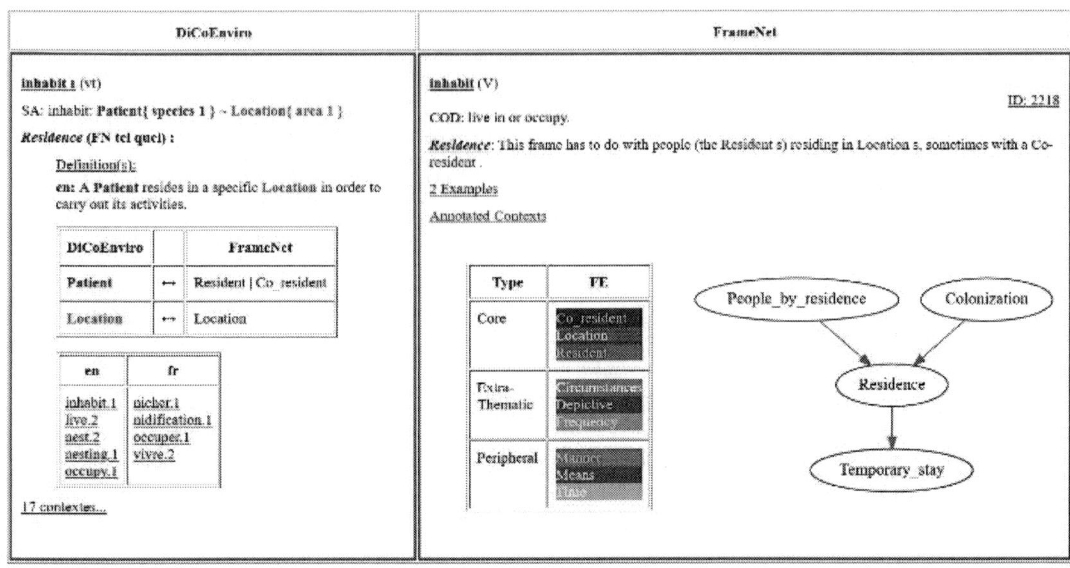

Figure 4. Comparison of terms and lexical units contained in FrameNet

and Location, and are instantiated by terms that denote living organisms and/or habitats (Patient; *animal, fish, species*, etc.; Location: *coast, environment, habitat, reserve*, etc.).

- Shared circumstantials (found in annotations).

Of course, shared participants are useful clues to identify terms evoking the same frame, but terminologists must define the content of frames based on much more information. Terms must denote the same general situation and share presuppositions about it (Ruppenhofer et al. 2016). Hence, based on our descriptions, we could establish that the terms *inhabit, live* and *occupy* evoke the same situation, whereby a living entity finds itself in a given location that should provide it with what it needs to feed, reproduce and survive.

To help them define frames, terminologists also refer to Berkeley FrameNet (2020). They look for corresponding data in the English data. To assist them in this process, a tool compares the XML versions of both resources (Figure 4), locates corresponding lemmas and extracts relevant information. If a frame was already encoded in FrameNet and that the data it describes fits the properties of the terms in the field of endangered species, the frame defined in FrameNet is used and adapted. For instance, this was possible for the terms *inhabit, live* and *occupy*. We thus based our frame on the one in FrameNet. Of course, many differences appear in the descriptions given in each resource (different lexical content, labels used for participants, etc., see Section 2). Furthermore, when we base our frame on an existing one in FrameNet, we use the same name and provide a link that will lead users to its description in the original FrameNet resource.[7]

Of course, there are many cases for which no correspondence can be established and we must also create frames that account for our specific data. More than half of the frames that appear in the Framed DiCoEnviro were defined specifically to account for situations in the field of the environment. For instance, a new frame needed to be created to account for the meaning distinction that was mentioned above for the verb *hunt*. In these cases, we create a name that attempts to be evocative of the situation that it represents.

3.7 Encoding of Frames

Once frames are defined, they are encoded in an entry that accounts for the following:

- The name of the frame.
- A definition formulated for the field of the environment and stating the obligatory participants.
- Example(s) for each of the languages described.
- An indication of the reference to FrameNet with a hyperlink to FrameNet wherever relevant.
- The list of participants (obligatory and optional ones).
- The list of terms that evoke this frame in different languages; hyperlinks to the DiCoEnviro are provided to visualize terminological entries and contextual annotations.

3.8 Definition of Relations Between Frames

Situations are connected in different ways, and frames that capture these situations can be linked so as to make these connections explicit. For instance, the SPECIES_COLONIZATION frame (with LUs such as *colonize,*

---

[7] Users can also view the similarities and the differences between frames as they are represented in FrameNet and those that appear

in the *Framed DiCoEnviro* when selecting the "Click here to see associated FrameNet infos". More explanations are given about this feature in L'Homme et al. (2016).

recolonization) is connected via a Causation relation with the ADDING_SPECIES_IN_LOCATION frame (with LUs such as *introduce, introduction, reintroduce*) (Figure 1). Relations described in the Framed DiCoEnviro are based on those defined in FrameNet (Inheritance, Perspective, Use, Subframe, Precedence, Causation, See also). However, two additional relations were introduced:

- Opposition: Is opposed to (e.g. **Removing_trees_from_location** Is opposed to **Adding_trees_in_location**). This relation captures domain-specific oppositions. It highlights oppositions such as reversiveness and contrastivity.
- Property: Is a property of, Has property (e.g. **Sustainability** is a property of **Human_activity**). Again, this relation captures recurrent domain-specific relations. It might be refined in the future when more data is described.

Once linked, frames can lead to larger scenarios that give an overview of how events are connected in the field of the environment. For instance, one scenario describes the different activities that species undergo or carry out (*live somewhere, feed, reproduce*, etc.) (part of this scenario is shown in Figure 1) as opposed to another one that accounts for human activities. Another scenario, called *Understanding life*, shows the different connections between living organisms according to the terms used to express them (*species, population, predator, offspring*, etc.).

4. Summary

This article presented a bottom-up methodology to compile FrameNet-like domain-specific resources. We applied this methodology to different environmental topics and to different languages. Our descriptions are first placed in a terminological resource, called *DiCoEnviro* (2020). Based on these terminological descriptions, we proceed to identify frames. Once a frame is identified and defined, terminological entries are linked to a frame module that is superimposed on terminological entries and that is visible in another resource called the *Framed DiCoEnviro* (2020). Up to now, 190 frames were defined.

We first applied our methodology to French and then extended it to English. Our infrastructure can easily be adapted other languages and entries in Spanish, Portuguese and Chinese are currently being added. However, the non-availability of tools can raise problems in certain languages. For instance, the term extractor TermoStat has not yet been adapted to Chinese. In this case, an alternative solution needed to be sought.

When defining frames, we refer to Berkeley FrameNet. In many cases, an existing frame can be used or adapted to our data. However, in many other cases (more than half), a new frame is created. More specifically, 112 new frames were created; 38 are used as such; 40 are slightly different (a different number of obligatory participants; a significant alternation, etc.). Table 3 gives an overview of the work carried out in different languages and of the frames defined up to now. Most of these frames were added to 17 scenarios.

	Frames	FR	EN	ES	ZH	PT
New	112	337	240	20	34	11
Unchanged	38	124	96	8	11	3
Differences	40	149	114	18	20	3
TOTAL	190	610	450	46	65	17

Table 3. Frames in the Framed DiCoEnviro and LUs in different languages

Table 4 gives a summary of the annotations that were revised up to now in all five languages. (Some annotated LUs have not been assigned to frames yet.)

	Annotated contexts
FR	12.262
EN	9,004
ES	2,267
ZH	1,150
PT	635

Table 4. Annotations in different languages

5. Future Work

The work reported in this article is ongoing. New terminological entries are added in different languages on a regular basis. Some of these entries can be assigned to existing frames or lead to the definition of new frames. We also extend the coverage of the DiCoEnviro by adding terms linked to new environmental topics.

Our methodology and infrastructure can easily be extended to new languages. However, as was mentioned above, some tools might not be available for some languages; in these cases, adjustments need to be made. As the descriptive work progresses in different languages, we should get a clearer picture of interlinguistic differences and the levels at which they occur (lexicon, frame).

The relationship with Berkeley FrameNet is visible through the Framed DiCoEnviro and this allows users to visualize similarities and differences between domain-specific and "everyday" situations to a certain extent. It would also be interesting to establish a connection the other way around, i.e. allow users of FrameNet to view how situations can be conceptualized differently in specialized areas of knowledge. For the time being, interrelationships between the two resources can only be made manually due to several methodological differences that exist between them. However, it would be useful to attempt to mitigate these differences in order to capture most of them automatically.

6. Acknowledgments

The authors wish to thank collaborators who work on the different versions of the DiCoEnviro and Framed DicoEnviro: Maria Francesca Bonnadona, Flávia Lamberti Arraes, and Zheng Ying. They also extend their thanks to two anonymous reviewers who raised many interesting points and whose comments helped clarify parts of the paper.

7. Bibliographical References

Cruse, D.A. (2011). *Meaning in Language*, Cambridge: Cambridge University Press.

Dolbey, A., M. Ellsworth, and J. Scheffczyk (2006). BioFrameNet: A Domain-specific FrameNet Extension with links to Biomedical Ontologies. In *KR-MED 2006. Biomedical Ontology in Action*, 87-94. Baltimore, Maryland.

Drouin, P. (2003). Term Extraction Using Non-Technical Corpora as a Point of Leverage. *Terminology* 9(1): 99–117.

Faber, P., P. León-Araúz, and A. Reimerink. (2016). EcoLexicon: New features and Challenges. In *GLOBALEX 2016: Lexicographic Resources for Human Language Technology in conjunction with the 10th edition of the Language Resources and Evaluation Conference*, ed. by I. Kernerman, I. Kosem Trojina, S. Krek, and L. Trap-Jensen, 73-80. Portorož, Slovenia.

Fillmore, C. (1982). Frame Semantics. In *Linguistics in the Morning Calm*, ed. by The Linguistic Society of Korea, 111-137. Seoul: Hanshin.

Fillmore, C. J., and B.T. Atkins. 1992. Toward a Frame-based Lexicon: The Semantics of RISK and its Neighbors." In *Frames, Fields and Contrasts*, ed. by A. Lehrer, and E. Feder Kittay, 75-102. Hillsdale, New Jersey: Lawrence Erlbaum Assoc.

Fillmore, C.J., and C. Baker (2010). A Frames Approach to Semantic Analysis. In *The Oxford Handbook of Linguistic Analysis*, ed. by B. Heine and H. Narrog, 313-339. Oxford: Oxford University Press.

Ghazzawi, N. (2016). *Du terme prédicatif au cadre sémantique : méthodologie de compilation d'une ressource terminologique pour des termes prédicatifs arabes en informatique*. Thèse présentée à l'Université de Montréal : Montréal.

Lamberti Arraes, F. (2019). DiCoEnviro, a Multilingual Terminological Resource on the Environment: The Brazilian Portuguese Experience. In *Electronic Lexicography in the 21st Century. Proceedings of the eLex 2019 Conference, ed. by* I. Kosem, T. Zingano Kuhn, M. Correia, J.P. Ferreria, M. Jansen, I. Pereira, J. Kallas, M. Jakubíček, S. Krek, and C. Tiberius, 291-304. Sintra, Portugal. Brno: Lexical Computing CZ.

L'Homme, M.C. (2015). Predicative lexical units in terminology. In *Recent Advances in Language Production, Cognition and the Lexicon*, ed. by N. Gala, R. Rapp, and G. Bel-Enguix. 75-93. Berlin: Springer

L'Homme, M.C., and A. Polguère (2008). Mettre en bons termes les dictionnaires spécialisés et les dictionnaires de langue générale, In *Lexicographie et terminologie : histoire de mots. Hommage à Henri Béjoint*, ed. by F. Maniez, and P. Dury. 191-206. Lyon: Presses de l'Université de Lyon.

L'Homme, M.C., B. Robichaud, and C. Subirats. (2014). Discovering frames in specialized domains, In *Language Resources and Evaluation, LREC 2014*, Reykjavik, Iceland.

L'Homme, M.C., C. Subirats, and B. Robichaud. 2016. A Proposal for combining "general" and specialized frames. In *Proceedings of the Workshop on Cognitive Aspects of the Lexicon*. 156–165, Osaka, Japan.

Malm, P., S. Mumtaz Virk, L. Borin, and A. Savera (2018). LingFN. Towards a FrameNet for the Linguistics Domain. In *International FrameNet Workshop. 2018. Multilingual FrameNets and Constructions. Proceedings. Language Resources and Evaluation (LREC 2018)*, ed. by T. Timponi Torrent, L. Borin, and C. Baker, 37-43. Miyazaki, Japan.

Mel'čuk. I., A. Clas, and A. Polguère (1995). *Introduction à la lexicologie explicative et combinatoire*, Duculot: Louvain-la-Neuve.

Pimentel, J. (2013). Methodological bases for assigning terminological equivalents. A Contribution. *Terminology* 19(2): 237-257.

Ruppenhofer, J, M. Ellsworth, M. Petruck, C. Johnson, C. Baker, and J. Scheffczyk, 2016. *FrameNet II: Extended Theory and Practice*. (https://framenet.icsi.berkeley.edu/fndrupal/index.php?q=the_book). Accessed January 27, 2017.

Schmidt, T. (2009). The Kicktionary – A Multilingual Lexical Resources of Football Language. In *Multilingual FrameNets in Computational Lexicography. Methods and Applications*, ed. by H. C. Boas, 101-134. Berlin/NewYork: Mouton de Gruyter.

8. Language Resource References

American National Corpus (ANC). (http://www.anc.org/). Accessed March 30, 2020.

British National Corpus (BNC). (http://www.natcorp.ox.ac.uk/corpus/index.xml). Accessed March 30, 2020.

Dicionário da copa de mundo (https://www.ufjf.br/framenetbr/dicionario/). Accessed February 18, 2020.

DiCoEnviro. Dictionnaire fondamental de l'environnement (http://olst.ling.umontreal.ca/cgi-bin/dicoenviro/search.cgi). Accessed February 21, 2020.

A Framed Version of DiCoEnviro (http://olst.ling.umontreal.ca/dicoenviro/framed). Accessed February 18, 2020.

FrameNet (https://framenet.icsi.berkeley.edu/fndrupal/). Accessed February 21, 2020.